Philippians and Colossians
Personal Workbook

Chad Sychtysz

Published by
Spiritbuilding Publishers
9700 Ferry Road, Waynesville, Ohio 45068

PHILIPPIANS AND COLOSSIANS
Personal Workbook
By Chad Sychtysz

ISBN: 978–1–96480–514–6

Spiritbuilding
PUBLISHERS

spiritbuilding.com

Table of Contents

The author of this workbook can be contacted at chad@booksbychad.com.

Cover design by Larissa Lynch

Introduction to *Philippians*

Historical Background: Philippi was the first Macedonian city into which Paul entered because of what has often called "the Macedonian vision" (Acts 16:11–12). It was built upon the banks of the Gangites River, about ten miles inland from the seaport of Neapolis. Philippi was originally named Crenides in the ancient kingdom of Thrace but was overthrown and re-named by Philip II of Macedon, father of Alexander the Great, in the mid-4th century BC.

Philippi became a Roman colony by an edict of Augustus (Octavian) Caesar, in commemoration of his and Antony's victory over Brutus and Cassius (42 BC). A Roman colony was a satellite of Rome itself, and its citizens enjoyed all the rights and privileges as did citizens of Rome. Philippi was free from taxation, had its own city government (rather than being overseen by a provincial ruler), and enjoyed autonomy as long as its own laws did not violate Roman law. It was comprised of three groups: the Roman colonists themselves; the native (Greek) Macedonians; and "a large group of [Eastern] Orientals, including Jews."[1] While its citizens spoke Koine Greek, Latin was Philippi's official language.

On his second missionary journey (ca. AD 52), Paul (and Silas) came to Philippi and sought out a synagogue of Jews, as was his practice in coming to a place that had not yet been evangelized. He found no synagogue, suggesting that there were not enough Jewish men to establish one (which required at least ten heads of households). He did, however, come upon Jewish women who were praying by the river, and to them he preached the gospel of Christ. One woman, Lydia, heard this gospel and obeyed it, and thus became the first known convert to Christianity on the continent of Europe (Acts 16:13–15).

After this, however, Paul encountered trouble that is well known to Bible students. A slave-girl who allegedly possessed the ability to divine the future began following Paul and Silas and disclosing their identity as "bond-servants of the Most High God." After "many days" of this, Paul finally had had enough and exorcised from her the demonic spirit that had been the source of this information (Acts 16:16–18). This, of course, ruined the steady income her masters had enjoyed until that moment. They took their anger out on Paul and Silas and dragged them before the city magistrates to face criminal charges. These charges were based upon spite and ignorance, since these men did not know or understand the gospel message that Paul preached. Nonetheless, the city officials had Paul and Silas beaten and imprisoned (Acts 16:19–24). Later, after the city officials found out that these evangelists were Roman citizens, they feared severe repercussions from Rome and begged that Paul and Silas leave them—which they did, but in their own time (Acts 16:35–40).

After this, Paul later visited Philippi again, and enjoyed a very favorable relationship with the church there. These were good people of solid character. The Christians at Philippi were extremely supportive of Paul and were among those who gave even to their own hurt because they first gave themselves to the Lord (see 2 Cor. 8:1–5, Phil. 4:15–16).

Authorship: There is virtually no doubt that Paul wrote *Philippians*. The personality of the author is consistent with everything we know about Paul; furthermore, his name is in the salutation. "This letter is so fresh, distinct, [and] inimitable in every way that forgery is impossible."[2] It is clear from internal evidence that Paul was in Roman prison at the time of writing but expected to be released soon (1:12–14, 2:17–28). There is no good reason to believe that this imprisonment was other than that which Luke mentioned at the end of *Acts*, where Paul spent "two full years" in prison while waiting for his official hearing before Emperor Nero (Acts 28:30–31). Given this premise, the writing is dated ca. AD 62, or about ten years after the founding of the church in Philippi. This letter was carried from Rome to Philippi by Epaphroditus, who had been sick for some time while he was with Paul (2:25–26).[3]

Purpose and Theme: The return of Epaphroditus gave Paul an opportunity to bring the Philippians up to date on his own circumstances, since they were concerned for him. This also provided an excellent occasion for Paul to express his deep gratitude for the gift(s) they had sent to him during his imprisonment. Paul also took this opportunity to impart to them whatever counsel, encouragement, and perspective he could provide as an apostle of Jesus Christ. These combined factors resulted in one of the more personal and letter-like writings of the New Testament (NT).

Rejoicing is a major theme of this epistle, and Paul wanted these people to find joy and cause for rejoicing even amid difficult circumstances (just as Paul did himself, even while in prison). The implication seems to be: if we (Christians) can rejoice during times of difficulty, we will learn to be joyful and content people in any circumstance (4:11–13). Thus, commentators often refer to Paul as the "optimistic prisoner" from this epistle.[4] "It breathes the language of a father, rather than the authority of an apostle; the entreaties of a tender friend, rather than the commands of one in authority. It expresses the affections of a man who felt that he might be near death, and who tenderly loved them; and it will be, to all ages, a model of affectionate counsel and advice."[5]

Philippi served as the retirement settlement for Roman officers and career soldiers. For this reason, and because of its Roman colony status, it was stable, disciplined, and relatively peaceful. Likewise, the internal character of the church itself was virtually trouble-free. This did not mean it did not have external challenges, however, such as those of the "false circumcision" (3:2–3)—i.e., Judaizing teachers—who tried to infiltrate any of the early churches. While the city prided itself on its Roman citizenship, Paul brought the Christians' attention to a far greater citizenship—that of heaven itself (3:20–21). In view of this, a "forgetting what lies behind and reaching forward to what lies ahead" theme (3:13) predominates this epistle.

General Outline of *Philippians*

- **Section One: Salutation and Opening Comments (1:1–11)**
- **Section Two: Expectations of Christian Living (1:12—2:30)**
  - Paul's Proclamation of the Gospel (1:12–20)
  - Encouragement to Live in a Worthy Manner (1:21—2:4)
  - The Pre-eminent Example of Christ (2:5–11)
  - Working Out One's Salvation (2:12–18)
  - The Coming of Timothy and Epaphroditus (2:19–30)
- **Section Three: The Heavenly Perspective (3:1–21)**
  - Gaining Christ through the Sacrifice of All Things (3:1–11)
  - Letting Go in Order to Move Forward (3:12–21)
- **Section Four: Reliance upon God (4:1–23)**
  - Dwelling upon Excellence (4:1–9)
  - The Philippians' Support of Paul (4:10–19)
  - Final Thoughts and Salutation (4:20–23)

SECTION ONE:
SALUTATION AND OPENING COMMENTS (1:1–11)

Lesson One
(Phil. 1:1–11)

Salutation (1:1–2): While the opening salutation is from both Paul and Timothy, Paul is clearly the writer of this epistle and the authority behind its content (1:1). The Philippians are well-acquainted with Timothy since he was with Paul when he founded the church there (Acts 16:1–10). At the time of writing, Timothy is accompanying Paul while he is in prison in Rome awaiting his trial before Emperor Nero. "Bond-servants" [Greek, *doulos*] indicates their humble position relative to Christ's own: He is the head of His church, and they are merely His servants. The exclusion of Paul's usual reference to his apostolic authority indicates that he is not writing to them to address problems, but that this is a more personal letter.

"To all the saints … including the overseers and deacons" is a unique address among the NT epistles. In the earliest days, church leadership came directly from the apostles; as time went on, however, this leadership was turned over to the appointed elders and deacons of each congregation. (Note the plurality of men in both groups.) In *Philippians*, however, Paul speaks to the entire group as one. "Overseers" is another word for elders or pastors (shepherds). "Grace to you and peace" (1:2): the source of all divine grace and spiritual peace is God the Father and His Son, Jesus Christ.

Praise and Prayers for the Philippians (1:3–11): Paul's daily prayers regularly included his gratitude and appreciate for the church in Philippi, as well as for other churches (1:3–5; see 1 Cor. 1:4, Eph. 1:15–16, Col. 1:3–4, etc.). Despite his lengthy imprisonment, Paul is particularly joyful and upbeat when speaking of the Philippians, partly out of sheer relief that they are relatively trouble free for the moment. He addresses a group that is neither divided nor fractured but is striving for unity (1:4). Also, the Philippians are not merely hearers of the gospel but are doers as well (1:5; see James 1:21–25). They take seriously their responsibility as fellow participants in the work of the kingdom, contributing financially to the needs of the saints abroad, and supporting Paul personally in his ministry to the churches. Thus, they do all things for the sake of the gospel, making them fellow partakers of it (1 Cor. 9:23).

Paul then expresses his confidence that God is actively at work within the church at Philippi (1:6). God never starts something that He does not intend to finish, yet the completion of this work requires the ongoing faith of those in whom He is working. Thus, Paul implies (as he will say directly later) that the Philippians need to continue in their faith so that God will continue to carry out His will in them. Given this, His divine activity has no limits, and will continue until Christ's literal appearance.[6]

Paul feels comfortable speaking so candidly about the Philippians in this way since he and they have mutual regard and affection for one another ("I have you in my heart") (1:7). His ministry to them and their support of his own ministry—despite all the trials and difficulties involved in both cases—have created a strong bond between the two. The church in Philippi witnessed Paul and Silas' unjust imprisonment for their sakes (Acts 16:22ff) and is aware of Paul's present imprisonment in Rome for the sake of the gospel. Likewise, his love for them is pure and genuine— so much so, that he calls upon God to be a witness of it (1:8).

Paul's prayers for the Philippians include an appeal on their behalf for increasing love and wisdom (1:9).[7] "Real knowledge" implies an increasingly *improved* knowledge—learning that is continuously refined and made more accurate through prayer and study. "All discernment" involves wisdom in dealing with spiritual matters, which includes the ability to judge between right and wrong (Heb. 5:14). The purpose for this knowledge and discernment is then stated (in 1:10–11).

- ❑ **"to approve of the things that are excellent"**: Excellent things must be properly appraised; the natural man of the world does not value them in the way that a spiritual child of God does (1 Cor. 2:11–14). The standard for our appraisal is the word of God; the application of this is in the Christ-like way we live.

☐ **"sincere and blameless"**: The Greek word for "sincere" literally means "(to be) judged by sunlight," that is, to be held up to the sun's rays and scrutinized for purity. In the case of believers, we are held up to God's word and exposed by the Light for what (and who) we really are (Eph. 5:7–13). If our character is consistent with God's expectations, we are sincere; if not, then we fail the test (2 Cor. 13:5). "Blameless" means "unoffensive," as in not bringing offense against God with our actions, and thus not incurring guilt and His condemnation. This does not mean that we are unable to sin, but that *when* we sin, we take the proper recourse and seek God's forgiveness (Col. 1:22, 1 John 2:1–2). "[U]ntil the day of Christ" indicates the duration of our seeking to be sincere and blameless: until death or the Second Coming, whichever comes first.

☐ **"having been filled with the fruit of righteousness"**: The power (or producing energy) of this fruit is the Holy Spirit; the believer's connection to this power is his fellowship with Christ. This alludes to the vine-branch analogy in John 15:1–9: because of our branch-like connection to the Vine (Christ), we can bear fruit (by the Holy Spirit; see Gal. 5:22–23). "[T]o the glory and praise of God" describes the ultimate benefit of this fruit-bearing process: not only do we receive salvation, but God is honored by our decision to serve Him.

Passages such as this (1:10–11) illustrate the full purpose of what Christians do and why we do it. While the world stumbles into the future without purpose, objective, or how to prepare for the afterlife, the Christian is to be informed, prepared, and looking forward to the full revelation of God's plan in the hereafter. It takes strong conviction to believe in things we have never seen, which is why "we walk by faith and not by sight" (2 Cor. 5:7).

Questions

1.) In 1:9–11, Paul clearly prayed for the Philippians with a specific purpose in mind. How does this compare to prayers that we often hear that simply say, "Lord, be with so-and-so"? Does Paul's example have something to offer us, or was this a special case?

2.) Are *all* Christians supposed to be "filled with the fruit of righteousness" (1:11)? What does this mean, exactly? How does this fruit manifest itself?

SECTION TWO:
EXPECTATIONS OF CHRISTIAN LIVING
(1:12—2:30)

Lesson Two:
Paul's Proclamation of the Gospel
(Phil. 1:12–20)

Instead of being a failed opportunity, Paul's Roman imprisonment has opened the door to those who might have never heard the gospel otherwise (1:12). The "greater progress" of the gospel indicates a pioneering direction that had not yet been taken. Thus, his circumstances have proven to be profitable for the cause of Christ (1:13). The "praetorian guard" (of the governor's palace) refers to the elite Roman guard that directly serves the emperor and provides for his personal safety.[8] ("Praetor" is Latin for "commander-in-chief.") These men are stationed in a special barracks in the actual palace of the emperor, whereas the rest of the soldiers are stationed outside the city.[9] This means that Paul is in a far more comfortable environment than before and has better proximity to Roman officials than he has ever had. "[A]nd to everyone else" indicates a wide array of access and opportunity to share the gospel. Furthermore, because of Paul's presence in the praetorian guard, "most of the brethren" in Rome are emboldened to speak of the gospel more than they might have done otherwise (1:14). They had someone on the inside, so to speak, opening doors and providing influence for them. "Courage as well as fear is contagious."[10]

Some Christians, however, "are preaching Christ even from envy and strife" (1:15). Likely, this refers to those Jewish Christians seeking to draw attention to themselves rather than allowing believers to sympathize with Paul and his circumstances. These men may have disparaged Paul's character ("If he were completely genuine, then why has he been sitting in prison for so long?") to magnify their own ("Since I am not being imprisoned, God looks more favorably upon me"). Thus, they envy Paul and strive against him rather than cooperate with him in their ministries.[11]

Thankfully, not all believers have responded this way: "some [are preaching] from good will." These brethren act out of brotherly love for Paul, as well as a godly love for reaching the lost (1:16). They understand and respect Paul's apostolic appointment to defend the gospel (Acts 9:15–16, Rom. 1:1–6). The others, however, seek to take advantage of his humiliating circumstances for their self-promotion. They preach the gospel of Christ—at least its *design*, but not its *love*—but they do so for the wrong reason and with impure motives, hoping to further diminish Paul's apostolic influence in the churches (1:17).

"What then?" (1:18)—or "How should I to respond to this?" In Paul's humble view, the preaching of the message of Christ is more important than having his character vindicated by other men. God Himself appointed Paul to be a steward of the gospel, and he answered to Him directly (1 Cor. 4:1–4). In the end, God will vindicate him; under the present circumstances, this is unnecessary.[12] Thus, regardless of the motives of those who preach, at least the gospel is *being* preached. This indicates that the transmission of information itself is accurate, even among those who preach it out of selfish ambition.[13] "Christ is proclaimed" is the real objective, and Paul sees this as reason for rejoicing.

At the time of writing, Paul had been in Roman custody for about two years. This long, grueling ordeal is near its end, however, and no doubt this fact contributes to his positive outlook on his ministry. His comments indicate confidence that he will soon be released, and he credits this prospect not only to God's providence but also the many prayers offered by the Philippian Christians on his behalf (1:19). On the other hand, "deliverance" carries another sense: he may be delivered from prison to continue his apostolic ministry, or he may be delivered from this life altogether—i.e., face execution by decree of Emperor Nero—to be with Christ.

The phrase "Spirit of Jesus Christ" is unique in the NT. This is not a different "Spirit" than the Holy Spirit of God but is one and the same (Rom. 8:9). The Holy Spirit, then, is "of God" as He is "of Jesus Christ," yet He remains one Spirit and an individual personality of the Godhead (Eph. 4:4).[14] "[A]ccording to my earnest expectation ... " (1:20)—the Greek word here indicates someone turning his head to see something important.[15] Paul eagerly anticipates that Christ will not allow him to be "put to shame" (or, have any cause for regret) for what he has suffered in His name (2 Tim. 1:12). Instead, he rightly believes that Christ will glorify His name through himself. "[W]hether by life or by death" does not mean he has no knowledge of the outcome of his imprisonment (see 1:24–25), but that Christ will be honored through him regardless of that outcome.

Questions

1.) One's imprisonment for his faith might seem to have a negative effect on fellow believers. Yet, Paul's imprisonment had a *positive* effect on the church. Why was this? Did Paul's personal attitude have anything to do with this—in other words, might the effect on others have been different if he had not been such an optimistic prisoner?

2.) Paul's attitude toward those who preached the gospel for the wrong motives was, in essence, "At least Christ is being preached" (1:15–18). Should we have this same attitude toward this same kind of preacher today? Is preaching with the wrong attitude the same thing as preaching the wrong message? Why or why not?

3.) Likely, we understand how Christ is exalted in a believer's life, but how would He be exalted in that person's *death* (1:19–20)? What bearing does one's *life* have to do with whether he (or she) can honor his Lord in his *death*?

Lesson Three:
Encouragement to Live in a Worthy Manner
(Phil. 1:21—2:4)

Having described his circumstances, Paul now uses these to draw practical lessons for the Philippian Christians. "For to me, to live is Christ and to die is gain" (1:21)—this is well-known verse serves as an excellent summary of the Christian's perspective. Regardless of whether Paul lives or dies, Christ is the object of his adoration; whatever the outcome, faith in Him works to a beneficial end. To "die" in the Greek (here) indicates an accomplished action; thus, it does not refer to the dying process, but what happens after death. If Paul remains upon this earth, he will continue to serve Christ and fulfill his ministry to Him; if he leaves this earth, he will forever be with the One whom he has loved for so long (1:22).

A Difficult Dilemma (1:23–26): But Paul admits he does "not know which to choose"—this does not mean that he has the luxury *of* choosing, but that he does not know which outcome will be in the best interest of all parties involved. We see him weighing out both sides in his mind (1:23). Certainly, to be with Christ would be "very much better" than to remain here on this earth, but Paul's heart is also with the Philippians and many others who would spiritually profit from the continuation of his ministry. Having considered both prospects, Paul selflessly accepts what he knows to be the case: he will "remain on in the flesh" for the benefit of the church and the spread of the gospel (1:24).[16] "Convinced" of this fact, Paul looks forward to contributing to the Philippians' progress and their collective "joy in the faith" (1:25). This serves as a positive answer to their prayers and is the basis for their "proud confidence" that they have in him (1:26). It is Paul's full intention to come to Philippi sometime soon after his release from Roman imprisonment to fulfill his joy as well as theirs.

The Philippians' Expected Conduct (1:27–30): Regardless of whether he does come to them, Paul admonishes the Philippians to live as godly people. "Only conduct yourselves in a worthy manner of the gospel of Christ" (1:27) follows a familiar theme throughout Paul's epistles: one's association with Christ demands personal responsibility and spiritual integrity (Eph. 4:1, Col. 1:10, 1 Thess. 2:12, etc.). Furthermore, Paul wants to hear that they are "standing firm" and "striving together" for the faith. "Standing" refers to a grounded, stabilized position (see Col. 2:6–7), as opposed to slipping, backsliding, or falling. To "strive together" indicates a cooperative effort toward a singular objective, rather than striving *against* one another (as in 1 Cor. 3:3). Christians cannot reach these positive objectives unless they are:

- ❑ **conducting themselves in a worthy manner.** The believer's lifestyle must be consistent with the expected behavior of a disciple of the Master (1 John 2:4–6). This also implies that if there is a "worthy" manner, then all "manners" that digress from or contradict *this* one are unworthy and inappropriate.
- ❑ **in one spirit.** This means, united by God's Spirit, even though the word "spirit" here does not specifically refer to Him. People can be united in one *human* spirit to do very bad things (e.g., when the Jews were of one "impulse" to kill Stephen—Acts 7:57), but people who are united with God's Spirit will glorify God and live as His people (Eph. 4:3).
- ❑ **with one mind.** While "in one spirit" implies a *spiritual* attitude conditioned by God's own Holy Spirit, "with one mind" indicates people working together for a common goal, as one sports team works together to defeat an opposing team. The "faith of the gospel" is the belief system based upon God's revealed word.

By working together in unity with God's Spirit, the Philippians will have no reason to fear the adversaries of the gospel (1:28). This does not mean that these opponents will not bother them, or that they will not enjoy a measure of apparent success. What it does mean is that believers should not shrink back from walking worthily, standing firm, and striving together because of their fear of these opponents (see Heb. 10:36–39). Paul does not identify the "opponents" here, but later he does warn the church of those of the "false circumcision" (see comments on 3:2–3). "[W]hich is a sign of destruction for them"—i.e., the faith of the gospel will reveal their opponents for what they are—enemies of God—and will speak to their ruin. The "sign [or, evidence]" here may refer to the historical example of all those who persecuted God's people in the past (i.e., in the Old Testament [OT] record). None of those antagonists escaped divine judgment; they were all destroyed (compare Deut. 32:35 and 2 Peter 2:3b). Thus, the same gospel serves to vindicate those who believe in it also condemns those who resist it (2 Cor. 2:14–16).

"For to you it has been granted … " (1:29–30)—on the surface, this supports the man-made Doctrine of Predestination (a.k.a. Calvinism), in which God allegedly foreordains the spiritual future of every person. Yet, as in every other case where he puts forward the concept of predestination, Paul speaks of the collective of believers (i.e., the church) rather than individual Christians (Rom. 8:29–30, Eph. 1:4–5, 11, etc.). In other words, *the spiritual body of Christ* is predestined (or, "granted" by God) to believe in Him *and* suffer for His name's sake (Rom. 8:16–17). A simple analogy will explain this: suppose you wish to go to Seattle by way of a bus, and so you talk to a certain bus driver. He says, "*This bus*"—referring to the one he operates—"is predestined to go to Seattle." This statement does not refer to what (or how many) people will be on the bus when it leaves, only that the bus is scheduled to go to Seattle. Whether *you* get on his bus does not change this fact. However, once you *are* on his bus, then you too—because of the vehicle you chose, not because you had no decision otherwise—will be going to Seattle. And, if the bus driver were to speak to those who are on the bus as it is *heading* to Seattle, then he could say, "You are all predestined to go to Seattle." This is true because of their present state of *being* rather than something *forced* upon them.

So it is with the church: God has foreordained that His church is headed for glory, regardless of which or how many human souls comprise this church. Whoever is in this church (and remains faithful to its head) will likewise be predestined for glory—not because he had no free will in the matter, but because he is on the only "vehicle" that God will save. To "believe" in Christ is what Christians do, and to "suffer" for the sake of Christ is what Christians must endure (Mat. 5:10–12, 2 Tim. 1:12). Thus, Paul is saying, in essence, "Remain faithful to the gospel in which you first believed and be willing to suffer for it, yet do not think that your suffering is something unusual or that it destroys the credibility of that gospel" (see 2 Tim. 2:9–10 and 1 Peter 4:12–16 for similar thoughts).

The Mindset of the Believer (2:1–4): "Therefore … " (2:1) indicates practical conclusions based upon what Paul has already said. If the Philippians are walking rightly, working in unity with God's Spirit, striving together for the gospel, and even suffering for the sake of Christ, then Paul should expect them to be of a certain "mind" or attitude. What follows (2:1–4) does not suggest that the Philippians are thinking otherwise, but Paul's admonition is to *keep on* pursuing a Christ-centered attitude, regardless of their circumstances or the opponents they face.[17] "If" in this section really means "since": *since* there are these things, a certain response is expected. The four clauses in this verse (2:1) are conditioned upon actions in the next verse being met (2:2):

❑ "encouragement in Christ" indicates any spiritual praise or reinforcement that Christians provide for one another that imitates that which they receive from the Lord.
❑ "consolation of love" refers to the comfort or support that Christian love offers when fellow believers act in the best interest of each other (compare 2 Cor. 1:3–5).
❑ "fellowship of the Spirit" means that believers who have communion with Christ also have communion with God's Spirit (2 Cor. 13:14), and that neither of these situations can exist without the other. This phrase can be taken two ways—fellowship *with* the Spirit and fellowship that is learned *from* the Spirit—and either way is fitting.
❑ "any affection and compassion" refers to any of the inward feelings that result from a common union with the Lord. "Compassion" can also be (and often is) translated as "mercy" in the NT and refers to the withholding of what one deserves (such as punishment) in anticipation of one's reform. Mercy is virtually always associated with patience, longsuffering, toleration, and forbearance (see Col. 3:12–15).

"[M]ake my joy complete" (2:2) does not mean the Philippians have not yet brought Paul any joy—quite the contrary, he speaks very highly of them (recall 1:3–8). Yet, he wants this joy to reach its fullest extent (1 John 1:4). Thus, while the Philippians have done well so far, he wants them to *continue* doing well (compare 1 Thess. 4:1). This requires the meeting of conditions defined in this passage:

- ❑ **"same mind"**—see comments above on 1:27. This does not mean "same opinions," because fellowship in Christ is not based on human opinions. It does not mean "same conclusions," because an entire group of people can be united in a conclusion that is entirely wrong. Thus, "same mind" requires that that "mind" be set on Christ, and if everyone involved *has* that mind then they will enjoy the fellowship that it produces.
- ❑ **"same love"**—not a selfish or selective love, but one based upon Christ's love for us (John 13:34–35, "as I have loved you"). It is popular for people to define "love" on their own terms and then use *those* terms in their religion. The "same love" to which Paul refers is defined by Christ, not any individual believer, church leadership, or congregation.
- ❑ **"united in spirit"** means what it says: united upon a common element—in this case, God's Holy Spirit—in order to reach a common goal.[18] Thus, Christians' unity is spiritual, not necessarily physical: a congregation—or the entire brotherhood of Christ—does not have to be literally assembled together to be "united," but *does* need to "be diligent to preserve the unity of the Spirit in the bond of peace" (Eph. 4:3).
- ❑ **"intent on one purpose"** indicates that Christians are to focus on something outside of (and bigger than) themselves—a transcendent, heavenly objective rather than a transient or personal one. The unity of inward or spiritual beliefs will be revealed through outward cooperation with those of like beliefs. When believers focus on Christ, they learn to work together for His sake and will overcome any difficulties they face along the way.

"Selfishness [or, rivalry]" and "empty conceit" have no place in the brotherhood (2:3–4). Such things are the seeds of division, not unity (1 Cor. 1:10). Thus, we are to consider one another with humility (or, lowliness of mind) rather than seeking to please ourselves (Rom. 15:2). Humility—the voluntary *lowering* of oneself while choosing to *raise up* (or defer to) another—is the opposite of pride. Human pride always seeks to exalt itself over another, exert itself against another, or extol itself in the presence of another. Pride always seeks self-gratification at the expense of someone else. Humility, on the other hand, regards others as more important than oneself. (This does not mean that every person *is* more important in every respect, but that this is how the humble person chooses to *treat* him.[19]) If Christ, being the Son of God, can regard us with such dignity and respect, then certainly we who are equals in His sight ought to treat one another with such humility (Rom. 12:10). Instead of seeking to promote our own views, our own agendas, or our own good points, we are to consider the interests of others first.

Questions

1.) Paul said, "For to me, to live is Christ" (1:21). What does the phrase "to live is Christ" mean? What does this necessarily imply that the believer's ideal view *of* his life ought to be?

2.) Notice that when Paul talks about the hereafter, he does not mention heavenly mansions or streets of gold, but about being with the Lord (1:23; see 2 Cor. 5:6–8). What is significant about this perspective? Does this mean it is inappropriate to look forward to the *glories* of heaven—like streets of gold and such? Please explain.

3.) To conduct ourselves "in a manner worthy of the gospel" (1:27) necessarily implies that there is a prescribed pattern by which God intends for us to live. Yet, suppose a person who identifies as a Christian chooses *not* to live according to that manner or pattern. Can he choose an equally acceptable manner, if he claims to be sincere and a good person?

4.) Does "being of the same mind" (2:2) mean:

    a.   we must all completely agree with each other on every religious topic?

    b.   any disagreement over our understanding of any Scripture must result in a break in fellowship with each other (until we all see things the same way)?

    c.   we are not permitted to challenge a fellow Christian's belief on his understanding of Scripture?

    d.   once our congregation (or elders) reaches a consensus, we dare not question this?

    e.   it is impossible to be "united in spirit" and "intent on one purpose" unless we all have the exact same beliefs, perspectives, and levels of spiritual maturity?

    f.   we must agree upon what is required for fellowship with God and His people, but we are entitled to individual convictions on things not required for this fellowship?

    g.   Or, how do *you* understand this phrase to mean—and must we all agree with you?

5.) If we are supposed to look out for "the interests of others" (2:4), does this mean that our own interests are unimportant, or that we must always sacrifice these for the sake of someone else? Who decides what or whose "interest" is to prevail?

Lesson Four:
The Pre-eminent Example of Christ
(Phil. 2:5-11)

Whatever disposition Paul requires of the Philippians is drawn from the pre-eminent example of the Master (Christ)—thus, "Have [His] attitude in yourselves [or, Let {His} mind be within you]" (2:5). The believer is not only to take on Christ's name, but also (to the best of his ability) His *heart*. This necessarily demands a proper attitude toward those who also belong to Him. Christ voluntarily chose to humble Himself for the sake of others on a level that exceeds human comprehension, since He (a divine Being) lowered Himself to human life (2:6ff). If the Lord can do this for us who are so undeserving, then *how much more* should Christians do this for each other, especially when we are all equals (both as humans and brethren)?

Christ "Emptied" Himself (2:6–8): In His pre-incarnate life, Jesus existed as a divine Personage of the Godhead (2:6; see John 1:1–3). While it is incorrect to identify Jesus as "the Father," it is entirely accurate to say that Jesus was (is) "God." This means both He and the Father share the same divine nature; they are both uncreated, eternal, and sovereign beings that are above the Creation in every respect. Equality (or unity) *with* the Father is not to be confused with having the exact same identity *as* the Father (John 10:30). God the Father has His identity; God the Son has His own separate identity; yet both are divine Personages of the triune "God" (or Godhead). If you struggle to wrap your head around all of this, you are not alone. We are not meant to fully comprehend all this; we are only to believe that it is *real* and *true*.

While our knowledge of Jesus' preexistence is considerably limited, this much we know for certain: before Jesus came to us in the flesh (John 1:14), He embodied the essential nature and character of God. He "did not regard equality with God a thing to be grasped"—i.e., it was not wrong for Christ to regard Himself as equal to God (see John 5:18–24);

it was also not wrong for Him to divest Himself of His heavenly glory in order to serve as our Redeemer.[20] It was necessary that Jesus be identified literally with those whom He came to save, as the following passages indicate:

- ❑ "And the Word became flesh, and dwelt among us, and we saw His glory, glory as of the only begotten from the Father, full of grace and truth" (John 1:14).
- ❑ "For what the Law could not do, weak as it was through the flesh, God did: sending His own Son in the likeness of sinful flesh and as an offering for sin, He condemned sin in the flesh … " (Rom. 8:3).
- ❑ "He [God] made Him [Jesus] who knew no sin to be sin on our behalf, so that we might become the righteousness of God in Him" (2 Cor. 5:21, bracketed words added).
- ❑ "But we do see Him who was made for a little while lower than the angels, namely, Jesus, because of the suffering of death crowned with glory and honor, so that by the grace of God He might taste death for everyone. For it was fitting for Him, for whom are all things, and through whom are all things, in bringing many sons to glory, to perfect the author of their salvation through sufferings" (Heb. 2:9–10).
- ❑ "For we do not have a high priest who cannot sympathize with our weaknesses, but One who has been tempted in all things as we are, yet without sin" (Heb. 4:15).

Christ did not need to continue to "grasp" onto (or, continue to cling to or maintain) His divine glory. At the same time, we could not have grasped His glory—or His role as our sacrificial Lamb—if He had come to us in His heavenly state of being. It is wrong to claim that Jesus gave up being God to become human, since this was not necessary and did not happen. It is accurate to say that when Jesus became a Man, He did not cease to be God. This is impossible for us to understand; it is like saying, "The apple became an orange without ceasing to be an apple." Lenski says, "Paul simply states the fact; he does not philosophize about its possibility. Facts are facts whether Paul or we are able to understand their possibility or not."[21] Yet, it was necessary that God (in the Person of Christ) die for His Creation, since no one else could provide the atonement necessary for human sin. Thus, "He emptied Himself" (2:7)—i.e., Christ divested Himself of His heavenly privileges, but not His essential nature.[22] He voluntarily relinquished—for the purpose that His coming to us "in the flesh" required—the rights and honor He deserved as the Creator (John 17:4, Col. 1:15–17) to save His Creation. He took on the form of an earthly "bond-servant" rather than retain His heavenly "form of God," the One worthy of being served.[23] Not only this, but He took upon Himself "the likeness of men," which was an unfathomable step downward from His equality with God.

Jesus not only assumed the form of a human bond-servant; He also subjected Himself to a human death, "even death on a cross" (2:8).[24] The cross was not just a painful, horrific, and torturous way to die; it was purposely designed to strip every shred of human dignity from the one being crucified. It was as if to advertise, "This person was not worthy to have ever lived!" In subjecting Himself to the cross, Jesus subjected Himself to a most demeaning, humiliating, and (for some) inexplicable death. The jeering, ridicule, and taunting contributed negatively to this awful experience, as did the beating with fists, pummeling with reeds, and contemptuous spittle of ungodly men (Mat. 27:27–30). Added to this were the crown of thorns and insinuations of being a false king and a false prophet ("Prophesy to us!"—Mat. 26:68).

Then there was the scourging—a brutal whipping with leather straps embedded with bone or bits of metal—which was purposely designed to draw blood and lacerate the body (Mark 10:34, 15:15). Instead of the sanitized, effeminate-looking images of Jesus with small trickles of blood coming down from the crown of thorns (that artists have handed down to us), it is likely that Jesus was beaten and bloodied beyond recognition. After all this, He was forced to lay upon His flayed back while Roman soldiers mercilessly pounded rough metal spikes through His wrists and feet and into His cross, then erected this cross and set it into a hole in the ground. To cap off this wretched experience, Christ was crucified between two men who in fact *deserved* to die—two common criminals who represented the offenders of all of humanity (Luke 23:33). For six hours, Jesus hung upon the cross, His back and sides horribly lacerated, His face bruised and swollen, His body covered with blood, spittle, sweat, and dirt, His heart pounding, and His lungs gasping for breath. This is not a nice, clean, sterilized picture of death; this is death in all of its unspeakable gruesomeness (Psalm 22:7–8, 13–18, and Isa. 52:14).

The Philippians are no doubt familiar with this scene. It is possible that retired soldiers who were members of the church in Philippi even participated in conducting a crucifixion. If not, then it is even more likely that these men have witnessed death by crucifixion, since this kind of execution is Rome's way of keeping law and order. Thus, Paul does not have to go into all the dreadful details of Jesus' death; they have seen this kind of death with their own eyes. (In contrast, most of us today probably would not have the stomach to witness an actual crucifixion.) Yet Paul does not focus only on the manner of Jesus' death, but more so the *injustice* of it. Being the Son of God, Jesus deserved to be honored and worshiped, never humiliated and tortured. He had committed no sin but was "obedient to the point of death"—He never committed a single crime and thus was not worthy of any punishment. Nonetheless, He died a truly innocent man, and His death became the most inhumane act and worst injustice that the world has ever seen: the Creation's murder of its own Creator.

God Exalts His Son (2:9–11): Having descended into the very darkest, most pitiful experience of what it means to be "human," Jesus then ascended from that place through His resurrection (John 10:18). Having walked out of His own grave, God then highly exalted His Son for His obedience, worthiness, and self-sacrifice (2:9). The Lamb of God had been slain, but now He lives again by His own power! His blood had been shed to redeem countless souls, but He bleeds and suffers no more (Rev. 5:6–10). In His human state, Jesus was made "a little while lower than the angels" (Heb. 2:9), but He is no longer human (2 Cor. 5:16), He is no longer humiliated, and now He reigns over all of heaven. The Name of Jesus—referring to His position, authority, and divine nature— is no longer a name of alleged weakness or reproach, as it seemed to those who crucified Him, but is a name of power, glory, and salvation (Acts 4:12).

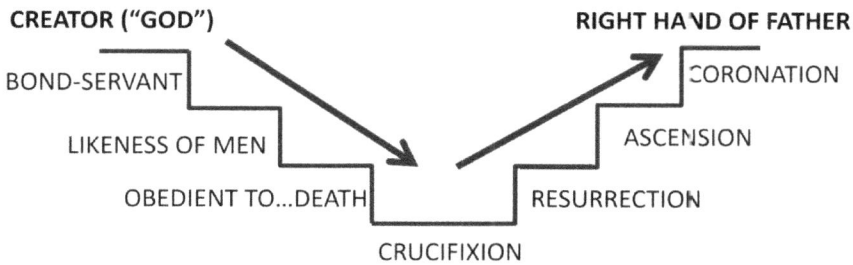

CREATOR ("GOD")   RIGHT HAND OF FATHER
BOND-SERVANT   CORONATION
    LIKENESS OF MEN   ASCENSION
        OBEDIENT TO...DEATH   RESURRECTION
                    CRUCIFIXION

"[A]t the name of Jesus every knee will bow" (2:10)—a quote lifted from Isa. 45:23 in reference to God Himself, which again makes Jesus an equal with God (as a divine Being). Paul refers to some future occasion, as in the Final Judgment, in which every authority that exists in heaven or on earth (Eph. 1:22–23, Col. 1:16) will profess submission and render homage to the King of kings and Lord of lords (2:11; see Rev. 19:16). Christ was a Servant to us to become our Redeemer, yet He is a Servant no more, but rules over all that has been created. "[T]o the glory of God the Father"—the ultimate purpose of Christ's servitude as well as His triumphant reign over the kingdom of God is to bring honor and praise to His Father.

Questions

1.) Can a Christian "empty" himself exactly as Christ did (2:7)? If so, what should this "emptying" look like? If not, why does Paul offer Christ as a model example of what we are to practice, if we cannot do this (2:5)?

2.) Notice that before Jesus was exalted *by* His Father and was glorified, He first had to undergo suffering *for* Him (2:7–9). Does this concept of suffering as a *route to* or as a *means of* entering glory also apply to Christians?

a.   What does obedience have to do with suffering (in this context)?

b.   What if one Christian suffers *more* than another—is it fair that they should both receive the same reward?

c.   What if a Christian goes through life with comparatively little "suffering"—will he (or she) still enter glory?

3.)   Will God exalt the faithful believer in the hereafter in a similar manner to how He exalted His Son? If not, what *do* we have to look forward to in that realm? If so, what will be the basis for such divinely bestowed praise?

Lesson Five:
Working Out One's Salvation
(Phil. 2:12–18)

Working Out One's Salvation (2:12–13): Returning to his earlier thought, Paul repeats his admonition to be faithful and obedient regardless of whether he comes to them soon (2:12; recall 1:27). "[W]ork out your salvation with fear and trembling" does *not* mean "Save yourselves by your own works," since Paul has taught elsewhere (e.g., Gal. 5:1–4) that human effort is unable to bring about spiritual salvation. Nonetheless, each believer is responsible to live obediently to the Lord since this is our "work" *as* believers. God is faithful to do His part; we must be faithful to do ours. Working out one's salvation requires a constant application of those things that make salvation real and anticipated.[25]

Thus, the Philippians must obey Paul's apostolic authority, but in the end each believer personally answers to God. This warning also implies the possibility of *failure* to maintain human faith; otherwise, the "fear and trembling" aspect is meaningless. "Fear" can mean reverence or terror, depending on the context; in the present case, both meanings apply. We ought to have great reverence for God and recognize our smallness in comparison to His greatness (Heb. 12:28). At the same time, we ought to be afraid of the power that God possesses to *destroy* those who are disobedient to Him (Mat. 10:28). Thus, "fear" has to do with God as much as it does the difficulty of the task laid before us. Despite our best efforts, we are still dependent upon the mercy and grace of God to compensate for our inadequacy.

Another reason to conduct oneself with "fear and trembling" is because "God … is at work in you" (2:13). It is an awesome and sobering realization to know that the God of heaven is directly intervening in one's life. No one can bring about his own salvation; only through the will of God actively working in one's life (and soul) can he be saved. It is not as though we are putting forth a little effort and God is doing far more; rather, it is that we are putting forward *all* our efforts and God is putting forth all *His* effort. Only when our will is in harmony with His, however, can the union of these two efforts—immensely unequal in performance, yet equal in necessity—bring about the perfect result. It is God's will and "good pleasure" that we are saved (1 Tim. 2:3–4).

The Believer's Responsibility (2:14–16): Perhaps *because* the Philippians have been doing so well, Paul needs to caution them against rivalries and competitions. "Grumbling" and "disputing" (2:14) may be the result of one person pitting his accomplishments against that of another, and the other person rebutting him. Such displays of worldly behavior only give opponents of Christians reason to criticize them. Instead, believers are to be blameless of any legitimate accusations of wrongdoing and innocence of evil (2:15; see Titus 2:6–8 and 1 Peter 2:12). "Children of God" must hold themselves to a far better and higher standard than that of sons of darkness (Eph. 5:7–13). Every generation of the unconverted is "crooked and perverse"; no generation is free from such moral blight.[26] It is our responsibility to provide "light" and "salt" to a lost and dying world (Mat. 5:13–16); we cannot do this if we imitate the world's selfish conduct. The "lights" here literally refers to cosmic luminaries—the sun, moon, and stars. Likewise, we are not merely to expose the deeds of darkness, but also to provide illumination for the *right* way in which to walk instead.

"[H]olding fast the word of life" (2:16) means to cling tenaciously to the gospel of Christ without letting go, but also holding it forth as a torch to light the path that leads to God. The word of God is a light to our own path (Psalm 119:105), but when we reflect this light, it becomes a source of illumination for others as well. "[S]o that ... I will have reason to glory"—i.e., Paul does not want to have his work among the Philippians to be in vain; he wants to give a favorable account of them when he stands before the Lord (compare 1 Thess. 2:19–20). For "the day of Christ," see comments on 1:6.

Paul's View of His Ministry (2:17–18): Yet, while Paul holds open the possibility that Christ will return in his own lifetime, he also holds open the possibility of his own execution (2:17). A "drink offering" (a.k.a. libation) alludes to the oil or wine that accompanied grain offerings prescribed by the Law of Moses (Lev. 2:1, 23:13, etc.). In one sense, Paul sees himself as an offering that is alongside (but not equal to) Christ's own offering (2 Tim. 4:6).

In another sense, Paul considers his life as a type of accompanying sacrifice for the brethren at Philippi and elsewhere. This latter sense is supported by what follows—"the sacrifice and service of your faith"—as though the two ministries (Paul's and the Philippians') worked together for one grand sacrifice of service to God. (In this view, Paul considers himself as the smallest part of the offering, and the Philippians' work as the main offering.[27]) If Paul must die for the sake of fellow believers, then it will be a worthwhile and noble death. In anticipation of this possibility, Paul has reason to rejoice and communicate his joy with them, since this will be a fruitful and rewarding conclusion to his apostolic work. This joy is, of course, to be reciprocated by the Philippians in their appreciation for all that Paul has done for them (2:18).

Questions

1.) How do we reconcile *working out* our salvation (2:12) and our having been saved by divine grace that is not dependent upon our *works* (Eph. 2:8–9)?

2.) If God is "at work" in us (2:13), then does this mean that there is *supernatural* activity going on in the life and heart of the believer (see Eph. 3:16–20)?

    a. If not, then how can that person claim to depend upon the grace of God—and why should he bother to pray for divine intervention?

b. If so, then (while this activity does not manifest itself in the form of visible miracles) can we give direct credit to God's Holy Spirit for bringing about one's spiritual transformation and renewal (2 Cor. 4:16 and Col. 3:9–10)?

3.) What exactly is our function or purpose as "lights in the world" (2:15)?

a. How can our light be of any value if it is hidden (Matthew 5:14–16) or does not expose what is in the darkness (Ephesians 5:7–12)?

b. Can we understand our role as "lights" to be not only a state of being but also a moral responsibility which we have accepted? Please explain.

Lesson Six:
The Coming of Timothy and Epaphroditus
(Phil. 2:19–30)

While we know of no internal problems within the church at Philippi, certainly these Christians faced external pressure and persecution from the Jews (as in nearly every place that churches have been established). They may have also experienced residual fallout from the same craftsmen who had Paul and Silas arrested (see Acts 16:16ff). Thus, Paul plans to send two men, Timothy (2:19) and Epaphroditus (2:25), to give them encouragement while he himself remains in prison. The Philippians know of both men and have a good rapport with them. Timothy will be sent to observe the true nature of the church in Philippi and will send a report of their "condition" back to Paul—a report that Paul anticipates will be positive (2:19).

Paul's High Regard for Timothy (2:19–24): Paul often dispatched Timothy, one of his most trusted protégés, to various hot spots within the brotherhood, as an extension of Paul's own influence. Paul has a fatherly affection for Timothy, calling him his "true child in the faith" (1 Tim. 1:2) and his "beloved son" (2 Tim. 1:2). But here he gives his greatest compliment to this fine man: "For I have no one else of kindred spirit … " (2:20). The phrase "kindred spirit" comes from a single Greek word [*isopsuchos*] which means "like-minded."[28] In Paul's estimation, Timothy knows Paul better than any other man knows him, and he shares Paul's passion for the Lord and his love for the brethren, making him an ideal representative of Paul: he will be as "genuinely [or, naturally]" concerned for the church's welfare as Paul is. This disposition of Timothy's contrasts with other brethren (who were with Paul at the time?) who sought their own interests, but not always the Lord's (2:21). The Philippians had already seen Timothy's character and his "proven worth" firsthand, so that Paul does not need to endorse him any further (2:22). In serving Paul, he is "like a child serving his father"—a fitting match, since Timothy's father is not a Christian (Acts 16:3) and Paul has no biological children. Paul plans to come to Philippi himself when he is released from prison, but at this point he is still waiting for a definite outcome to his circumstances (2:23–24).

Paul's Commendation of Epaphroditus (2:25–30): Meanwhile, Paul has also sent Epaphroditus—the assumed bearer of this epistle—because he also is a very capable man, and because of his personal interest in the situation at Philippi (2:25). Paul calls Epaphroditus "my brother and fellow worker and fellow soldier"—a compliment of high praise, especially coming from a Christian soldier like Paul. Furthermore, he refers to him as "your messenger and minister to my need," indicating a man who is trustworthy and not afraid to serve.[29]

Epaphroditus had come *from* Philippi (at an indefinite time in the past), having delivered a gift from those Christians to Paul (see 4:18). Now, Paul is returning the favor by sending this valuable worker back to them for their spiritual encouragement. Likewise, Epaphroditus himself wants to go to Philippi, since the news of his personal illness has brought added distress to the Philippians and he wants them to know that he has recovered (2:26–27).[30] This must have been a severe sickness, one "to the point of death," but God spared him to continue his ministry to Paul and the churches. For this, Paul is thankful since the news of Epaphroditus' death would have dealt a strong blow to his own state of mind. "[S]orrow upon sorrow" indicates the sorrowfulness that Paul has already experienced as a prisoner—the only dark expression in this otherwise bright and optimistic epistle.

"Receive him ... and hold men like him in high regard" (2:29)—a statement like what Paul has written elsewhere (see 1 Cor. 16:15–16 and 1 Thess. 5:12–13). Those who devote their lives in service to the Lord and His churches are worthy of honorable reception and high reputation. Particularly, those who put their own lives on the line for the brethren are to be commended for such self-sacrifice (Rom. 16:3–4, 2 Cor. 11:23–28, etc.). "Minister" (2:25) and "service" (2:30) come from the same Greek root word which indicates a priestly service or spiritual ministry.[31]

Questions

1.) By referring to Timothy as a "kindred spirit" (2:20), Paul implied
that he was closer to him (and his personality) than were other
Christians. Is it appropriate, then, for *us* to be closer to some
Christians than others? Do these closer relationships constitute
a "clique" or division within the church, or is this natural and
expected? Please explain.

2.) Paul was an expert at dispatching the right people—like Timothy
or Epaphroditus—to the right place for dealing with demanding
situations in the brotherhood. Can any of us do this today—dispatch
skilled help to where it is most needed in the brotherhood—or was
Paul's administrative work unique because of his apostleship?

SECTION THREE:
THE HEAVENLY PERSPECTIVE (3:1–21)

Lesson Seven:
Gaining Christ through the Sacrifice of All Things
(Phil. 3:1–11)

"**F**inally" (3:1)—lit., "as to what remains"—is often used to indicate the closing of a letter. Paul may have *meant* to close the letter here originally, but then thought it necessary to add the following material (an entire chapter's worth!). He appears to pick up later (in 4:4) where he leaves off here.

An Encouragement and Warning (3:1–3): In any case, Paul's mind has clearly transitioned to different subjects than what he has just covered. His encouragement to "rejoice in the Lord" (3:1) is exceptional, coming from a man imprisoned for two years. The cause for or source of this rejoicing has nothing to do with his circumstances, however, but is "in the Lord." Many people in world rejoice over things that are not of God (e.g., Rom. 1:32); yet Christians alone are able to rejoice "in the Lord" over whatever will advance the cause of Christ. Rejoicing, then, is a personal expression of gratitude and satisfaction for one's participation in the work of God. Likewise, "joy" is second among Paul's description of the "fruit of the Spirit" (Gal. 5:22–23), indicating its importance and relevance in the Christian's walk *with* the Spirit. This is not the first time in the present epistle that Paul has focused on "joy" or "rejoicing" (recall 1:25); yet he sees no difficulty in the healthy repetition of this thought.

"Beware of the dogs ... " (3:2–3)—this is Paul's assessment of those Jews who pride themselves on their heritage, conformity to the Law of Moses, and controlling interest over Gentile converts (Gal. 6:12–13). People in the ancient world did not regard dogs as household pets as they do today, but as useless and expendable scavengers. They often roamed through the countryside in packs as wild animals (like jackals or dingoes). The Jews habitually regarded Gentiles as dogs (Mat. 15:26) or worthless people. In a sad reversal of fortune, Jews who reject the gospel (which many Gentiles have readily received) become "dogs" instead, having repudiated the message that came from heaven (compare Acts 13:46).

In the present passage (3:2–3), "dogs," "evil workers," and "the false circumcision" all refer to the same people: Jewish teachers who either wholly reject the gospel of Christ or malign it with their imposed teachings of Law, rituals (like circumcision), and justification by works. Such men consider themselves to be pious and righteous to God, yet Jesus calls them "a synagogue of Satan" (Rev. 2:9; compare John 8:44–47). "False circumcision" refers to a circumcision that really does not accomplish anything.[32] The "{true} circumcision" refers to an action that Christ performs upon the human heart—i.e., the removal of the condemnation of God (Col. 2:11–12)—thus, transformation of the heart versus cutting of the flesh. Physical circumcision no longer has any spiritual significance; it no longer serves as a sign of a covenant relationship between men and God (as before; see Gen. 17:10–11). Spiritual circumcision is a matter of the heart, not the human body; one's confidence is no longer on what he does in the flesh, but what Christ does for him (Rom. 2:28–29). Only such people can "worship in the Spirit of God" because they seek to worship Him in spirit and truth (John 4:23–24) rather than seeking to justify themselves through physical works.

Paul Recalls His Past (3:4–6): Even though Paul has just warned not to put any confidence "in the flesh," he draws upon his own personal experience as a rising star in the Jewish world as being far more sincere and impressive than these other Jews (i.e., "dogs") who flaunt their own heritage and status (3:4; compare 2 Cor. 11:21–28). Paul's point is to show how hopeless it is to put confidence in human achievement as a means of self-justification. It is as if to say, "If anyone ought to boast, it should be me—yet all that I once relied upon is useless in comparison to what I have gained in Christ." Nonetheless, for the sake of argument, Paul lays out his credentials (3:5–6):

- "circumcised the eighth day"—i.e., a valid, covenant-bound member of the nation of Israel, according to the Law of Moses (Lev. 12:3). Paul's point here is to demonstrate his (former) loyalty to the covenant and the Law, to rebuff accusations that he was a traitor to these.
- "of the nation of Israel"—i.e., not a proselyte, but a full-fledged, pure-blooded Jew.
- "of the tribe of Benjamin"—Paul is able to trace his lineage to one of the founding patriarchs of the nation of Israel, by way of genealogical records.
- "a Hebrew of Hebrews"—i.e., not a Hellenist (i.e., a Greek-cultured Jew), but one immersed in Hebrew law, customs, and religion since his youth. This does not mean he has not been educated in secular history, but that he has always stringently maintained the purity of his ancient roots (Acts 22:3).
- "as to the Law, a Pharisee"—referring to one of the strictest sects among the Jews. "Pharisee" is believed to have come from a word meaning "separate." Accordingly, they separated themselves from the common Jews, whom many Pharisees believed were ignorant of the Law and its meaning (John 7:49).[33] Paul states, then, that he is the son of a Pharisee, was a devout Pharisee himself, and was fully committed to that sect's beliefs (Acts 23:6).
- "as to zeal, a persecutor of the church"—i.e., his zeal for defending the Law (as a Pharisee) necessarily led him to silence all those who, in his own mind, violated the Law in order to pursue their blasphemous religion. He was not passive in this defense, but aggressive (see Acts 26:9–11 for his own graphic depiction of this). In this respect, Paul virtually single-handedly instigated an area-wide persecution against the church, which was far more than any of his contemporaries had done.
- "as to righteousness ... , found blameless"—i.e., regarding ceremonial and legal righteousness. If any person were to scrutinize Paul's pre-Christian life, he would see that he was a man who meticulously, piously, and fervently obeyed the Law's smallest details. Like many Jewish teachers, Paul sought righteousness through law-keeping rather than through grace (Rom. 10:2–4), yet at the time did not realize his huge mistake.

Such is the character sketch of a man who justified himself before God, and who defended His honor and His laws more tenaciously than all others. Paul was not an outwardly arrogant man, but in his pre-converted state of mind he did place full confidence "in the flesh," seeking to be justified by his status and credentials rather than by the grace of God.

Counting All Things as Loss for Christ (3:7–11): "But … I have counted [those things] as loss for the sake of Christ" (3:7). This statement marks the crucial turning point in Paul's thinking as well as his life. Indeed, the church and the entire world have never been the same since this great conversion. Though blinded temporarily on the road to Damascus (Acts 9:1–16), his spiritual sight became clearer than ever. He could now see that to which his self-righteousness had previously blinded him. All that he so strenuously pursued through Jewish pride and law-keeping suddenly paled in comparison to what he had discovered in Christ. To count something as "loss" here means to regard it as valueless *in comparison to* or *in exchange for* something else. Thus, Paul's Israelite parentage, Jewish heritage, Pharisaic training, etc. simply could not do for him what Christ alone could do.

"More than that," he continues, "I count all things to be loss … " (3:8)—i.e., not only things pertaining to his religion, but he counted *all* things in *whatever* context as "loss."[34] We must keep in mind that Paul is making *comparative* statements ("This is better than that") rather than *evaluative* statements ("This is worthless; that alone is valuable"). His Jewish upbringing, rabbinic training, life experiences, etc. did not suddenly become valueless since he draws upon these heavily in his apostolic ministry. However, they cannot accomplish for him what he hoped they would do. In comparison to Christ, they are "rubbish" [lit., dung or refuse]; thus, Christ is *worth* the "loss of all things." All of Paul's earthly status and accomplishments (as an Israelite, as a Pharisee, etc.) cannot overcome his sinful disposition before God; despite all his previous efforts, he remained a condemned sinner. Christ, however, changed everything: now he can serve God with a clear conscience and in genuine righteousness.

To "gain Christ" does not merely mean "to be a Christian." It is not merely a change of status (from "sinner" to "Christian") but also implies the establishment of a new relationship with God based upon the intercession of Christ. This more accurately defines "knowing Christ Jesus my Lord" (3:9)—Paul personally identifies *with* Him rather than merely having a fact-based knowledge *of* Him. Likewise, to "be found in Him" (3:10) means to have fellowship with Him and enjoy all the privileges of that fellowship (up to and including salvation itself). "[N]ot having a righteousness of my own … but that which is through faith in Christ"—i.e., not trying to obtain righteousness through works (of law) but in demonstrations of his faith in Christ (Rom. 1:17). The change of heart from a strict, self-righteous Pharisee to an obedient Christian that sought justification by grace was immediate; the fruits of this change would manifest themselves over time.[35] Paul then summarizes the broader scope of this fellowship (3:10–11):

- ❏ "that I may know Him"—personally, experientially, and in a life-transforming manner.
- ❏ "and the power of His resurrection"—the power to raise Jesus from the dead is the same power (and comes from the same Source) that justifies the sinner before God.
- ❏ "and the fellowship [or, sharing] in His sufferings"—i.e., any suffering for His sake and the sake of righteousness (Mat. 5:10–12; see Rom. 8:16–17).
- ❏ "being conformed to His death"—not, "equating my experiences of suffering with His," but, "suffering for the same cause—to do the will of God—as exemplified and epitomized in Christ's own death." Paul "conformed" to Christ's death in his baptism (Rom. 6:3–7), but he continues to conform to that death every time he suffers personal loss and puts to death the will of the flesh for the Lord's sake.
- ❏ "that I may attain to the resurrection from the dead"—or, in the present context, "that I myself may participate in (the) resurrection, just as Jesus did." Paul clearly understands that *all* believers will experience a physical resurrection from the dead in the likeness of Christ's own physical resurrection (Rom. 6:5, 1 Cor. 15:21–23, 1 Thess. 4:13–17, etc.). Thus, "knowing Christ" naturally leads to a

realistic expectation of this resurrection, which will be shared with all those who have been made "worthy" to participate in it (see Luke 20:35).

Questions

1.) Ideally, Christians are to "put no confidence in the flesh" (3:3). But what does this mean, in everyday terms? Since physical circumcision is no longer an issue (as it was in Paul's day), what might be comparable illustrations of a Christian putting confidence in the flesh today?

2.) To gain Christ, must a person truly give up *everything* and count *all things* as "loss" (3:8)? (Consider Mat. 16:24–26 and Luke 14:25–27, 33 in your answer.)

3.) Given the context, why does Paul put so much emphasis on conformity to Jesus' death and resurrection (3:10–11)? Should we also put great emphasis on these things, or should we instead emphasize Jesus' *life* and *virtuous behavior*?

Lesson Eight:
Letting Go to Move Forward
(Phil. 3:12–21)

While Paul's objectives are great, he admits that he is still a work in progress. "Not that I have already obtained {it}" (3:12)—"it" is necessarily implied, but refers to all the things he had just mentioned. "[B]ut I press on so that … "—in essence, "I keep striving to obtain the very thing which Christ made possible for me to obtain." This does not contradict what he said earlier (about not seeking a righteousness of his own—recall 3:9) but emphasizes his own part in this process of being perfected. God does not perfect His saints *apart* from their own effort, but they must fully cooperate *with* Him to this end.

Pressing Forward in Christ (3:13–16): While perfection in Christ is Paul's goal, he remains realistic and practical about how this happens. He will not be saved by an epiphany or mere confidence alone, but through a process of letting go of what hinders him to pursue what will be in his best interest. Thus, "I do not regard myself as having laid hold of it yet"—a restatement of what he just said (in 3:12), yet with renewed emphasis. "[F]orgetting what lies behind and reaching forward to what lies ahead" (3:13) provides a God-given strategy for spiritual maturity. Unfortunately, some Christians may not follow this apostolic instruction. Instead, they try in vain to "reach forward" while *not* forgetting "what lies behind." In other words, they may:

- ❑ choose to be obsessed with their poor decisions or personal failures of the past.
- ❑ allow hurts, offenses, and injustices of the past rob them of joy in the Lord.
- ❑ allow the damaging words of people in their past to discourage their hope for the future.
- ❑ blame others for "why I can't be more spiritual" or "why I can't draw near to God."

- be unwilling to forgive their offenders (or at least cultivate a Christ-like heart *of* forgiveness—Col. 3:12–15).
- cling to brooding anger, bitterness, resentment, and even cynicism as a means of coping with all the wrongs that have been committed against them.
- resign themselves to a "that's just that way I am" disposition—and thus ruin any opportunity for positive change, personal growth, or spiritual maturity.
- refuse to let go of sinful behavior, addictions, and attitudes.
- choose to remain in a pattern of self-destruction and self-limitation.
- make excuses for their *lack* of growth rather than do what it takes to *grow*.
- refuse to "add" to their faith (2 Peter 1:5–7) and then are disappointed when their faith remains small and unproductive.
- be unwilling to believe in the power of the gospel (Rom. 1:16, 1 Cor. 1:18) and its life-transforming message.
- be unwilling to believe in the willingness and/or ability of Christ to overcome their seemingly insurmountable obstacles to salvation.
- refuse to study God's word (2 Tim. 2:15).
- refuse to be devoted to prayer (Col. 4:2).
- refuse to participate in the assemblies of the saints (Heb. 10:24–25).
- try to outsmart God by doing what He said *not* to do but hoping they will be successful anyway (e.g., Mat. 6:24).
- try to hold onto this world while claiming to seek the things above (Col. 3:1–3, 1 John 2:15–17).
- be unwilling to let go of religious or family traditions to embrace "sound doctrine" (or, erroneously think these traditions are *on par with* sound doctrine).
- resist the guidance of the Holy Spirit (Gal. 5:16–17).
- refuse to do the will of the Father (Mat. 7:21).

The point is: we cannot think we are drawing near to God while our heart remains anchored to this fallible life. To "forget" what lies behind does not mean we pretend that the past did not really happen. It means to dwell upon that past no longer; refuse to allow it to dictate the future; refuse to obsess over it at the expense of one's future life with God. "Let us not spend our time either in pondering the gloomy past, and our own unfaithfulness, or in thinking of what we have done, and thus becoming puffed up with self-complacency; but let us keep the eye steadily on the prize, and run the race as though we had just commenced it."[36]

Once we let go of what lies behind us, then we can successfully pursue—by the grace of God—what lies before us. "I press on toward the goal … " (3:14)—the implication is that of an athlete giving everything to win the race, straining forward to cross the finish line, looking to the prize ("the crown of righteousness"—2 Tim. 4:8). This is an "upward call" because it leads the believer heavenward and does not allow him to remain fixed upon the things here below (see Col. 3:1–3). This "call" is "of God in Christ Jesus"—i.e., God has called us with a heavenly calling (Heb. 3:1) through His Son's ministry of reconciliation (2 Cor. 5:18–21).

Thus, "as many as are perfect [or, mature]" will have this attitude of forgetting what lies behind and pressing forward to the upward call (3:15). This instruction compares the mature in Christ to those with far less maturity; thus, "perfect" in this context is relative, not objective.[37] To paraphrase 3:15b: "If your attitude is different than what I have just described, in time God will disclose to you this error (and you will be expected to correct that) [implied]." Even so, we are to live according to what we *presently* know to be true until Scripture reveals otherwise. For this reason, "[L]et us keep living by that same standard to which we have [thus far] attained" (3:16, bracketed words added). This standard (or rule) is the same as what Paul taught in all the churches (1 Cor. 4:17).

The Need to Follow the Pattern (3:17–19): Paul does not just tell others what to think or how to live, but he practices what he preaches. Several times in his epistles he puts himself up as an example for others to follow (1 Cor. 4:16, 11:1, 2 Thess. 3:7–9, etc.): "Brethren, join in following my example … " (3:17). He instructs these Christians to "observe those who walk according to the pattern" that Christ has revealed to Paul. This "according to the pattern" concept has its roots in the Law, where God told Moses to follow the explicit pattern He gave to him concerning the construction of the tabernacle (Exod. 25:9, 40; see Heb. 8:5). The pattern for one's Christian life is far more important than that of a primitive tent of worship; our "temple" is a living thing, not a lifeless structure (1 Cor. 6:19–20). Likewise, the entire spiritual body of Christ is a living organism ("a holy temple in the Lord") that is built according to a specific heavenly pattern (Eph. 2:19–22).[38]

Not everyone who claims to be "of God" walks according to this pattern, however. Those who refuse to comply with this heavenly pattern "are enemies of the cross of Christ" (3:18), since no one can walk contrary to Christ and still be a friend of God (Mat. 12:30, James 4:4). Instead of reaching forward to the upward call of God in Christ, such people fixate on things of this world, which includes their human pride and self-sufficiency (as what we see in the Judaists who preach Christ but trust in "the flesh," as discussed earlier). Their end will be "destruction"—the self-inflicted ruin of their soul—because they resist the word of the cross (1 Cor. 1:18ff). Paul adds a brief but potent threefold description of such people (3:19):

❏ First, their god is not God the Father but their own "appetite [or, belly]." This refers to things that are of this life, temporary in nature, and destined for destruction (Rom. 6:13, 1 John 2:15–17). These are base and dishonorable "animal passions."[39]
❏ Second, they glory in that which is shameful, having repeatedly perverted what is good and honorable (Isa. 5:20). Lack of shame reveals a calloused conscience that no longer discerns between right and wrong: it has been violated so many times that it has lost all moral sensation.
❏ Third, they "set their minds on earthly things"—and thus they have their reward in full, however small and pathetic it is (compare Mat. 6:1–2, 5).

Citizenship in Heaven (3:20–21): In sharp contrast, Christians who follow the God-given pattern are no longer citizens of this world, but "our citizenship is in heaven" (3:20). To be a citizen of heaven (or sons of the kingdom—Mat. 13:38) indicates one's favorable standing with

God and anticipates an eternal fellowship with Him. No wonder, then, that those who have this priceless citizenship "eagerly wait for a Savior" whose return will be to take them home to this heavenly glory (2 Peter 3:11–12, Heb. 9:27–28). When He appears, Christ will "transform" the physical bodies of believers into a glorified state that is in conformity with His own (3:21; see 1 John 3:2).

This brief description leaves questions unanswered, but it is not meant to be comprehensive or even explanatory. It only intends to bring the discussion full circle: while Christ has endured suffering and humiliation as a means of achieving glory, so we also must endure the fellowship of His sufferings (recall 3:10) before entering a glorified state of existence. Paul does not say anything (in the present text) about the resurrection of the righteous or the wicked (compare John 5:28–29) but only to those who are alive at His coming: such people will be transformed and thus prepared for a glorified existence (see 1 Cor. 15:50–53). It is clear, however, that this transformation must also be made possible for those who have already died and will be bodily resurrected, especially since some believers had died in the Lord even during Paul's own lifetime (1 Cor. 15:6, 1 Thess. 4:13–14).

Yet how will Christ do this? How will He *raise* a body that has so decomposed that it is *no longer* a body? Our immediate answer is: If God can fashion dust into a pristine human being (as in Adam's case), then He most certainly can *re*-fashion our "dust" into a new living being. "If he [Christ] can subject *even all things*, the totality of all the powers of the universe, unto himself … , will he not be able to refashion our lowly body so that it will have a form like his own glorious body?"[40] The point is: we tend to focus on logistics, technical details, and natural processes, when all we are *told* to focus on is a belief in an all-powerful and all-knowing God with whom "all things are possible" (Mat. 19:26).

Questions

1.) Please review the bulleted list above (in comments on 3:12–13). Why are some (or many?) Christians unwilling to let go of what *hinders* their walk with God? If anyone deliberately refuses to do what it takes to "press forward," will God save him anyway?

2.) As we strive for spiritual maturity, we are to maintain the "standard" or "pattern" given to us through God's revealed word (3:16–17). Is this pattern required or optional? Must it remain exactly as it was handed down to us or is it amendable? If it *is* amendable, what was the point in giving it to us at all?

3.) Christians must regularly interact with those whose god is their appetite, who glory in shameful thinking and behavior, and who set their minds only on earthly things (3:18). What must we do to resist this persistent negative influence? What are we supposed to do with those of our *own brotherhood* who have embraced these characteristics?

4.) Paul wrote, "our citizenship is in heaven" (3:20). What are some benefits of *citizenship* that enhance our understanding of and connection to the spiritual realm in which Christ dwells?

Section Four:
Reliance upon God (4:1–23)

Lesson Nine:
Dwelling upon Excellence
(Phil. 4:1–9)

P aul's use of "beloved brethren" (4:1) again emphasizes his deep affection for the Christians in Philippi (recall 2:12). At Christ's coming, whenever it happens, Paul hopes to hold the Philippians up as one of the excellent highlights of his ministry. His repeated admonition to "stand firm" (recall 1:27) is a standard theme in all his epistles.

A Call for Peace between Two Believers (4:2–3): "I urge Euodia and … Syntyche … " (4:2–3)—this is a (rare) personal appeal to two women (deaconesses?) who have been of great assistance to Paul's ministry, but now apparently are at odds with each other. We do not know the reason for the disagreement, only that they are to work it out "in harmony in the Lord." Paul asks a "true companion" to mediate in resolving the friction between these two women, but he does not identify this "companion."[41] He also asks this companion to help "Clement and the rest of my fellow workers" there in Philippi, though we do not know of these people other than what is mentioned here. "[W] hose names are written in the book of life"—a reference to God's record of the faithful (see Luke 10:20, Rev. 20:12, and 21:27). In the ancient world, Roman "free" cities had a roster that contained all the names of those who resided there and thus had a right to citizenship. Here, Paul speaks of a much greater roster (or book; recording) of those who have citizenship within the kingdom of God, since "the Lord knows who are His" (2 Tim. 2:19).

Rejoice, Pray, and Find Peace (4:4–7): Earlier in the epistle, Paul wrote, "Finally, my brothers, rejoice in the Lord" (3:1). Now he resumes that thought and expounds upon it: "Rejoice in the Lord always; again I will say, rejoice" (4:4). Joy and rejoicing are obviously major themes of this epistle, and ought to be major themes of the Christian life. "Let your gentle {spirit} be known to all men" (4:5)—the word for "gentle" can be translated here "moderation," "forbearance," or "big-heartedness."[42] These all refer to the same kind of "spirit"—a word not in the text, but necessarily implied—i.e., one who lives in a Christ-like manner among believers and non-believers alike ("all men").

What motivates this behavior is the fact that "The Lord is near." This can refer to the nearness (in time) of Christ's actual appearance (recall 3:20–21); or, figuratively, it can mean that the Lord's presence is always among believers, and He sees all things (as in Mat. 18:20 or Heb. 4:12). The first meaning is the most natural, but then creates an alleged problem among believers: if Paul said that "the Lord is near," and yet 2,000 years have passed, how are we to believe in his credibility?

Jesus made it clear—and Paul underscored this (1 Thess. 5:1–2)—that God has not revealed to us the "times or epochs" that pertain to the future, except in the most general sense (Acts 1:7). We know that Christ will come again; we do not know in what age, year, day, or hour He will come. Paul likely does not mean "near" as in "at any moment," but "His coming is not indefinitely prolonged." Technically-speaking, the Lord *is* "near"—i.e., since we do not know when He will come, His coming is *always* "near." This creates a perpetual anticipation among believers who wait for their visual redemption (1 Thess. 5:4–6). All said, we must take Paul's words in the context of what he was able to know rather than using them to pinpoint a definite time in history when Jesus would come. One thing is clear: when Jesus *does* come, it will be unmistakably evident, and will usher in the end of the physical system (2 Thess. 1:6–9, 2 Peter 3:3–10, and Rev. 1:7).[43]

"Be anxious for nothing … " (4:6)—or, "Do not be troubled with cares or your thoughts," which is a common problem among all people. Jesus addressed this same thing and gave the same antidote as Paul: turn everything over to God (Mat. 6:25–34). "Prayer" is a general term; "supplication" implies calling upon God to *supply* something. In the exercise of prayer, the believer is to leave his anxious fears and concerns with the Lord and make requests of Him ("because He cares for you"—1 Peter 5:6–7). All such requests are to be "with thanksgiving," because God deserves our gratitude, and we do not deserve His kindness. This does not mean that we should only thank Him for things that seem beneficial to us, but we should thank Him for "everything."

Our prayers are not to inform God of anything since He already knows all things (Mat. 6:8). Rather, prayer is an act of faith and a testing of our confidence in His ability to act. In place of our anxious thoughts and apprehensions, God responds with peace "which surpasses all comprehension [lit., the human mind]" (4:7)—i.e., a heavenly, soul-calming, indescribable assurance that God is in control and will not abandon the one who looks to Him in faith (Heb. 11:6, 13:5–6). This calm assurance is available only for those "in Christ Jesus"; God will only guard the heart and mind of those in fellowship with Him.

Thinking on and Practicing Excellence (4:8–9): "Finally, brethren … " (4:8)—the following prescription is the antidote for fear, worry, anxious thoughts, and the dread of one's circumstances. It also cultivates a positive attitude that looks beyond this unstable and fickle world and trusts instead in the stability and certainty of God's world. The "whatever" of this verse includes all things that fit the description of its counterpart. Thus, the things upon which we are to fix our attention include "whatever" is:

- ❑ "true"—truth is what God reveals to men and is the foundation of the Christian's belief in God (John 4:24). It is also the basis for spiritual freedom (John 8:31–32) and the certainty of one's heavenly future.
- ❑ "honorable"—lit., venerated for its character; dignified; upstanding.[44]
- ❑ "right"—in essence, "righteousness," or that which exactly conforms to God's holy nature. Whatever is "right" with God will be beneficial to the human soul; the person who is "right" with God will have nothing to fear in the age to come.

- ❏ "pure"—blameless, innocent, and free from moral corruption.
- ❏ "lovely"—acceptable, pleasing, or welcome (to God); lit., "friendly toward."[45]
- ❏ "of good repute"—or, that which is well-spoken of; words befitting a child of God (as opposed to the gutter language or profanity of worldly people—Eph. 5:3–5).
- ❏ "excellence"—or virtue (same word as in 1 Peter 2:9 and 2 Peter 1:3, 5). In classical Greek literature, this referred to manliness, moral courage to do what is right (regardless of the consequences), or moral goodness of any kind.[46] NT writers have taken this thought to its highest level in defining it as a divine attribute which we are to imitate.
- ❏ "worthy of praise"—lit., exemplary, commendable, or approved (by God).

These are the things upon which the believer is to set his mind, and which will thus govern his good behavior. "Dwell" here means to meditate heavily; take seriously into account; make a reckoning of (with the purpose of drawing conclusions).[47] In another sense, we might think of ruminating upon these things (like a cow chewing its cud) thoughtfully, quietly, and unhurriedly.

The believer is not merely to dwell upon good thoughts, however; he is also to put into practice those things upon which he has given such serious attention (4:9). Christ's church cannot be filled with people who merely think good thoughts; He needs those people to be active servants and living witnesses as well. On the other hand, good behavior begins in the heart. "We grow like our thoughts; we cannot entertain impure thoughts without becoming corrupt, and we cannot think good thoughts without becoming pure. Meditation precedes, and works follow."[48] Once again, Paul offers himself as a model example of how he intends for the Philippians to conduct themselves (recall 3:17). After all, "The preacher is the interpreter of the spiritual life and should be an example of it."[49]

Questions

1.) "Rejoice in the Lord always; again I will say, rejoice!" (4:4). What *reasons* do Christians have to "rejoice in the Lord"? If what He offers us is so good, then why do we need to be instructed to "rejoice"? Might this imply that we can allow things to *interfere* with or even *altogether obscure* our joy in the Lord? Please explain.

2.) By turning all our anxieties, concerns, and problems over to God, are we absolving ourselves of all responsibility in these matters (4:6)?

    a. When we pray to God about what makes us anxious, does this mean that all our concern simply evaporates, and we experience carefree joy instead?

    b. In other words, do we need to have a *realistic* and *biblical* understanding of what Paul teaches on prayer and faith in this section? Please explain.

3.) In this passage (4:6–9), what *conditions* must we meet to receive the peace of God? Are there any other conditions that must be met as well?

4.) Why is it critical that Christians *dwell* upon pure and excellent things? Why is it also critical that we *practice* such things (4:8–9)? Why is it impossible to fulfill our discipleship to the Lord successfully or genuinely by only doing one without the other?

Lesson Ten:
The Philippians' Support of Paul
(Phil. 4:10–19)

The Secret of Contentment (4:10–13): Paul abruptly changes the subject here as he winds up this epistle (4:10). The Philippians had supported Paul at an earlier time, but then "lacked opportunity" to do so for a while after this. Now, they have revived or refreshed their resolve to give him financial assistance, which is the underlying meaning of their "concern." "Not that I speak from want," Paul clarifies (4:11), since he has learned how to be content in all circumstances. "Content" here literally means self-sufficient; possessing enough to require no aid or support; independent of external circumstances.[50]

Obviously, Paul's self-sufficiency refers to physical needs, not spiritual. Instead of trying to protect an earthly lifestyle to which he had become accustomed (which is what many Christians do), he instead has learned to adapt to whatever situation in which he finds himself. His "I have learned" statement indicates that contentment is indeed a *learned* perspective, not a natural one (see 1 Tim. 6:6–8). In other words, Paul looks forward to the Philippians' help, but he can also survive without it. In the next verse (4:12), he briefly expounds on this thought. Whether destitution or prosperity, having enough to eat or going hungry, or having abundance or suffering need, "I have learned the secret" of how to find contentment in all circumstances. Again, "I have learned" indicates a perspective acquired over time, maturity, and experience.

"I can do all things through Him [i.e., Christ] who strengthens me" (4:13) means, "Whatever God needs me to do, Christ is the source of my strength for doing it" (Eph. 3:20, Col. 1:29). Many *think* this means, "Whatever I want to do for God, Christ will 'strengthen' me to do it!" This latter view justifies any feel-good endeavor that a person wants to pursue, as though obligating Christ to "strengthen" him for it. This is not what Paul is saying. It is Christ who commissions the work, and (then) it is Christ who strengthens the person He so commissions. It is not our place to tell God what we will do for Him ("And You will like it!"); instead, He calls each of us to whatever ministry He has planned for us (Eph. 2:10).

The Philippians' Generous Sharing (4:14–19): The Philippians "shared" in (or "communicated with") Paul's afflictions by sending him gifts of money or provisions (4:14). This was an honorable act of compassion on their part. Christians are to "Remember the prisoners [who are imprisoned for their faith], as though in prison with them, and those who are ill-treated, since you yourselves also are in the body [of Christ]" (Heb. 13:3, bracketed words are mine). In fact, this has been the Philippians' endeavor since they heard the gospel preached to them (4:15). When Paul left Philippi and traveled south to Corinth, they contributed to his financial support even to their own hurt (2 Cor. 8:1–5). Even while Paul was still in nearby Thessalonica, the Philippian church sent gifts to him (4:16). In so doing, these Christians set a high standard for all other churches—a point Paul makes to the Corinthians—regarding generosity toward Paul's ministry to the Gentiles.[51] "Not that I seek the gift itself … " (4:17)—in other words, the money is not nearly as important to Paul as the *spiritual increase* it brings to those who supplied it *and* to the kingdom in general (2 Cor. 9:10–11, Heb. 6:10).

While Paul did not "seek" (or personally request) the "gift" itself, he certainly did appreciate it (4:18). Because of the Philippians' generosity, "I have received everything in full and have an abundance; I am amply supplied … ." Paul refers to these gifts as "a fragrant aroma, an acceptable sacrifice, well-pleasing to God"—i.e., not so much a gift to him as it was a pleasing sacrifice to God. "Sacrifice" here alludes to the animal sacrifices that the Levitical priests offered properly and in faith (Lev. 3:5, for example). The language here also is reminiscent of what Paul has said about Christ's own sacrifice (Eph. 5:1–2)—not that the two are equal in what they accomplish, but that they are both "pleasing" to God (Heb. 13:15–16). "And my God will supply all your needs … " (4:19)—i.e., just as He has supplied Paul's needs, even though he is in difficult circumstances, God will supply the Philippians' needs, even though some of them faced "deep poverty" (cf. 2 Cor. 8:2). Since Christ has unlimited resources and offers providential help to those who believe in Him, He is more than able to take care of them.

Questions

1.) According to Paul's inspired perspective (4:11–13), what is the true "secret" for contentment? Does being "content" mean that we *like* or happily *welcome* every experience or adversity that we face in this life? If not, then what *does* it mean?

2.) When Paul wrote, "I can do all things through Him who strengthens me" (4:13), did he mean that no matter what he chose to do for the Lord, Christ would empower him to perform it?

    a. Is Christ like an electrical outlet into which we plug ourselves for energy to do what we choose? Or is He like a tree to which we are connected as branches in order to bring about what *He* chooses *for* us (recall 2:13)?

    b. How are these two perspectives so different?

3.) What should be the believer's attitude toward providing financial support for the ministers of God's word (4:15–19)? What benefit does the giver receive for such contributions? (Consider Luke 6:38 and 2 Cor. 9:6–15 in your answer.)

Lesson Eleven:
Final Thoughts and Salutation
(Phil. 4:20–23)

A Brief Doxology (4:20): Overall, this has been a most positive letter. Paul has dealt little with negative matters and has had no need to correct any doctrinal errors among the Philippians themselves. His concluding remarks then, while brief, are also positive and cheerful. "Now to our God and Father ... " (4:20)—in the preceding verse, Paul referred to God as "my God"; here, it is "our God." In other words, the God that Paul originally revealed to the Philippians through his gospel is the same God in whom they have come to believe. "[To Him] be the glory forever and ever. Amen"—a fitting but brief doxology (hymn of praise). Since God is a self-existent eternal Being, He is worthy of such praise.

Greetings and a Final Exhortation (4:21–23): "Greet [lit., salute; welcome[52]] every saint in Christ Jesus" (4:21): every person who is "in Christ" is a saint to God (compare 1 Cor. 1:2). While Paul asks the Philippians to greet Christians whom they meet, he likewise sends his greetings from those who are with him in Rome, including "those of Caesar's household" (4:22). Likely, this refers to any of the servants and guards who directly or indirectly served or protected Emperor Nero himself (ruled AD 54–68). "The term can apply to slaves and freedmen and even to the highest functionaries."[53] It is possible that these people had learned of Paul (and subsequently heard his gospel) through connections with Philippi, a Roman colony. Or, simply by proximity to Paul's imprisonment, some had heard the gospel and then brought others to him over time (recall 1:12–13). In any case, this statement is an example of how far the gospel had penetrated Caesar's own inner circle. It is possible—though we will never be able to confirm it—that Nero himself heard the gospel of Christ.

"The grace of our Lord Jesus Christ be with your spirit" (4:23)—a common but sincere exhortation designed to draw the reader's attention back to the source of his strength and spiritual success (as in Gal. 6:18).

Christ will not give His grace to those who remain outside of His fellowship but He only imparts it to those who live faithfully in covenant to God *through* Him.

Sources Used for *Philippians*

Barnes, Albert. *Barnes' Notes*, vol. 12. Grand Rapids: Baker Book House, no date.

Barnett, Paul. *Jesus & the Rise of Early Christianity*. Downers Grove, IL: InterVarsity Press, 1999.

Coffman, James Burton. *Commentary on Galatians, Ephesians, Philippians, Colossians.* Austin, TX: Firm Foundation, 1977.

Cogdill, Roy E. *The New Testament: Book by Book.* Marion, IN: Cogdill Foundation Publications, 1975.

Conybeare, W. J. and J. S. Howson. *The Life and Epistles of St. Paul.* Grand Rapids: Eerdmans, 1964.

Hendriksen, William. *New Testament Commentary: Galatians, Ephesians, Philippians, Colossians and Philemon.* Grand Rapids: Baker Books, 1995.

Hester, H. I. *The Heart of the New Testament.* Liberty, MO: Quality Press, Inc., 1963.

Jamieson, Robert, Andrew Fausset and David Brown. *Jamieson, Fausset, and Brown Commentary: Commentary Critical and Explanatory on the Whole Bible (1871).* Database © 2012 by WORDsearch Corp.

Lenski, R. C. H. *Commentary on the New Testament: The Interpretation of St. Paul's Epistles to the Galatians, to the Ephesians, and to the Philippians (vol. 8).* Peabody, MA: Hendrickson Publishers, 1998.

Lipscomb, David. *A Commentary on the New Testament Epistles, volume IV: Ephesians, Philippians and Colossians.* J. W. Shepherd, ed. Nashville: Gospel Advocate Co., 1976.

Robertson, Archibald T. *Word Pictures in the New Testament*, vol. 4. Grand Rapids: Baker Book House, no date [orig. published 1931].

Strong, James. *Strong's Talking Greek-Hebrew Dictionary*, electronic edition. Database © WORDsearch Corp.

Sychtysz, Chad. *The Holy Spirit of God: A Biblical Perspective.* Waynesville, OH: Spiritbuilding Publishers, 2010.

$\sim$ **End of *Philippians Personal Workbook*** $\sim$

Introduction to *Colossians*

The City of Colossae: Colossae was one of three sister cities on the Lycus River in ancient Asia Minor (modern-day Western Turkey). The other two cities were Laodicea and Hierapolis (4:13); Ephesus was located about 100 miles to the west of these cities. Colossae had long been inhabited by pagan believers who worshiped various gods, as was common in the Phrygian region. Around 200 BC, Antiochus the Great brought about 2,000 Jewish families from Mesopotamia and Babylon to Lydia and Phrygia. This monotheistic influence no doubt had some positive influence on the indigenous population, but the Jews seemed more interested in the clothing industry and the "wines and baths of Phrygia" than in promoting their unique religion of Jehovah worship.[54] After 133 BC, the entire region came under control of the Roman Empire. In the 7th and 8th centuries AD, the Saracens invaded the area and devastated Colossae. The population moved to another place and deserted the city; by the 12th century AD, Colossae had disappeared.

Historical Background of *Colossians*: Likely, Paul did not establish the church in Colossae, although he might have passed through the city on his way to Ephesus prior to its establishment. Epaphras (4:12–13) is believed to be the founder of the church in Colossae and Laodicea and one of Paul's converts (see Acts 19:9–10). He may have been a native of Colossae, and was a man of great energy, a hard-worker, and highly regarded by Paul. While Paul was under house arrest in Rome, Epaphras went to see him—a land journey of over 1,000 miles—and brought to him a report of the condition of the church in Colossae. The report was overall favorable, yet there were also reports that external teachings and philosophies threatened the spiritual stability of the group (2:8)—to be discussed below.

Authorship: Paul's authorship of this epistle has seldom been questioned. Several early church "fathers" (Justin Martyr, Theophilus, Irenaeus, Clement of Alexandria, etc.) quote liberally from this epistle, and all of them cite the apostle Paul as its author. No observant Bible student can help but notice the strong commonality between Paul's epistle to the Ephesians and the one to the Colossians. Paul wrote both letters from his Roman imprisonment which stemmed from his arrest in Jerusalem a few years earlier (4:3, 18); for this reason, both are considered "prison epistles" (along with *Philippians* and *Philemon*). Likely, Paul wrote these letters near the end of this imprisonment (ca. 62 AD) since he seems optimistic about his release. Tychicus seems to be the bearer of both letters to their intended destinations by (4:7–8).[55]

Nonetheless, while *Colossians* does resemble *Ephesians* on first examination, its style and emphasis are unique. In *Ephesians*, Paul emphasizes the spiritual church of Christ; in *Colossians*, he emphasizes the Christ of the church. While these two approaches overlap, each has its own particular characteristics. Furthermore, there are several Greek phrases that appear in *Colossians* that appear nowhere else in the New Testament (NT).[56]

Purpose and Theme: The reason for Paul's writing this epistle appears to be self-evident. First, he wanted to give his general encouragement to these Christians. Having spent so much time in nearby Ephesus, Paul had developed several associations with believers from Colossae, some of whom are mentioned in the closing remarks and salutations. Second, Paul wished to develop in writing—as a permanent record—what has become the most detailed information on the deity of Christ (a.k.a. Christology in scholarly writings) in the NT.

Certain teachers were persuading the Colossian church to believe that Christ was beneficial, but not beneficial enough, and that Christians needed to practice asceticism and other works of human effort as well to obtain righteousness before God. This idea is often referred to as the "Colossian Heresy," since it departs from the gospel that Paul taught. (A "heresy" is a human teaching, doctrine, or opinion, which departs from the divinely revealed gospel of Christ.) This teaching—i.e., that the heavenly message of the gospel can successfully be married to any earthly or man-made doctrine of justification—needed to be nipped in the bud (2:8).

This alleged heresy explains Paul's exposition on the divine nature of Christ *and* the all-sufficiency He provides for His church. He does so with diverse and often unique descriptions. In *Colossians*, Paul refers to Christ as the:

- Son of God's love (1:13).
- redeemer of all saints (1:15).
- visible (or incarnate) image of God (1:15).
- "firstborn" (or pre-eminence) of all Creation (1:15).
- architect of all Creation (1:17).
- head of the body (church) (1:18).
- beginning of all things (1:18).
- firstborn of the (resurrected) dead (1:18).
- embodiment of the fullness of God (1:19).
- agent of reconciliation between God and men (1:20).
- sources of all riches and wealth for men (1:27 and 2:3).
- mystery of God (2:2).
- embodiment of the fullness of the Godhead (2:9).
- head of all authorities, principalities, and powers—visible and invisible (2:10).
- One who circumcises the heart of the believer and makes him alive to God (2:11–13).
- One who removes the condemnation of law (2:14).
- substance of all the "shadows" of the Law (2:16–17).
- One who sits at the right hand of God (3:1).
- One who will be revealed with us in glory (3:4). substance of one's "new self" (3:10–11).
- forgiver of those who sin against Him (3:13).
- rewarder of those who serve Him (3:24).
- content (or substance) of Paul's gospel (4:3).

This is an impressive array of descriptors by any account. There can be no doubt that the central character and subject of Paul's thoughts here is none other than Jesus Christ, the Son of God. This, and subjects related to it, reverberates throughout. "In Him," "with Him," and "through Him" are common prepositional phrases that highlight Christ's direct involvement in the believer's conversion, transformation, and completion (1:28, 2:10, etc.). In any case, it is difficult to read *Colossians* without being impressed with the grandeur, loftiness, and transcendent nature of both Paul's writing and the subjects he covers. This epistle is yet another showcase of both inspired eloquence and the divinely revealed insights into the doctrine of God. Its profound character simply cannot be duplicated today without copying what Paul has already written.

General Outline

SECTION ONE:
SALUTATION AND PAUL'S PRAISE (1:1–12)

Salutation
(Col. 1:1–2)

Paul opens this epistle characteristically by identifying himself as an apostle of Christ (1:1). This decision to be an apostle was one he made on his own, but Christ appointed him according to God's will. The reason for this introduction is twofold: first, it establishes the authority by which he speaks; second, it identifies him and his office to those at Colossae who may not know him. "Timothy" is Paul's beloved protégé, his "kindred spirit" (Phil. 2:20), "true child in the faith" (1 Tim. 1:2), and "beloved son" in the Lord (2 Tim. 1:2). While the letter is from both men with respect to their collaborative ministries, it clearly is written with Paul's apostolic authority. Timothy, though a co-worker with Paul, is not to be regarded as having equal authority with him.

"Saints" and "faithful brethren" (1:2) are the same people: saints [lit., holy ones] are—in the ideal sense of the word—faithful brethren; those who are faithful brothers and sisters in Christ must necessarily be saints. "Brethren" is an old expression that comes from a Greek word [*adelphos*] which refers to those (brothers) who have come from the same womb. In a spiritual context, all who are in Christ are "brethren" (regardless of gender) since we have been born again through the same process, for the same reason, by the same divine intervention, and into the same family (John 1:12–13). In a sense, the same water that served as our "grave" in which the "old man" was buried also symbolizes the watery womb of our spiritual rebirth. "Grace to you and peace"—grace and peace being divine virtues extended to those in fellowship with God.

Lesson One:
Paul's Praise for the Colossians
(Col. 1:3–8)

W hile Paul and Timothy have never visited the church in Colossae, they nonetheless have prayed often for their welfare (1:3–4).[57] The two ministers have "heard" of their faith in God and acts of love "for all the saints" without ever having seen these demonstrated in person. Thus, as we say today, the Colossians' reputation has preceded them—in a good way. "God the Father of our Lord Jesus Christ" does not mean that God is Jesus' Father in the sense that Jesus, a Divine Being, originated from Him. As a Personage of the eternal Godhead, Jesus has *always* been in the presence of the Father (John 1:1–3). Yet in His earthly, incarnate role as the world's Redeemer, the Holy Spirit conceived Him (Luke 1:31–35) and thus He became God's "only begotten Son" (John 3:16).[58]

Paul now speaks to how the Colossian Christians received their salvation. Their "hope" is the result of their having "heard the word of truth," which is "the gospel which has come" to them through those who preach it (1:5–6; see 1 Cor. 15:1–2). They could not have had any *hope* in God apart from hearing—and, by necessary implication, *obeying*—the "word of truth" (compare Eph. 1:13–14). "Truth" here (in 1:5) cannot refer to any single fact or detail, but involves the entire message of God-given facts that, when received and responded to, produces salvation. Likewise, one cannot bear "fruit" *for* God unless he is in fellowship *with* God; apart from Christ no one can bear good fruit (John 15:5). Thus, Paul says, in essence, "The reason that you have this hope is because you believed in the gospel truth; and the genuineness of your obedience is manifested in the faith and love you express in your lives."

The one who originally preached this truth to the Colossians seems to have been Epaphras, whom Paul honors as "a faithful servant of Christ" (1:7–8).[59] It is through Epaphras (and others, as we will see) that Paul learned of the Colossians' faith and love. We also safely assume that it is from Epaphras that Paul has heard of the doctrinal concerns among that congregation, and the worldly philosophies that threaten to infiltrate it. The phrase "in the Spirit" (1:8) can also read "in spirit" or "in Spirit." It is far more natural—and is consistent with Paul's typical inclusion of all three Personages of the Godhead in his references to salvation—that the Holy Spirit is meant here. Thus, these brethren's love has been shown to one another, but is not limited to the physical church. The genuine source of their love is God Himself.

Questions

1.) According to 1:4–5, does obedience to the gospel have a direct effect on one's "hope laid up for you in heaven"? If obedience is missing (or ceases to exist), will one's hope also disappear?

2.) The natural result of the internalization of "the word of the truth" is *fruit* (1:5–6). What if someone has not heard or obeyed this "word"—can he bear fruit for the Lord? How should we respond to someone who claims to have obeyed, yet bears no such fruit?

Lesson Two:
Paul's Prayer on Their Behalf
(Col. 1:9–14)

Paul obviously has been impressed with the report he has received concerning the Colossian's faith in God and love for the brethren. "For this reason," he offers an ongoing intercessory prayer for them—a prayer that he had earlier only alluded to (in 1:3). The specific requests of his prayer include the following:

- **Knowledge of God's will (1:9).** This knowledge is superior to all human knowledge because it comes from a higher source; it is not bound by human limitations; it is uncorrupted from error; it is uncompromised from self-serving interests; it leads a person to the truth which will set him free (John 8:31–32). "The maxim, 'Knowledge is power,' is true in spiritual life more than anywhere else. When a person grows in the clear knowledge of God, his strength and courage increase."[60] Divine wisdom is from above; earthly wisdom is from below; the one is infinitely superior to the other (James 3:13–17). Furthermore, "*Right* conduct cannot be the product of *wrong* knowledge."[61] While men boast in the "wisdom of the world," it is inescapably true that all such wisdom has never led anyone closer to God (1 Cor. 1:20–21). Knowing—and acting upon— God's eternal purpose brings a person to his full potential, inviting him into fellowship with the Godhead.

- **Walking in a manner worthy of the Lord (1:10).** Knowledge by itself is nothing until one puts it into action: the *practice* of knowledge manifests itself in visible behavior. "Walk" (in this context) refers to a lifestyle or everyday conduct that leads to a certain end—i.e., it is not aimless or directionless, but purpose-driven and goal-oriented. The word of God never instructs the Christian to choose his own "walk," since "a man's way is not in himself, nor is it in a man who walks to direct his steps" (Jer. 10:23). Rather, the "manner" or behavior of one's walk *in* the Lord must be consistent *with* the Lord (1 John 2:4–6). Whenever God has asked believers to do something in His name, He has also provided the way

He wants that action carried out. In other words, He does not only tell us *what* to do, He also tells us *how* to do it and gives us the *ability* to do it.

- **Pleasing God in all respects (1:10).** Striving to please God is in direct contrast with striving to please oneself (or, one's own agenda). Jesus said that "true worshipers will worship the Father in spirit and truth; for such people the Father seeks to be His worshipers" (John 4:23). In other words, God has revealed in His word that those who seek after Him in a worthy manner also are pleasing to Him. "[I]n all respects" means that there are no "off limits" realms in a person's heart that do not have to surrender to His will. One who knows of God *and* walks in a manner worthy of Him will relinquish control of every aspect of his life to please the One who has redeemed Him.

- **Bearing fruit in every good work (1:10).** In Jesus' own words, He is the Vine, we (believers) are branches, but our *objective* is not merely to serve as an ornamental fixture on the vine but to be bearers of good fruit (John 15:1–6). It is impossible to reconcile a fruitless "branch" with someone who is pleasing the Lord in all respects. It is through good works that we honor God before others (Mat. 5:16), and it is for this very purpose that we have been created anew in Christ (Eph. 2:10). We are not saved *by* works, but we cannot prove our faith in God *without* them, either (James 2:17).

- **Increasing in the knowledge of God (1:10).** Godly knowledge is not only important to have, but it needs to increase over time. The Christian must continually infuse his faith with knowledge (of God's word). Failure to increase in knowledge naturally leads to spiritual atrophy and a deterioration of one's faith in God (2 Peter 1:8–11). As disciples of the Master, we are also supposed to be students of His teaching. We can accurately handle the word of God only if we know what it says and how to teach it (2 Tim. 2:15). Paul's prayer for the Colossians, then, is that they will be constantly increasing in knowledge of God rather than trying to marry human knowledge (or philosophy) with spiritual wisdom.

- **Strengthened with all power (1:11).** There is no reason to think that Paul here refers to miraculous gifts in this expression. Instead, he refers to whatever the Holy Spirit does for the human soul in preparing it to overcome worldly temptations *and* minister to God.[62] It is not necessary that we know or understand *how* the Spirit strengthens the human soul; it is only important that we believe that He *does*, and that we ask God for this strengthening (Eph. 3:16). A Christian is not the source of his own strength; none of us can improve or even sustain ourselves (spiritually) for walking the path of righteousness. Rather, we are instructed to "be strong *in the Lord* and in the strength of *His* might" (Eph. 6:10, emphasis added), fully believing in what this divine power accomplishes within us.

❏ **Attaining steadfastness and patience (1:11).** Endurance and patience (or longsuffering) are the results of the impartation of God's strength. While God's word teaches Christians to endure in their faith (Luke 21:19, Heb. 10:36, etc.), this does not mean we possess all the energy required for this endurance. If we could empower ourselves with what is necessary to continue our walk of faith, it would not *be* faith that we would be exercising but reliance upon our own resources. "Patience" is a voluntary restraint toward something or someone in anticipation of a better outcome than one's present situation. In this way, God is patient to hold off His judgment against the world in anticipation of more people coming to repentance (2 Peter 3:9). Likewise, the believer *in* God restrains from giving in to the world, or giving up on his faith, in hope of a future reward *from* God.

❏ **Joyously giving thanks to the Father (1:11–12).** This is as much a part of Paul's prayer for himself as it is on behalf of the Colossians. Even though living by faith in this world has its attending trials and hardships, fellowship with God is joyful and enthralling. One is external and temporary; the other is internal and everlasting (2 Cor. 4:17–18). To give thanks to God for all that He has provided the believer, one must first recognize the joy of living in fellowship with Him (John 15:11). Likewise, one cannot truly be filled with joy who will not also give thanks for the source of his joy. Thus, "giving thanks" is not a mere obligatory or formal response to divine blessings but an outpouring of the soul's deep appreciation for the undeserved gifts it has received from a generous and benevolent God.

God "has qualified" the believer for glory—he is never self-qualified or able to obtain such a future based upon his own merits (1:12). Christ's church will inherit the riches and glory that Christ Himself now enjoys. He has received all such honors as the only begotten Son, but He is willing to share these with those who have become "sons" of God by adoption (Gal. 4:4–7). The saints' inheritance is in "in light"; in contrast, unbelievers are engulfed in a realm of spiritual darkness and ignorance (compare Eph. 4:17–20). "Light" is always associated with virtue or the divine nature of God, and expresses all that is excellent, pure, upright, and truthful. Not only does this speak of God's character; it defines God Himself (1 John 1:5). Our inheritance, then, is not just *from* God, but is *in* God; in reality, our inheritance *is* God.

A Great Change of Allegiance (1:13–14): God's salvation of human souls must be viewed as a *rescue operation* for those who will indeed be forever lost if they are *not* rescued. The "domain of darkness" indicates a realm in which Satan has authority over an organized and active kingdom of his own. Those who sin against God are given over to this authority, and thus to Satan's blinding and deluding influence (2 Cor. 4:3–4). This is *not* to say that people become prisoners of Satan in the literal sense—i.e., Satan does not own anyone's soul or have authority to send anyone to hell. However, it is accurate to say that one's sins against God warrant His condemnation, and such people are made prisoners (so to speak) of Satan's *deceptions, accusations,* and *wicked influence.*[63]

The "kingdom of His beloved Son [or, the Son of His love]" refers not specifically to His church but speaks instead of a *change of allegiance* from one master to another. Those who are in darkness have (consciously or not) made Satan their master; those who are in (or, who give allegiance to) God's kingdom have consciously made Christ their Master. Christ is King over *all* Creation, but this does not mean that all Creation acknowledges His rule or authority. Those who *do* acknowledge this (through their obedience to Him) are thus brought into the sanctuary of believers within the kingdom of God—His church.

This transference, then, from one domain to another refers to a change in status (or state of being) rather than a literal release from Satan's captivity. While in our condemned state of being, Satan tormented us with guilt, feelings of inadequacy, the fear of death, and the awful judgment that follows death. Christ liberates us from such torment, having removed from us the condemnation (of God) that created such incapacitating fear in the first place (Heb. 2:14–15). He has taken us *out* of one state of being (condemnation) and put us *into* another (salvation). Those condemned by God have no inheritance; they only have wages according to what they deserve—spiritual death (Rom. 6:23). Those "transferred" or translated into the kingdom of God's beloved Son receive an inheritance because they have received sonship through adoption (Acts 26:15–18).

Once, we were fellow prisoners of darkness, awaiting our sentencing to our well-deserved condemnation. Now, however, "we have redemption" in Christ since His blood has provided the atonement for our sins and has released us from our condemned state of being (1:14; see Eph. 1:7 and Heb. 9:11–12). Thus, "having now been justified by His blood, we shall be saved from the wrath of God through Him" (Rom. 5:9). No one can receive forgiveness apart from a life-giving offering, because "without shedding of blood there is no forgiveness" (Heb. 9:22). No other blood has the qualities or properties that Christ's blood alone possesses; no other blood but His can impart life or redeem the human soul. Christians are redeemed because we are a blood-bought people (Rev. 5:9).

Questions

1.) Imagine a congregation that provides regular Bible study discussions involving spiritual concepts, biblical principles, and moral lessons of God's word. Yet, no one in the group ever changes, no one's faith grows, and no one does anything different than they did before. What did this group miss from what Paul taught the Colossians (1:9–10)?

2.) In 1:10 we learn that Christians are to "walk in a manner worthy of the Lord." In 1 Cor. 11:27, we learn that it is possible that Christians can conduct themselves in "an unworthy manner." What does this tell us about:

    a. The necessity of a universal *standard* (to know the difference between "worthy" and "unworthy")?

    b. The fact that there are *right* and *wrong* ways to "walk" as Christians?

    c. The hopeless pursuit of modern "feel-good worship," "progressive religion," or the imposition of man-made ideas upon the divinely revealed pattern of God's word?

3.) The effect of God's *spiritual blessings* upon the believer is supposed to result in that person's endurance (in faith), patience (in doing what is good), joy in the Lord, and overflowing gratitude (1:11–12).

a. Given this, why do some Christians hang their heads, mope about as if already defeated, and complain about their day-to-day troubles?

b. In such cases, is God's power insufficient to overccme the trials of life and the difficulties of discipleship? Or are such people failing to understand and appreciate what they *have* in the Lord? Please explain.

4.) In 1:13–14, Paul uses several terms to describe the believer's salvation: "rescued," "delivered," "transferred," "qualified," "redemption," and "forgiveness." How does each of these terms illuminate our understanding of what Christ has done for us?

SECTION TWO:
THE DIVINE NATURE OF CHRIST (1:15–20)

Lesson Three:
The Pre-eminence of Christ in the Old Creation
(Col. 1:15–17)

Having spoken of the redemption that is *in* Christ, Paul now turns his attention to the pre-eminency *of* Christ (1:15–17). The power and authority that Christ possesses is exactly what we need for the task at hand. "He is the image of the invisible God" (1:15)—not a reference to Christ's earthly glory, but to His glorified state following His resurrection and ascension to heaven (John 17:4–5). While the Father is invisible to us, and Christ is invisible to us now (2 Cor. 5:16), Christ remains the only historical visible expression of God (in personal form) that humankind has ever seen (2 Cor. 4:4). "He is the image" of God in His pre-incarnate state (John 1:1–2), His earthly state (John 14:7–10), and His present glorified state. It is true that Christ has never been anything *less* than this "image" in His heavenly glory regarding His divine nature (Heb. 1:3). Yet, Paul speaks of Christ's glory as it is *now* rather than His earthly ministry, and the fact that He is above all other glories or powers.

"[T]he firstborn of all creation" (1:15) *does not* and *cannot* mean that Christ was the first to *be* created. Throughout the NT, Christ is defined as one of the three Persons of the Godhead; He is a Divine Being, not a part of the Creation; He is the Creator, and the Creator cannot also be a part of the Creation—He did not create Himself.[64] Anything that is not of the Godhead has been created; the Godhead has no beginning point, but the Creation does; as an ever-existent Being, Christ is superior to any being that has *come into* existence at some point in time.[65]

Given all this, "firstborn" must mean something different here than it does in its application to ordinary human procreation. In this context, Paul refers to Christ's place before God regarding His incarnate existence. Even in His fleshly existence, He remained pre-eminent to (i.e., the premier of; in the forefront of) all that *has* been created. Thus, in this one verse (1:15), Paul expresses two sides of Christ's nature: as a Divine Being, He is the full expression of the Father; even in His human form, He remains above all other humans—and all that has been created in heaven or on earth.

"For by Him … "—that is, by Christ the Creator (1:16). We are familiar with the *Genesis* account of Creation, in which "God" is the Creator (Gen. 1:1). Now we have an even clearer revelation: Christ *as* God is the Creator and is the reason *for* the Creation (John 1:3, 2 Cor. 8:6, and Heb. 1:3). He has created all things in the physical (or earthly) realm as well as whatever exists in the spiritual (or heavenly) realm. While Christ's authority far surpasses all earthly authority, there are thrones, dominions, rulers, and authorities that exist outside of our earthly view. These cannot be defined by us with any certainty: we know that they exist, but we do not know exactly what or who they are, how much power they have, or what they preside over.[66] Paul's purpose here is not to expound on the *identity* of these rulers, only that Christ (as God) is over *all* of them.

The prepositional phrases "by Him, "through Him, and "for Him" indicate the authority, source, and purpose for all that has been created. Nothing has been created apart from Christ's direct involvement and expressed purpose. Some of us may have been conditioned to think that God the Father created humankind, and then sent His Son to redeem our fallen race.[67] However, Christ created humankind *for* His Father, and then offered *Himself* to redeem the fallen. In this way, He (Christ) could present to His Father an incomparable and priceless gift: a great assembly of blood-bought worshipers who have *chosen* to serve Him forever.

"He is before all things" (1:17)—this is Christ's pre-eminence re-stated. This also helps to define the "firstborn" reference used earlier. He is not *of* the Creation but is "before" it in every respect: in importance, authority, power, glory, and knowledge. Christ has no equal in the

Creation; nothing that is created *by* the Godhead can be comparable *to* it.[68] In a real sense, Christ sits on His throne of glory at the right hand of His Father (Heb. 8:1–2), and all Creation bows to Him or *will* bow to Him in due time (1 Cor. 15:25–28, Phil. 2:9–11). "[A]nd in Him all things hold together"—the Greek present tense indicates that this is an ongoing, perpetual state of being.[69] Christ did not only *once* hold "all things" together (in bringing the Creation into existence) but continues to do so with His authority and power as God. *How* He holds all things together is not disclosed to us, only that He *does* this by His own sovereign will.

This much we do know: regardless of how intricately we explore the smallest atom, the most immense galaxy, or even the essence of human life, there remains a certain force that binds all things together and keeps everything in motion toward a certain end. This force is inexplicable to the scientist, physicist, astronomer, and physician; it eludes the comprehension of moralists, philosophers, and even Christians. In other words, there is a connective and cohesive element to all that has been created that holds our world together. This binding force is not something visible, quantifiable, or even comprehensible; indeed, it is something otherworldly and supernatural. This is *not* to reduce Christ's binding power to a kind of "glue" that keeps the universe intact. On the other hand, it seems clear that there is more than meets the eye, and that this invisible, binding force is nothing short of the power of the One who created all that exists.

Questions

1.) In Gen. 1:1, it clearly states that *God* is the Creator of the heavens and the earth. Yet, Paul states unequivocally that *Christ* is the Creator of all that exists. Do you see this as a contradiction? Are there good reasons why it was not disclosed to humankind "in the beginning" that Christ is our Creator?

2.) Having studied this section (1:15–17), has your perspective of Christ's position relative to *all that exists* changed or improved? If so, how?

   a. Can you see how Christ is not only the *beginning* (or inception) of all things, but also the *summing up* of all things (Eph. 1:9–10), and why He identifies Himself as "the Alpha and the Omega, the first and the last, the beginning and the end" (Rev. 22:13)?

   b. If you are in fellowship with Christ—the One who presides over all that exists—then how does this benefit you in this life? In the life to come?

3.) While Paul has revealed some things about Christ's role and authority that we could not know otherwise, there remains a tremendous amount of information that we do *not* know about Him. Do we need to know *everything* about Christ to believe in Him, or is what we *do* know sufficient for this belief?

Lesson Four:
The New Creation in Christ
(Col. 1:18–20)

The Head of His Church (1:18): Not only is Christ before "all things" of the physical Creation, but He is also before all things spiritual (1:18). The "head" indicates the source of all intelligence, will, design, and creativity for the "body." The body does not tell the head what to do, but the head informs and directs the body. The head provides life and direction for the body and the body serves the head and carries out its will. As this is true in the natural world, so it is true in the spiritual world: Christ has supreme authority over His church; He commands, and the body responds; He defines and directs, and the church submits and obeys (Eph. 1:22–23).

Not only is He the *headship* of His church, but Christ is also its *origin* or *life-source*: His church could not have existed without Him, just as the physical Creation could not have come into existence without its Creator. "The church" does not mean "a" church (such as the church at Colossae), but "the" church—the entire body of those redeemed by the blood of the Redeemer, both living and dead. This church includes those who walked by faith before the church was built as well as those who have walked by faith ever since. This great assembly stands before God the Father and Jesus the Son amid all the angels of heaven (Heb. 12:22–24).

"He is the beginning" of His church in every respect: there is nothing in or about the establishment of His church for which Christ is not responsible. He is the summing up of all things, including all things regarding His church (Eph. 1:9–10). "[T]he firstborn from the dead" has two concurrent meanings: Christ was the first to rise *from* the dead (without any human involvement), and He is pre-eminent over and incomparable to all those who *will be* raised from the dead. This alludes to His physical resurrection (1 Cor. 15:20–24) as well as the future resurrection of those who have died "in Christ" (1 Thess. 4:13–17). The existence of Christ's church rests upon the reality and success of Christ's resurrection from the dead. The church's future glory is guaranteed by the same power which Christ exercised to overcome His own death (John 10:18, Phil. 3:20–21). Thus, Christ has "first place in everything": He is pre-eminent over all that exists in the first Creation, as well as that of the second (or spiritual) creation.

The One Who Reconciles Us with God (1:19–20): The reason for Christ's "first place in everything" is so that He can reconcile all things to the Father (1:19). In His earthly state of existence, Christ embodied the essential nature of God within Himself: God the Father was revealed, personified, and explained through the man Jesus Christ (John 1:18). The indwelling of this "fullness" was necessary because the sacrifice required for reconciliation between God and man could be satisfied only through divine effort. God's "eternal purpose" has been to provide universal salvation through His Son (Eph. 3:11–12). Through this fullness of God, Christ became not only the Creator of the old creation (i.e., the physical domain), but also of the new creation (i.e , the born-again spiritual life of believers). Thus, the "new heavens and a new earth" are realized in the spiritual context of man's fellowship with God through Christ (e.g., Isa. 65:17 and 2 Peter 3:13).

"Reconciliation" necessarily implies that a relationship *once* existed that is now restored.[70] We once enjoyed fellowship with God in our moral purity as children, having been born into innocence and not guilt.[71] Having "fallen" from God's holiness through having sinned (Rom. 3:23), we alienated ourselves from God and our fellowship with Him died (Eph. 2:1–3). Only through "the blood of His [Christ's] cross" are we cleansed of our sins and therefore released from divine condemnation. No longer enemies of God, we now have peace with God (or, are made sons of God by faith) (Rom. 5:8–9, Gal. 3:26–27).

Thus, Christ is the source and power of one's reconciliation to God, and every blood-bought soul has its access to (or fellowship with) God through Him. This is what Paul means whenever he speaks of being "in Christ": we enter a covenant relationship with God through Christ. In this new relationship—which we enter through being "born again" (1 Peter 1:3)—we enjoy saving grace and all spiritual blessings (Eph. 1:3). We have fellowship with the Father that is superior to what we had (in our ignorance and naivete) prior to our having sinned against Him. Our relationship with Him is restored—better than before—and will continue into eternity if we remain faithful to the covenant while we are here on earth.

Christ is the centerpiece and substance of this reconciliation; without Him, fellowship would be impossible. Peace with God comes through "the blood of His cross"—the blood which Jesus deliberately, willfully, and lovingly shed in providing Himself as a sin offering for all of humankind. His blood represents His life, since "life of the flesh is in the blood" (Lev. 17:11), and "without shedding of blood there is no forgiveness of sins" (Heb. 9:22).

To clarify: *we* are reconciled to *God*—He is not reconciled to us. God has not moved, changed, or declined in any way, but *we* have through the act of our sin. Yet, this reconciliation is what God has always wanted (Isa. 53:10–12) and is what human beings have always needed (Rom. 5:10–11, 2 Cor. 5:18–19).[72] "[W]hether things on earth or ... heaven" (1:20)—i.e., whatever sin had unbalanced in the lives of men on earth or the souls of men in heaven is corrected through Christ's redemptive work. This redemption of sinful people also corresponds to the redemption of all Creation (Rom. 8:19–23): as individual believers are redeemed, so the entire Creation—i.e., the *purpose* for which the Creation came to be—is fulfilled.

Questions

1.) If God has given the church (Christ's "body") all the instructions it needs to organize, function, and grow, what need does it have for a "head" (Christ Himself) (1:18)?

    a.   What does Christ's headship provide for those within His "body"?

    b.   Can (or does) Christ provide this headship to those *outside* of His "body"?

2.) Reconciliation is a huge subject in the context of salvation, yet it does not always receive due attention. What are the *tremendous benefits* of reconciliation to God? What if one is *not* reconciled to Him—where does that person stand?

3.) How does Christ's blood make "peace" between the Father and sinners (1:19)? If Christ had not provided His blood for this reason, could we have peace with the Father through some other way?

SECTION THREE:
STANDING FIRM IN CHRIST (1:21—4:1)

Lesson Five:
Paul's Ministry to Christ's Gospel
(Col. 1:21—2:5)

Having clarified what God has done to secure our reconciliation to Him, Paul now turns to the believer's personal responsibility in the matter. First, our separation from God due to sin is *real* and *humanly insurmountable* (1:21). Paul uses three terms or phrases to depict this.

❏ **"alienated":** This means to be estranged to or a non-participant (with someone).[73] Sin is the cause for separation between man and God; yet separation could not have occurred unless a relationship had once existed. The sin that created the breach is *personal*—i.e., no one's fellowship with God can be corrupted because of another person's sin (see Deut. 24:16 and Ezek. 18:23, in principle).

❏ **"hostile in mind":** This hostility (or enmity) comes from a decision to seek friendship with the world at the expense of one's relationship with God (Rom. 8:6–8, James 4:4). In other words, the sinner does not exist in a neutral or compatible state of existence with God but has become His opponent and is antagonistic to His will (Mat. 12:30). "In mind" does not soften the effect of this hostility toward God: the damage is not merely a conceptual one but is real and—if not properly addressed—eternally ruinous.

❏ **"{engaged} in evil deeds":** The practice of evil deeds—however small or insignificant they might seem to the one responsible for them—only underscores the reality of the problem. Just as good fruit cannot come from a bad tree (compare Mat. 7:16–20 and 12:33–35), so "fruit of the Spirit" (Gal. 5:22–23) cannot come from an enemy of God.[74]

Reconciliation Remains Conditional (1:22–23a): "Yet now" indicates a radical change in this former state of being (1:22). The *point of reference* for our reconciliation with God is the real, historical, and atoning sacrifice that Christ made upon His cross. If He had not literally died on that cross, no change in our state of being would be possible; we would still be enemies of God.[75] Christ did not just offer blood (recall 1:20), but also His entire body; thus, the sinner is reconciled not through the body *or* the blood, but through both the body *and* the blood of Christ (Heb. 10:5–10). Thus, the two thoughts run concurrently in Scripture: "In Him we have redemption through His blood, the forgiveness of our trespasses, according to the riches of His grace" (Eph. 1:7) and "By this will [of God] we have been sanctified through the offering of the body of Jesus Christ once for all" (Heb. 10:10, bracketed words added).

"[I]n order to present you … " (1:22) indicates the *purpose* for this reconciliation. We cannot make ourselves holy, blameless, or beyond reproach; these are things that God alone does for us. God is the One who credits a person with righteousness based upon that person's obedient faith in Him (as in Rom. 4:3 and Gal. 3:6). Christ is the One who "presents" us before the Father, not angels, not the church, and not even ourselves. We have no ability, authority, or permission to stand before God apart from Christ's personal intercession.

The small word "if" (1:23a) has tremendous bearing upon the long-term success of the one who comes to God for salvation. "If" means this relationship with God is conditional: *if* one remains faithful, it continues perpetually; *if* he does not, however, then he forfeits all that God has promised him. Such language defeats the fictional belief of being "once saved, always saved" or an infallible "preservation of the saints"—teachings of popular religion but not of Scripture. If salvation is dependent upon *any* human effort, then it is conditional and not irrevocable.

God's *promises* are guaranteed and cannot change; yet the believer's faith is the variable that can change the imparting of those promises. The expression "in the faith" here (1:23a) does not merely mean "faithful" (without a specific point of reference) but faithful *to* something mutually valued by both parties (i.e., the Christian and God). In this case, "the faith" refers specifically to the gospel which has been preached throughout the Roman Empire—"in all creation under heaven" being a broad phrase that simply means "everywhere."[76] The believer is to remain "firmly established and steadfast" (or, grounded and settled) in this gospel—i.e., constantly increasing in knowledge, maturity, and demonstrations of faithfulness (see comments on 2:6–7).

Paul's Ministry and Proclamation (1:23b–29): At this point (1:23b), Paul shifts his discussion from the details of the gospel itself to familiarize the Colossians with his part in the preaching of that gospel. "I, Paul, was made a minister"—not, "I appointed myself" or "the church ordained me," but (by implication), "Someone with authority greater than men commissioned me to be a spokesman for this message." The purpose of this information is not to boast or assert any personal merit, but to provide *authority* and thus *credibility* to that which he writes. Since he has never met many of the Christians at Colossae, it is necessary that they know who he is and what business he must write to them concerning doctrinal matters and other instructions.[77]

No doubt, too, the news of Paul's troubles and persecutions (as a direct result of his commission to be a minister of the gospel) has already reached the ears of the church in Colossae (1:24). A natural question might be, "If Paul's message is from God, then why is he facing such resistance?" Historically, the prophets of God have always faced resistance from those who oppose His will, but this fact may not be understood by Gentile believers (unfamiliar with the OT) as well as it is with Jewish believers. Thus, the need for clarification and explanation is in order.

Paul responds, in essence, "I do suffer for what I preach, but my suffering *benefits* you—it does not in any way detract from the *genuineness* of the message" (paraphrase of 1:24a). While Christ was crucified in the flesh, Paul also suffers in the body—not equally to Christ's suffering, but as a complement or an accompaniment to it (compare Phil. 3:10). Christ suffered in the flesh to establish and build His spiritual church; Paul suffers to propagate the work of that church and preach its gospel. Put another way: Christ suffered *in* His body for the salvation of believers everywhere; Paul suffers *for* His body (Christ's church) to propagate this salvation through his ministerial work. "[F]illing up what is lacking in Christ's afflictions" (1:24b) cannot mean that Christ did not suffer enough (and Paul must complete what He did not finish); such logic contradicts the once-for-all redemptive work of Christ (Heb. 10:10, 1 Peter 3:18, etc.). What it means in this context is that Paul viewed his suffering (and that of all genuine ministers) as being supportive of and necessary for the overall preaching of Christ's gospel (see 2 Tim. 2:8–10 and 3:12).

Thus, Paul was made a minister of Christ's church to provide to others what Christ had revealed to him (1:25–27). This revelation was once a "mystery"—a message that remained hidden until the time it was to be unveiled—but now it has been made known (or manifested) to believers everywhere. The mystery does not only involve the terms and conditions of the gospel itself, but specifically the universal salvation offered to "the Gentiles" as well as the Jews (see Eph. 3:1–12). "Mystery" is thus set opposed to revelation: the word of God was once obscure, but now it has been revealed "to His saints." Moses and the prophets revealed only shadows, types, and glimpses of what was to come; Christ and His apostles have declared the substance of God's salvation to humankind. "Gentiles" refers to all people who are not Jews: prior to the revelation of Christ's gospel, fellowship with God was proclaimed only through the Jews and their Law. Now, however, God invites *all* people into His fellowship through the same message, same method, and same Savior (Rom. 1:16).

"[W]hich is Christ in you" (1:27) indicates the indwelling of Christ, which is not a separate indwelling than that of the Spirit but speaks of the same action: the divine presence of God in the heart and life of the believer (Rom. 8:9). No one can have Christ "in" him without also having God's Spirit: if one Personage of the Godhead abides in Him, so must the others.[78] Christ is "in" those who believe in, love, and obey Him (Gal. 2:20). Thus, Christ abides in those who give allegiance to Him, and they also abide in Him (John 15:7–10, 1 John 3:24, 4:16, etc.). "[W]e proclaim Him"—"proclaim" is from the same Greek root word from which we get "evangelism"; "we" refers to Paul and all other evangelists who announce the revealed word of God to men. This word serves several purposes (as in 2 Tim. 3:16–17):

❑ As an admonition (or warning) for those whose souls stand in jeopardy with God. The warning here is to repent of sin while there is still opportunity, and not to allow the heart to grow hardened by the deception of sin (Heb. 3:12–15).
❑ As the source of sound teaching (or doctrine) according to the revealed wisdom of God, even though this appears inferior to those who resist it (1 Cor. 1:18–21).
❑ As the preparation for one's presentation before God. Christ does His part in atoning for and sanctifying the human soul (recall 1:22), but each believer is to do *his* or *her* part as well. We are never asked to do what Christ alone can perform; yet Christ does not do for us what we are to perform in faith.

No person ("man") is "complete in Christ" apart from *learning* and *implementing* the revealed instruction that comes from heaven—no exceptions (1:28). "Complete" means mature, full-grown, or perfect (depending upon the context). The source of this completion lies outside of the believer's own ability to achieve it. "In Christ" is one of Paul's favorite expressions throughout his epistles. It refers to living in union or fellowship with God the Father through Christ the Son. This is accomplished when both parties (God and the believer) enter a covenant agreement, the terms of which are spelled out in the gospel.

Paul labors to bring about God's word to whomever will hear it, but he does not work according to his own power. Instead, he strives to fulfill his ministry "according to His power, which mightily [or, powerfully] works within me" (1:29). Paul may refer here to the *miraculous* power that works within him, yet when we compare this with similar passages

(Eph. 3:20, Phil. 1:6, 2:13, etc.), this can easily mean the everyday work of divine grace in the heart of the believer. Paul's "striving"[79] is not against *God's* will but is against all those forces or people that would oppose it (2 Cor. 10:5). We are never told to strive against God, but we most certainly must strive to conform to Him.

Paul's Concern for Those Whom He Does Not Know (2:1–5): Many of the Christians at Colossae had not met Paul, yet he has exerted a great deal of effort on their behalf (2:1). He tells them this not to boast or gain sympathy, but so that they can support him (through prayer, encouragement, and whatever other means) and so that they will respect his authority. In other words, "Even though we have not met, I want you to know that I, as an apostle of God, am interested in you and seek your best interest through prayer and the preaching of Christ's gospel."

This preaching has not been a passive interest, but a "great struggle" (or, strenuous conflict), some of which is detailed in 2 Cor. 11:25–29. Paul's purpose is not to divide, which is the agenda of false teachers (in separating believers from the word and dividing believers from each other). Rather, it is to unify (or "knit together") all believers in "the wealth that comes from the full assurance of understanding" the word of God (2:2). In other words, the purpose of an evangelist is not to keep Christians in the dark and teach only limited information, but to declare the "whole purpose of God" (Acts 20:26) and to immerse them in what Christ has revealed from heaven. Encouragement and understanding, not sophistry or power struggles, are proper objectives. This results in increasing understanding of Christ Himself, in whom are priceless treasures of *knowledge* (as facts and information) and *wisdom* (as the proper application of that knowledge) (2:3). These treasures, though "hidden" in Christ, are meant to be discovered by those who draw near to Him in faith.

Paul clearly states his purpose for writing to the Colossians (2:4–5): he does not want them to be seduced by (or, overtaken with) any "persuasive argument" that would oppose the gospel that he preaches. These foreign persuasions, which no doubt posed as having apostolic authority, had infiltrated Colossae, Laodicea, Hierapolis, and other cities of Phrygia and Asia Minor. "Paul is here referring to the false teachers, who attempted to mix Oriental theosophy, angel worship, and Jewish asceticism with pure Christianity."[80] "Stability of your faith" indicates a faith that is not wavering, failing, or filled with contradictory teachings. This thought leads into the next section, which deals with *how* one's faith is stabilized and made steadfast.

Questions

1.) For a person to be "alienated" and then "reconciled" (1:21–22), what had to have existed *prior* to these states of being? In other words, were we born in sin, or did we fall from innocence? (Note: we could not have done *both*.) Put another way: were we born guilty of someone else's sin, or are we condemned once we commit our *own* sin against God?

2.) Christ will reconcile us to God through Himself *if* we continue in the faith of the gospel (1:23). But what if we do *not*? Is Paul teaching here that salvation is conditional or unconditional?

3.) Paul says that he rejoiced in his sufferings for the sake of the Colossian Christians (1:24). What did he mean by this, exactly? What was the objective *of* his suffering for their sakes?

4.) Suppose a person says, "I am complete in Christ" but is ignorant of the teaching *concerning* Christ (1:28)? Can *anyone* be "complete" in Christ apart from knowing and obeying "the word of truth" (recall 1:5)? Please explain.

Lesson Six:
Christ Is the Substance of One's Regeneration
(Col. 2:6–15)

Walking and Growing in Christ (2:6–7): "Therefore …" (2:6) indicates a new thought built upon the previously laid foundation. Paul refers to the Colossian Christians' reception of Christ in the past tense: now that it has happened, a certain kind of thinking and lifestyle is to follow ("so walk in Him"). There must be union or harmony between one's inward profession of faith and his outward conduct. "[H]aving been firmly rooted" (2:7) seems to jar against the "so walk in Him" concept, as if Paul has just unwittingly mixed his metaphors. How can a person "walk" and be "firmly rooted" all at once? This question is resolved when we understand that Paul is talking about two different things. What is "firmly rooted" (in this context) is the believer's *faith*—i.e., it is not going anywhere—while the "walk" refers to his *conduct*. This person's faith has taken root downward in Christ for stability, and thus is able to grow upward toward heaven. (We are not to take the "downward" and "upward" directions literally, of course.)

The believer's "walk" will be the outward and visible demonstration of his inward faith. One's faith is like a living, breathing, growing organism; one's Christian life is like a healthy, rhythmic cadence of activity that leads toward a certain goal—a journey that winds through this life and into the life to come. "[J]ust as you were instructed" indicates the uniformity and consistency of the doctrinal basis for this indwelling and walking. The Colossians did not hear a different gospel than did all other believers but the same message that led to the same inescapable conclusions (recall 1:5). This walk is to be "overflowing with gratitude," indicating the necessary attitude the believer must have to appreciate and embrace all that God has done for him. No one can enjoy Christ's indwelling by his own volition; no one can walk the pathway to heaven by his own strength. Gratitude certainly involves the giving of thanks but also necessarily implies reverence and respect.

Avoiding Worldly Philosophies (2:8): While the Colossians are established in Christ (as though rooted in sacred ground), the possibility remains that they could be taken prisoner to somewhere else (as though uprooted and taken captive to a foreign land). This seems the clearest and most natural flow of thought from the preceding verses to the present one (2:8). If the believer does not remain completely grounded in Christ, then he will become the prisoner (or spoil) of someone else's inferior teaching. Paul mentions several dangers of which the Christian must beware:

- ❏ **philosophy** [lit., love of wisdom]. Likely, this refers to Jewish philosophy (or sophistry), which involves extra-biblical teachings, mystical superstitions, strict asceticism, rituals of purification, and other man-made teachings intended to impart greater wisdom upon the one who accepts them. Human philosophy has long paraded itself as the key to higher wisdom and (often) moral superiority, even though it rests upon the finite perspectives and flawed thinking of men.

- ❏ **empty deception.** This broad category covers any human teaching that claims to impart enlightenment, wisdom, secret knowledge, etc., yet is devoid of anything useful or practical. Such teachings claim to bring one closer to God (or one's version of "God") yet stand opposed to what He has in fact revealed.

- ❏ **tradition of men.** "Tradition" here means any teaching transmitted from one person to another, whether by word of mouth or writing.[81] Likely, Paul refers either to Jewish traditions (wrongly put on par with the teachings of God; see Mat. 15:1–9) or those of Greek philosophers, rhetoricians, and other promoters of human wisdom.[82]

- ❏ **elementary principles of the world.** "Elementary" refers to the first things (in a series) from which all other things (in that series) are derived. Our modern vernacular would read, "The ABCs of language," or "The simplest and primary physical components of the universe."[83] In a sense, Paul refers to the simple, child-like, and rudimentary building blocks of human knowledge (as in Gal. 4:3). While philosophers are prone to tout their teachings as being wise and profound, Paul discredits these as being nothing more than infantile understandings in comparison to what the believer discovers in Christ.

Christ and His revealed wisdom is the ultimate standard against which all man-made teachings are to be compared (1 Cor. 1:30). The "rather than" phrase indicates making a deliberate choice between Christ and human wisdom. Comparatively, it matters little what men produce on their own; no amount of human logic or wisdom can erase a single human sin or redeem a single human soul. "Christ is the measure for all human knowledge since he is the Creator and the Sustainer of the universe."[84]

Spiritual Completion Is "in Him" (2:9–10): The *reason* why Christ and His gospel are superior to this world is because He Himself was not entirely *of* this world (2:9). "In Him" in this specific context means "in the physical person of Christ on earth," His bodily manifestation before men (John 1:14–18, 1 John 1:1–3). The "fullness of Deity"[85] refers to "the totality of God's nature and person."[86] Jesus was not half-God and half-man; rather, He was a very real Personage of God dwelling in a very real person of this world. He was the Son of God, and at the exact same time He was the Son of Man—the fullness of the Godhead as well as the fullness of (what it means to be) a human being. Such information is not meant to be humanly comprehensible, but Paul provides this to prove that it is far *superior* to whatever people produce otherwise.

"[A]nd in Him [i.e., Christ] you have been made complete" (2:10a)—which means, *apart* from being "in Him," a person remains incomplete and thus unprepared for his presentation before the Father (recall 1:22). The "in Him" phrase *here* now is meant spiritually, since Paul is no longer dealing with Jesus' physical body but His spiritual body (the church—recall 1:18). (Paul is the one who has changed the context, not me or us.) Thus, we see both sides of the picture: "in Him," the believer receives what is necessary for his salvation; at the same time, he is in the constant state of *achieving* completion through the constant nourishment of his faith (recall 1:28). The one (salvation) is dependent upon the other (genuine faith), yet both are made possible only through Christ's direct intercession.

"[A]nd He is the head of all rule and authority" (2:10b)—a reiteration of what Paul said earlier (in 1:16–17; compare Eph. 1:22–23). If Christ possesses the power to bring the Creation into existence and rule over it with absolute authority, He certainly has the power and authority to redeem the human soul that trusts in Him for salvation. Likewise, if Christ is above any created being (whether angels or men), it is foolish to worship the creation above or instead of the Creator (Rom. 1:22–25). If Christ is sufficient for one's salvation, it is unnecessary to look outside of Him for something else for one's completion. Christ is not merely a participant in the process of one's salvation; He is the reason for and substance of it.

Spiritual Circumcision of the Heart (2:11–12): Having defined the way things are *presently* for the Colossians, Paul then reminds them of the way things *were* (2:11). It is true that the Colossian church was comprised mainly of uncircumcised Gentile believers, yet the "circumcision" he mentions here is spiritual in nature, not literal. The Judaists—those who tried to impose ordinances of Israel's Law of Moses upon Gentile converts—insisted that all male believers be circumcised. Yet, this was not required by the gospel of Christ and did nothing for one's justification.[87] In Christ, *every* believer is "circumcised"—men and women, Jew and Gentile, master and slave—but not with human hands, and not in the flesh. Instead, all are "circumcised" by the (symbolic) cutting away of the "old self" in order that a new life can begin.[88] This is an action only Christ can do, since it requires supernatural power and authority to perform it. No person can remove the corrupted "old self" of another, nor can he remove his own corrupted self. This must be carried out by One whose authority and ability far exceeds any human effort.

When did this "circumcision" occur? Paul explains it precisely: upon one's water baptism into Christ (2:12). In other words, Christ does in baptism what only He (as God) is able to do, yet He is not baptized for us and He will not "circumcise" us if we are not baptized. It is incorrect to say that "baptism replaces circumcision," for this confuses what Christ does with what the believer does. Believers must be baptized in water to be "in Christ"; Christ circumcises the heart *of* each believer in this physical demonstration of his faith in Him.[89] Christ's "removal" of the "body of the flesh" is not accomplished by mere immersion in water; likewise, immersion in water means nothing without one's spiritual circumcision by Christ. Nonetheless, the two actions—what Christ does for the believer and what the believer does for Christ—happen simultaneously. Thus, the one being baptized believes that Christ does for him what he could not do for himself: salvation is by divine grace, but through his faith. The outward or visible sign of the believer's faith is his baptism.[90]

One who *is* baptized no longer belongs to himself but to God. His baptism is the visible demonstration of his having entered into a covenant agreement with Him. This covenant comes to life by the blood of Christ (Mat. 26:27–28, Heb. 9:15–25) and becomes binding upon the believer in his baptism. (We can baptize people, but we cannot *un*-baptize them: the decision, once made, is for life.) Through baptism, the believer calls upon the name of the Lord to save him (Acts 2:21, 4:12, 22:16, etc.); in the process of baptism, Christ performs His supernatural work upon that person's heart. Thus, we see both aspects of one's salvation: that which the believer performs, and that which God alone can perform (John 3:3–5 and Heb. 10:19–22). By participating in a symbolic death, burial, and resurrection process of our conversion, we are united with Christ in the likeness of His own death, burial, and resurrection (Rom. 6:3–7, 2 Tim. 2:11). Our baptism is literal, even though our "death" is symbolic (or, spiritual in nature); Christ's death was literal, even though His characterization of it as a "baptism" was figurative (Mark 10:38). As necessary as it was that Christ died and was resurrected, so it is necessary that the believer share in that process to identify with Him.

The Believer's 'Debt' Is Canceled (2:13–15): "[W]hen you were dead" (2:13) indicates the believer's pre-converted state of being (see

Eph. 2:1–3). Even though human perception does not fully comprehend this deadness, it is real, nonetheless. Paul speaks here of the soul's condemnation before God: he is as a dead man—he has no future life with Him; he is dead to *God* even while he lives in this *world* (Eph. 4:17–19). (Paul specifically refers to Gentiles here, since they are regarded as the "uncircumcised"; however, the application in principle extends also to Jews who face the same condemnation.) The only way to escape this condemned state of being is to put that condemned "man" (the "old self") to death and begin a new life "in Christ."

God's condemnation of the sinful soul is the "certificate of debt" that was "hostile" to that person's spiritual well-being (2:14). This certificate (or handwriting) refers to all the decrees or details of transgressions which the sinner has incurred. Jesus nailed this decree of condemnation to His cross: in effect, He absorbed in Himself, by means of His own sacrificial death, the penalty incurred by the sinner.[91] "Canceled" here is based upon a Greek word that describes the washing of ink from a papyrus, thus effectively removing the record of any debts written upon it (as in Acts 3:19).[92] This figurative washing is twofold for the believer: first, the record of his sins is "washed" away by the atoning blood of Christ; second, he himself is "washed" in a symbolic, born-again process (i.e., his baptism—see Acts 22:16 and 1 Peter 3:21). Another figure Paul employs here is that of "nailing" the certificate of death to the cross as a means of canceling it.

What, exactly, was "nailed ... to the cross"? If we say that Christ nailed the Law of Moses to the cross, this makes it look like the Law itself was the problem, and that Jesus came to remove it. This transfers the problem from the *sinner* to what God *provided* him. Paul says elsewhere that "the Law is holy, and the commandment is holy and righteous and good" (Rom. 7:12). And Jesus came to *fulfill* the Law of Moses (Mat. 5:17–18), not terminate it—certainly not to kill it (by nailing *it* to the cross). The cause of spiritual death is not the laws of God; it is the *violation* of such laws. This is what Paul says in 1 Cor. 15:56: "The sting of death is sin, and the power of sin is the law ... ." The "sting" is divine condemnation for having violated the law; it is not the law that is sin, but the "power of sin" comes through violation of law. Thus, the *sinner* gives power to sin when *he* commits it. The debt he creates by *having* committed sin—i.e., God's condemnation of him—is what is nailed to the cross, not the law he violated. God's law is not cursed, but human souls are cursed for having sinned against it.

"[W]hen He disarmed the rulers and authorities … " (2:15)—a reference to Jesus' authority over those who supposed that *they* exercised control over *Him* (John 11:47–53, 19:10–11). The facts are otherwise: Jesus orchestrated the very events that led to His own sacrificial death and exercised complete mastery over the occasion of His arrest, trials, and crucifixion. The entire event was foreknown and prearranged. This does not remove the freewill of those involved; rather, it demonstrates the omniscience and omnipotence of God over all human effort and interference. God foreknew that if He sent His Son to *those particular people* at *that particular time* and at *that particular place*, the result would be His crucifixion. God's role of prearrangement was to bring all these conditions together, not to override the hearts of the ones who crucified His Son.

After Christ's resurrection, and as the gospel began to be proclaimed, it became clear that the rulers and authorities were clueless as to their assessment of who Christ was and what He came to do (see Acts 2:22–23, 3:17–18, and 1 Cor. 2:6–9, for example). Thus, Jesus proved Himself innocent to those who accused Him of being worthy of death. In effect, He exposed them as being wicked and/or ignorant while at the same time vindicated Himself through His self-resurrection from the dead.

Questions

1.) Christians are supposed to be "overflowing with gratitude" (2:7). Does gratitude *toward* God require reverence *for* Him? Can we properly express one without the other?

2.) Regarding fellowship with God, how are human philosophy, traditions of men, and elementary principles of the world corruptive to the human mind (2:8)? How (or why) is the gospel of Christ superior to these things?

3.) If a person is not buried in baptism with Christ (2:11–13), then:

    a. When did he receive the spiritual circumcision that only comes from Christ?

    b. How was the "body of [his] flesh"—i.e., the representation of his sinful life—removed (see Rom. 6:3–7)?

    c. How was he "raised up with Him [Christ] through faith"? In other words, why should he expect Christ to raise him up if he has not yet acted *in faith* to what Christ asked of him?

d. How is he "made alive" or forgiven of his sins, having not yet obeyed what Christ requires of him *for* his regeneration or forgiveness?

e. Is he not still dead in his transgressions and in the "uncircumcision" of his flesh?

f. Is he even converted, having not yet *obeyed* what is required of him *for* his conversion? In other words, is he even a *Christian*?

4.) Christ nailed our condemnation to His cross (2:14) by fulfilling what that condemnation *required* of us (i.e., He gave His life for our life—1 Peter 3:18). Even so, He still requires that we put our faith in Him to receive the benefits of this life-for-life exchange.

a. Why doesn't Christ just forgive *everyone on the planet* because of His sacrifice on the cross? Why does He require that we have faith in Him?

b. If we *must* put our faith in Him to have *our* certificate of condemnation removed through His death on the cross, what if we choose *not* to put our faith in Him? Will we be saved anyway?

Lesson Seven:
Warnings against Self-imposed Religion
(Col. 2:16–23)

"Therefore ... " (2:16)—what follows is based upon the foregoing text. This means:

- ❑ The believer has been forgiven of his sins "in Him" (1:13–14).
- ❑ Christ has all power and authority over anything that has begun to exist (1:15–17); even while He was on earth, the fullness of God dwelt within Him (2:9).
- ❑ Christ is the "head" of His church, which is His "body" (1:18).
- ❑ Christ prepares the believer to stand righteously before His Father (1:21–22).
- ❑ The believer has been "made complete" in Christ (1:28, 2:10).
- ❑ In baptism, Christ circumcises the believer with a spiritual circumcision that cannot be performed by men (2:11).
- ❑ Through the symbolic rite of baptism, the believer has put to death his old self and has been reborn (or, raised from his death) by Christ's power and authority (2:12).
- ❑ The decree that spelled spiritual death to the believer has been removed by his appeal to Christ's redemptive work on the cross (2:13–14).
- ❑ Even in His death, Christ showed mastery over everyone involved in it, proving His own innocence, *and* vindicating His every word to be true (2:15).

In other words, if one is "in Christ," there is no need for him to be "in" anything else, since Christ is everything he needs to stand complete before God. Furthermore, there is no need for him to follow the commands, convictions, or decrees of mere men, since no man has authority over another man's soul; and no man can impose his personal beliefs upon a servant of God (Rom. 14:4–8, 1 Cor. 7:23). (These refer to commands dealing with one's relationship with God, not commands concerning employment, law, government, etc.) These latter conclusions are the subject of Paul's letter from here to the end of chapter 2.

Shadows and Substance (2:16–17): "[N]o one is to act as your judge" (2:16)—i.e., since Christ is the head of His church, and all who are "in Christ" are equals (Gal. 3:28), no believer has the right to dictate the beliefs or lifestyle of another. "Judge" here implies one who not only imposes his "law" upon another but also condemns the person who does not comply with it (as in Mat. 7:1–2 and James 4:11–12). Yet, no one has the right to sit on God's throne and pronounce either salvation or condemnation upon another by his own authority.

The particulars that Paul cites here—food, drink, festivals, new moon, and Sabbath day—all refer to dietary restrictions, ritual feasts, or ordinances of the Law of Moses.[93] In other words, he refers to Judaizing teachers who impose requirements of the Law upon Gentile Christians. These things *were* important for the purpose they once served, but that purpose has been fulfilled in Christ and thus they are no longer necessary.[94] Such things were mere "shadows" of what was superior and enduring (2:17; see Heb. 10:1); no one is to follow the *shadow* once he has been shown the *substance* that created it. By following mere shadows, people reveal their ignorance of (or lack of concern for) the true substance of the Christian faith, which is not ritual observances or holy days but Christ Himself. The Levitical priesthood, sacrificial offerings, temple services, and all the ordinances of the Law itself pointed forward and prophesied of Christ.[95] To cling to the prophecies rather than the One who has fulfilled them is an approach that is both backward and inferior. Paul speaks forcefully and directly against any such thinking.[96]

Seeking Completion Outside of Christ Is Useless (2:18–23): Having spoken positively about Christ and how He is the believer's completion, Paul now speaks against other alleged sources of completion (2:18–19). Apparently, some men are imposing upon the Colossians to accept parallel forms of worship. "Self-abasement" is a form of asceticism in which a person inflicts hardship or deprivation upon himself as a means of forced humility and drawing near to God. Similarly, in the case of angels, some believe that one's humility before God is so great that he needs to make appeals to Him through angels rather than praying to Him directly.[97] Likewise, "visions" indicates that, because some had seen special revelations from God, therefore these revelations themselves are considered a route to deeper piety ("I know what I saw—God *showed* it to me specially!").

In each case, the worshiper indirectly draws attention to himself by emphasizing his personal humility, and the one who trains him to do so delights in his control over this person. Paul states that such beliefs or practices are useless in seeking fellowship with God. Instead, the believer is to "[hold] fast to the head" of the body—in other words, he is to cling tenaciously to Christ rather than anything or anyone else. From the head comes all the wisdom and instruction that is necessary for the body to operate properly. The ligaments and joints of the body connect every member together, so that the head can communicate its will to every part of the body. So it is with the church: Christ is the head that controls His spiritual body of believers; there is no need for another source of wisdom or instruction. Being connected to the head (Christ) provides for "a growth which is from God" rather than the semblance of growth which is man-made or self-determined (compare Eph. 4:15–16).

Paul then poses a rhetorical question to the Colossians (2:20–22). "If you have died" really means "*Since* you have died," because no one can become a Christian without uniting with Christ in the likeness of His death (Rom. 6:3–5). One's burial in water in his baptism symbolizes this "death" (recall 2:11–12). And, since this is true that the Christian has given full allegiance to Christ (having died to all other allegiances), it is impossible for him to give equal allegiance to "elementary principles of the world."[98]

The "decrees" mentioned here are not instructions from God (such as, "Do not drink blood"—Acts 15:29) but are human decrees or traditions forced upon believers and considered on par with the laws of God (i.e., the "commandments and teachings of men"—see Mat. 15:1–9). These decrees intended to bring the believer away from his contact with the world to draw closer to heaven. The *problem*, however, is the emphasis on personal righteousness (or justification) rather than seeking righteousness through Christ. In other words, this other approach is an inferior and worldly repackaging of the Christian lifestyle. It promotes a salvation-by-works theology that denies the power of divine grace (Gal. 5:1–4). Furthermore, one cannot find heavenly completion through things which belong to this transient world (or that will "perish"—see 1 John 2:16–17).

Since the church began, men have tried to improve upon God's system of salvation by adding to it their own systems of righteousness and personal piety. Such alleged improvements "have … the appearance of wisdom," but are the products of self-made religion and are unable to compare to God's gospel of grace (2:23). Human-designed salvation is really no salvation at all; asceticism ("self-abasement and severe treatment of the body") is not the means by which a person overcomes spiritual temptations or brings about moral purity; "Neglect of the body will never cure the soul."[99] Only by clinging to Christ and following God's Holy Spirit can a person truly draw near to God and overcome the effects of this world upon the human soul. All other attempts or so-called solutions are hopelessly dependent upon flawless human behavior, which is impossible to produce. If Christ is who completes us, then we cannot become *more* complete in something less than Him. To teach otherwise is illogical as well as unbiblical.

Questions

1.) If a person clings to the "shadow" of something rather than its "substance"—especially when he knows (or ought to know) better— what does this say about his belief system (2:16–17)? If a person gives attention to your shadow on the sidewalk rather than to you, what does this say about his regard for you personally?

2.) Christians sometimes gravitate toward "peripheral worship"— worship that focuses on side issues and self-gratifying religion rather than Christ. In such cases, what are they defrauding themselves of (2:18–19)? Will such people truly grow in the Lord, or will any "growth" they experience be artificial and unprofitable? Please explain.

3.) How does man-made religion have the *appearance* of wisdom (2:23)? However, what is this kind of religion unable to do for the human soul?

Lesson Eight:
The Transcendent Christian Perspective
(Col. 3:1–4)

Seeking the Things Above (3:1–2): Having dealt with the external pressures to conform to man-made teachings, Paul now turns to the inward transformation that is expected in the one who belongs to Christ (3:1). "If you have been raised up" means "*Since you have been raised up*": all Christians *became* Christians by through a symbolic resurrection from the watery grave of baptism (Rom. 6:3–5). "[K]eep seeking the things above" indicates an ongoing and active process rather than limiting it to a historical event in the past. The "things above" indicates those things (or truths) that are far superior to the things of the world below. In other words, rather than seeking completion in the things *below*, one should strive to seek completion in the things *above*, which transcend the created world.

There is no higher authority (outside of the Father's own authority) than to be "seated at the right hand of God" (3:1). Since antiquity, the "right hand" has been a symbol of power and pre-eminence. To sit at the king's right hand indicates a position of power and glory second only to the king himself (compare Gen. 41:39–44). This is the position that Christ holds in heaven: He is above all that He has created, and only the Father Himself is exempted from His power (1 Cor. 15:27–28). Consider the several passages that speak of this (all bracketed words are mine):

❑ "Therefore having been exalted to the right hand of God, and having received from the Father the promise of the Holy Spirit, He has poured forth this which you both see and hear" (Acts 2:33).
❑ " … Christ Jesus is He who died, yes, rather who was raised, who is at the right hand of God, who also intercedes for us" (Rom. 8:34).
❑ "These [riches] are in accordance with the working of the strength of His might which He brought about in Christ, when He raised Him from the dead and seated Him at His right hand in the heavenly places, far above all rule and authority and power and

dominion, and every name that is named, not only in this age but also in the one to come" (Eph. 1:19–21).

- " … When He had made purification of sins, He sat down at the right hand of the Majesty on high, having become as much better than the angels … " (Heb. 1:3–4).
- "Now the main point in what has been said is this: we have such a high priest, who has taken His seat at the right hand of the throne of the Majesty in the heavens … " (Heb. 8:1).
- " … But He, having offered one sacrifice for sins for all time, sat down at the right hand of God … " (Heb. 10:12).
- " … Fixing our eyes on Jesus, the author and perfecter of faith, who for the joy set before Him endured the cross, despising the shame, and has sat down at the right hand of the throne of God" (Heb. 12:2).
- "[Christ] is at the right hand of God, having gone into heaven, after angels and authorities and powers had been subjected to Him" (1 Peter 3:22).

This is a substantial list of references. Whenever God keeps repeating the same truth over and over, we are to sit up and take notice of its importance. Christ, entrusted with kingship over His Father's entire kingdom, has all authority, all rule, and all power over all Creation. God has also given Him headship over the church (recall 1:15–18). There is no need for secondary or supplemental powers or authorities; Christ has no rivals, competition, or challengers to His throne. This is the message Paul communicates to the church in this passage (3:1). While the believer no longer lives to the world, he is made alive through the power of the One who reigns over it.

Since Christ is at the right hand of God and is the object of our faith, this is where we must place our rapt attention (3:2). To "set your mind [or, be intent on]" indicates a personal and deliberate decision (as in Mat. 6:33), not an automatic or reflexive one. It also indicates an internal focus despite whatever external troubles or conflicts might be present. Christ's love, power, and holiness draw us to Him; our faith in Him draws Him to us. "For you have died" (3:3)—to become a Christian, one must "die" to his old self and be re-born ("born again") as a child of God (John 3:5, 2 Tim. 2:11, and 1 Peter 1:3).[100] This spiritual rebirth also recalibrates our thinking, perspective, and conduct differently than those who still remain in the old creation (i.e., having been born of blood, the will of the flesh, and the will of man—John 1:12–13).

A Life Hidden in Christ (3:3–4): While we remain visible to the world, our spiritual union with Christ is (for now) invisible, since we have not yet seen it fully realized. Thus, our life with Christ in God is "hidden" (3:3), even though it is real and functional. Our spiritual life is hidden for now, but it will not always be so: "When Christ ... is revealed" (3:4), our life with Him will also be fully revealed "in glory." The context will not allow this revealing to be anything other than the Second Coming of Christ (see 1 Thess. 3:13, 4:16, Titus 2:13, 1 Peter 1:13, 1 John 2:28, etc.).

In a future day, Christ will reveal Himself in glory to the entire world. For those who belong to Him, this will be a day of triumph and divine vindication; for those who do not belong to Him, this will be a day of divine wrath and vengeance (2 Thess. 1:6–9). He will glorify those who belong to Him and they will join Him and His throng of angels; "and so we shall always be with the Lord" (1 Thess. 4:17). This is the Christian's hope, but it is not a weak or wishful one. As real as Christ's Coming will be, so will be our future glory with Him. Yet this is contingent on our seeking the things above and keeping our eyes fixed upon Him (Heb. 12:1–2).

Questions

1.) "If you have been raised up with Christ" (3:1) necessarily demands that one has *died* with Christ (3:3; recall 2:11–13, 20). When and how did this death occur? Can one die with Christ *or* be raised up with Him simply by asking Him into his heart to be his personal Savior, as is popularly taught today?

2.) When Paul says, "Set your mind on the things above, not on the things that are on earth" (3:2), did he mean that we should no longer be responsible for anything in this life? Or can this mean that we will be even *more* responsible than before? Please explain.

3.) For now, the believer's life is "hidden with Christ in God," yet in time his life will be revealed when Christ Himself is revealed (3:3–4). Why is our spiritual life yet "hidden"? In what manner will it one day be "revealed"? (Consider 1 Peter 1:3–5 in your answer.)

Lesson Nine:
The "New Self"
(Col. 3:5–11)

Bringing One's Body in Subjection to Christ (3:5–7): If the believer has died to the world and now lives to God in Christ, then it makes sense that "the members of your earthly body" must conform to this great transition (3:5). "Members" is not figurative language but refers to the believer's actual body that is under the control of his head (or heart).[101] Just as Jesus is the head of His church, and the church is thus to conform to the will of the head, so the body of the believer is to conform to the converted and transformed heart of the believer (Rom. 6:11–13).

This conformity is not automatic, however. The body has a physical connection to this world and is conditioned by its wicked influences, carnal appetites, and satanic desires. This creates an inevitable conflict and persistent tension between the spiritual believer in Christ and his physical presence in the natural world. These two natures are not merely incompatible but are antagonistic toward each other (Gal. 5:16–17). While the members of one's body are to be regarded as "dead" to sin, worldly desires and sinful cravings (immorality, impurity, passion, etc.[102]) continue to exert their pull and influence on the believer's heart. While one cannot put these desires or forces to death in the entire world, he can and *must* put them to death within himself (Rom. 8:12–14).[103]

This means all Christians are consciously to suppress these wicked desires from influencing our heart *and at the same time* choosing to fill our mind with the things of God instead (Phil. 4:8–9). "Greed" and "idolatry" (3:5) go together, since one's god becomes that for which his heart is greedy. One who belongs to God in Christ has no business giving attention to any other god (or, object of worship). This other god can be in the form of a lifestyle, behavior, belief, spouse, child(ren), male or female human being, or anything or person that reigns over a person's heart. "A man really worships that on which his heart is set, which is the chief end of his labor in life. That which man most ardently desires, he worships; and the service he renders in obtaining it is worship."[104]

"[T]hese things" (3:6)—namely, immorality, impurity, etc.—stand opposed to God and therefore incite His holy wrath (see Rom. 1:18–20). This "wrath of God" refers to divine anger (or vengeance) that will consume those who defiantly oppose the very source of their own existence. Such wrath is not merely the *separation* from God, but also necessarily implies His divine *punishment*. It is true that those who experience His wrath will be separated from Him; it is also true that those who are thus separated will consciously experience divine punishment in their separation. Such talk about God's "wrath" is unpopular and unsettling yet cannot be ignored: it is a consistent and conspicuous teaching of Scripture.[105]

"[S]ons of disobedience" (3:6) are in direct contrast to "sons of God" (Gal. 3:26) and "children of light" (Eph. 5:8). Such people are not predestined to be disobedient (as if against their own free will) but have chosen this course through their rejection of God. Likewise, no one becomes a son of God or child of light apart from his own decision to pursue this. "[A]nd in them you also once walked … " (3:7)—i.e., because you (Christians) were once sons of disobedience, you also incurred God's wrath. "Walked" indicates one's daily conduct; "living" implies the pattern that dictates this walk. Believers had to come out of the sinful world to walk with God: only by separating themselves *from* the world can they be separated *to* God (2 Cor. 6:16–18).

Putting on the New Self (3:8–11): "But now … put them all aside" (3:8)—"them" referring to the behaviors mentioned in 3:5, as well as those he now mentions: anger, wrath, malice, slander, etc.[106] These things reveal the god that is being served: not the God of heaven, but the god of this world (2 Cor. 4:3–4). Such a character is satanic or demonic in nature, as well as self-serving and self-ambitious (James 3:15–16). People led by Satan also act and speak like him; those led by Christ will act and speak like *Him*. The fact that we can put satanic behavior "all aside" necessarily implies that we have control over—and thus are responsible for—our conduct. Paul is not accusing the Colossians of engaging in these things, but he is saying that such conduct is incompatible with their walk in Christ.

"Do not lie [or, Stop lying] to one another … " (3:9)—lying, in any form (deception, evasion, distortion of the facts, etc.), is evidence of one's having given himself over to a wicked influence. This kind of behavior has no place in the new self (3:9–10). The "old self" was "laid aside" (as though in a grave) in baptism; it has no right to exercise control over the Christian. Having died to sin, the believer also died to its mastery over him. Nonetheless, if he chooses to dabble in the sins in which he once lived, then those evil influences will *control* him rather than be "laid aside" *by* him.

Being dead to the world and alive to Christ does not refer only to one's conversion experience. In sharp contrast to the "old self," the "new self" (3:10) is in a constant state of renewal and reflects the very nature of God Himself. This "new self" enjoys the "true knowledge" that God has revealed—that which is not only *known* but also practiced in a visible manner. There is a very real sense of a *new creation* here, as though the physical Creation is spiritually replicated in the life of each believer. The Creator in both cases remains the same: the Christ who has created the physical world (recall 1:15–17) is He who gives life to the "new creation" in Him (2 Cor. 5:17). While the physical world has been irreparably corrupted and lies under a curse, the believer basks in the glory of his Creator and lives according to the promise of an inheritance in light (recall 1:12). Thus, the believer is indeed "Christ-like"—a *Christian.*

In this "renewal" (or spiritual regeneration), all physical, ethnic, national, and former religious distinctions are irrelevant (3:11).[107] Likewise, all social statuses are meaningless, such as the status of a slave or a free man. This does *not* mean these distinctions are no longer in existence, since most of these cannot be changed, but that *in Christ* they have no purpose. Christ's body is a singular, unified, and interrelated assemblage of believers who all have the same mind, are led by the same Spirit, and answer to the same head. While this oneness is spiritual in nature, it must also bear directly on how we regard one another and thus treat one another (Phil. 2:3–5). "[B]ut Christ is all, and is in all"—i.e., just as Christ holds the physical world together by His own power and authority, so He unites the spiritual church into one cohesive body.

Questions

1.) If we have died with Christ and the members of our body are "dead" to sin and vice (3:5), how are we still tempted with wickedness? Does this mean that our conversion did not "take"? Does this mean we have to deal with these things differently than we did before? Or … what do you think?

2.) There is a great deal said about the "wrath of God" in the Old Testament, but comparatively little in the New Testament. Why do you suppose this is?

   a. Does God still have "wrath" toward sin and impenitent sinners (3:6)?

   b. If so, is this wrath actual *punishment* or simply God's harmless *displeasure*?

   c. If there is no punishment for sin, then what is the point of obedience? Put another way: if there is no consequence (or personal loss) for breaking a law, what is the point of having that law in the first place?

3.) Notice that *we* (not God) are responsible for laying aside the behaviors of the "old self." Likewise, while God *provides* the "new self," *we* are responsible for putting it on (3:9–10). In other words, we are saved by the power of God (Rom. 1:16) but we also have a personal responsibility in our *being* saved. Why is it critical to understand both sides of salvation? What errors do people fall into when they give attention only to one side or the other?

4.) In 3:11, Paul teaches that our mutual fellowship in Christ *transcends* whatever earthly distinctions or statuses that might otherwise separate us. How does this transcendent perspective manifest itself in our dealings with one another? In other words, what should we *see* in our conduct toward one another because of this? What should we *not* see?

Lesson Ten:
Results of the Transformed Life
(Col. 3:12–17)

Those who identify with God (in Christ) must conduct themselves accordingly. There is no excuse for improper, ungodly, or illicit behavior; on the contrary, we are to live to a much higher standard than that of the unconverted world (3:12). Christians are "chosen of God"—i.e., they belong to the church that has been predestined for glory (compare Rom. 8:29–30 and Eph. 1:3–5).[108] This group is "holy and beloved": "holy" refers to its conformity to the nature of God; "beloved" refers to the intimate relationship it has with Him.

What Christians Are to Put on (3:12–14): "[P]ut on a heart of compassion, etc."—earlier (recall 3:5, 8, and 9), the Colossian Christians were told to "put aside" or "lay aside" their worldly thinking and behavior; here, they are told to "put on" something. In every case where the word of God instructs Christians to put *off* one thing, it also teaches us to put *on* something else (compare Titus 2:11–12). The things we are to "put on" (3:12) begin as attitudes of the heart but ultimately and necessarily must become our visible conduct.[109] They describe the gentle and humble disposition of Christ (Mat. 11:29) and are the opposite of anger, wrath, malice, slander, and abusive speech that Paul mentioned earlier (recall 3:8).

"[B]earing with ... and forgiving each other" (3:13)—i.e., exhibiting a desire for *reconciliation* and *restoration* rather than separation and condemnation. Forbearance describes one's patience toward another person's inexperienced, immature, or unintentional conduct. Forgiveness refers to the proper dealing of a person's past offenses or sins. The first deals with unwise choices; the second, with definable sins against another person—and thus, against Christ. We are never told to be forbearing toward sin, and we are never told to forgive what is merely a matter of poor judgment.[110] "In differences in which we feel that we are right and our brethren are wrong, we should be gentle and patient, not quick to assert our rights, or to avenge the wrongs others committed against us."[111]

"[J]ust as the Lord forgave you … "—i.e., those chosen of God are to imitate the same kind of mercy and forgiveness Christ has already shown to them (Rom. 15:7). One who refuses to forgive his brother also refuses to show love to him; one who will not love his brother in Christ has no fellowship with God (see 1 John 2:9–10 and 4:19–21).[112] This is essentially a recap of what Jesus had already stated in His sermon on the mount (Mat. 6:14–15). All these virtues are bound together by God's love for His church and the believer's love for God (3:14). This "perfect bond of unity" is linked to the "unity of the Spirit in the bond of peace" (Eph. 4:3). Peace and fellowship with God's Spirit are visibly reflected in the Christian's virtuous treatment of his brothers and sisters in Christ.

What Is to Rule and Fill Our Hearts (3:15–17): Instead of being led or driven by self-serving and satanic impulses of the world, the believer is to be controlled by Christ (3:15). The word "let" (in 3:15 and 3:16) indicates that one's personal decision to comply with this instruction will be consistent with God's expectation of him. The peace He brings to the believer's heart, and the resulting peace that the believer himself pursues with others, mirrors the peace that exists between Christ and His Father (John 17:20–22). This peace characterizes the church's holy fellowship with Christ, so it is only right that each member should allow it to rule over him. "[A]nd be thankful"—those who are at peace with God will respond with thankfulness; those who are ungrateful for or indifferent toward the salvation He offers are not at peace with Him.

"Let the word of Christ richly dwell within you … " (3:16). The internalization of the gospel of Christ ought to reveal itself in one's personal conduct *toward* others and his songs of praise *with* others. "Psalms" refer to poems or odes set to music; "hymns" refer specifically to sacred songs in praise of God; "spiritual songs" are all religious songs used as a form of worship *and* that provide teaching about God to one another. "Singing" is the form of teaching and admonishing that Paul instructs here. Thus, these songs are not for entertainment or to highlight the vocal talents of select individuals. Rather, they serve a purpose like that of preaching and the exposition of God's word. These songs do not communicate mere music, but also teaching and admonition.

Music is the vehicle here, not the objective; educating and encouraging the church *and* honoring God are the objectives. Singing is a unique form of collective activity among the saints that allows for *many* voices to be joined into *one* voice (or song). The blending of various voices (and the various ages, talents, statuses, etc. of those who give them) illustrates the kind of unity and fellowship that is to be exercised within the church in all other areas. These songs are not merely to be sung *at* fellow believers (as though from a choir) but are to be sung *by* all believers.

Today, most congregational vocal singing has been either overtaken or altogether replaced by instrumental music—an impossible position to maintain from what Paul teaches here. Edification and admonition are no longer objectives, but entertainment and personal enjoyment reign supreme. Churches that use instrumental music (especially, that employ a band to provide their music) will all claim to be worshiping God, but true worship (John 4:24) is not to be determined by the preferences of the worshipers but the One being worshiped.[113]

Singing is a form of worship to God ("singing with thankfulness in your hearts to God") as well as means of collective fellowship with His church. "Whatever you do ... , do all in the name of the Lord Jesus" (3:17)—a general instruction that applies across the board to every activity, whether in the context of spiritual worship or in everyday conduct. To do something in Jesus' name means to follow His word, His character, and His regard for those who belong to Him (see 1 John 2:6). "[I]n the name of the Lord" defers to His authority rather than one's own; the believer seeks His approval over that of anyone else. Again, gratitude ("giving thanks") must be an ingredient in one's devotion to Christ.

Questions

1.) After reading 3:12–17, ask yourself: is it enough to *be* "chosen of God" or are believers expected to *live* like those who are "chosen of God"? What are the *rewards*—both now and in the hereafter—for choosing to live in this way?

2.) We are to be forgiving, just as Christ is forgiving toward us (3:13). Does Christ forgive you apart from you taking responsibility for *your* sins against *Him*? Should you forgive those who refuse to take responsibility for *their* sins against *you*? (Even if they do not do this, should you have a *heart* of forgiveness, regardless?) Please explain.

3.) How is godly love a "perfect bond of unity" (3:14)? Can one's unity with God exist in the absence of his Christian love for his brothers (see 1 John 2:9–10 and 4:20–21)?

   a. Can we be (spiritually) united with those whom we do not love? Or can we love *as brethren* those who are not "in Christ"?

   b. In other words, what is the necessary connection between *love* and *unity* in the context of our fellowship in Christ?

4.) Why is *singing together* an excellent (and unique) form of collective fellowship?

    a.   However, are we in fellowship with God just because we sing about Him?

    b.   Should we unite in spiritual songs with those whom we have no spiritual fellowship?

Lesson Eleven:
Relationships in the Lord
(Col. 3:18—4:1)

Having spoken all Christians in general, Paul now turns his attention to specific roles that would be typically found in any congregation: spouses, children, fathers, slaves, and masters. This is hardly a comprehensive coverage on any one role and is briefer than parallel instructions in *Ephesians*.[114] The purpose here is not to belabor the point but to provide practical application of the general truths he has already discussed. If the believer has his heart fixed upon Christ, who sits at the right hand of God (recall 3:1), he (or she) must reflect that attitude in his behavior toward his wife (or husband), in the family, and in his occupation. In other words, the Christian belief system is not limited to the context of worship services, church functions, or the company of fellow believers. It extends into and permeates all realms of one's life, however secular or non-spiritual they may seem otherwise. Since Christ has purchased us with His blood, He owns us entirely—we are His possession (1 Cor. 6:19–20). This means He owns every part of us and every aspect of our lives, and thus governs every relationship to which we belong.

Instructions to Spouses (3:18–19): "Wives, be subject . . . as is fitting in the Lord" (3:18). A wife's subjection to her husband is not a separate matter from her subjection to Christ. Her spiritual subjection to the Lord *conditions* or *governs* her subjection to her husband. Subjection is not a demeaning evaluation of a person's worth; it is merely a comparison of one's rank (or position) to another's, as in the military. God has made the husband the head of the household; God expects the wife to honor and support her husband's position. The husband's position of authority in the home is over that of his wife's position. This does not make him a superior person, or his wife an inferior one, but simply recognizes the difference in roles or responsibilities that God has assigned to these two people. The phrase "in the Lord" means "what the Lord would approve of," exclusively for those who are "in Christ."

"Husbands, love your wives … " (3:19)— Paul does not direct this command to "love" only to husband (see Titus 2:4), but husbands should take the leadership role in demonstrating godly love in the marriage. Christ's love for His church must be the pattern for a husband's love for his wife (Eph. 5:25), which is selfless and sacrificial in nature. As with a wife's subjection, a husband's love for his wife is not a separate matter from his love for the Lord. His love for Christ ought to *condition* or *govern* his love for his wife. While the husband is the head of the marriage, love puts him in a servant role to his wife (just as Christ is also the head of His church yet serves His bride selflessly). "[A]nd do not be embittered against them"—i.e., do not be irritated with or indignant toward them. While love is selfless and noble, bitterness is selfish and worldly in nature. This does not mean a man can never be angry toward or upset with his wife (or vice versa), but that this reaction cannot serve as a ruling principle for his behavior and must not continue for long (Eph. 4:26).

Instructions Regarding Children (3:20–21): "Children, be obedient … for this is well-pleasing to the Lord" (3:20). Are these children *Christians*, or merely children of Christian parents? Either scenario would apply equally, if they are still under the roof of their father's house. Clearly, Paul is not speaking of very young children (say, single-digit aged) but children who are old enough to be responsible for their behavior yet remain subject to their parents' oversight. (Adult children who no longer live with their parents cannot be obedient in this same context.) "Obedient" means following the rules (of the house) that do not conflict with the transcendent laws of God. God has always expected children to honor their parents (Exod. 20:12, Eph. 6:1–3), and for good reason: one's honor of his earthly source of life parallels the proper honor of his Creator. "Waves of lawlessness sweep over the world because the child was not taught to obey."[115]

"Fathers, do not exasperate your children … " (3:21)—lit., do not infuriate, enrage, or overwhelm with frustration (Eph. 6:4). Fathers have the responsibility to manage their household (1 Tim. 3:4–5), but this position can easily be abused or used in a self-serving manner.

It is in the best interest of the children for fathers to lead them to the Lord, not incite anger, bitterness, or ill-feelings due to the father's poor representation of Him. Jesus declared that those who deliberately or carelessly drive their children away from the Lord will answer for this (Mat. 18:5–6, 10). This instruction is brief yet significant: the father's abuse of his authority or his perversion of justice (within the home) is a source of provocation for children. This would be the case if he:

- puts stumbling blocks in the (spiritual) path of his children (Mat. 18:6).
- fails to be consistent in the administration of rules, justice, rewards, or punishments.
- is a hypocrite—i.e., he portrays himself in one manner when with Christians, but in an entirely different manner when in the privacy of his home.
- makes no effort to live what he preaches to his children (Rom. 2:21–24).
- fails to prepare them for life, setting them up for future failure.
- is overprotective and does not allow his children the ability to exercise responsibility.
- is neglectful and gives little time or attention to his children.
- is abusive, either mentally or physically.

Instructions Regarding Slaves and Masters (3:22—4:1): The instructions for "slaves" are general ones that might be loosely applied to modern employees who work under a boss (or "master") in some company or corporation. In the ancient world, "slaves" had broad application, and not all slaves engaged in hard labor or dangerous occupations.[116] Many slaves were educated men who, because of circumstances beyond their control, found themselves under the authority of a master. Likewise, not all masters were the same: some were fair, decent, and humane; others were unjust, abusive, and crooked.[117] In any case, the Christian "slave" has a moral obligation to God to serve in a manner that rightly represents Him, even to his own hurt. This service is not to be good when "the boss" is looking but unproductive when he is not; rather, it is to be always good, regardless of who is watching. This is because *God* is always watching and expects His servants to be always consistent and honorable. The word "heartily" [lit., from the soul[118]] indicates that a Christian slave's *work* is to reflect the faithful disposition of his *heart*. Because he has devoted his heart to Christ, his work will demonstrate that devotion in his service to his earthly master.

"Whatever you do ... as for the Lord" (3:23) is a principle that extends well beyond the sphere of one's employment (although this is the immediate context in this passage). This means that even in times of rest or recreation, or in the company of friends, the Christian is to conduct himself in a manner that is consistent with his profession of faith in Christ. His spiritual inheritance depends upon the genuineness of his earthly conduct (2 Cor. 5:10). If he conducts himself well in this life, he will reap the benefits of this in the life to come; if he says one thing but does another, then he will reap the consequences of that duplicitous life (3:24–25; see Rom. 2:9–11). In other words, how a believer chooses to conduct himself in his earthly circumstances, regardless of how blessed or difficult those circumstances might be, directly impacts the "reward of [his] inheritance."

"Masters, grant your slaves justice and fairness ... " (4:1). The primary abuse among masters of slaves in the ancient world was that of injustice through an abuse of their authority. While Christian slaves are to be just in their service to their masters (whether these masters are believers), Christian masters are to be just in the treatment of their slaves (whether these slaves are believers). In the modern application, all Christians who are in positions of authority over others are to exercise that authority with a view to their spiritual relationship with God: "you too have a Master in heaven." From Christ's point-of-view, all believers are equal (Gal. 3:28); thus, we cannot allow our earthly circumstances to contradict or circumvent this spiritual perspective.

Questions

1.) What is the intended *benefit* to wives for being submissive to their husbands (3:18)? (There are several answers.) In the case where a wife's husband is not a good head of the household, is she permitted to ignore her subjection to him? Please explain.

2.) Will a husband who refuses to love his wife enjoy a favorable relationship with God (3:19)? Will a husband who *does* love his wife automatically have a favorable relationship with God (apart from his obedience to Christ)? What is Paul's point with this instruction?

3.) Why must children "obey" their parents whereas wives are to "be subject" to their own husbands (3:20)? In other words, why are children not told to "be subject" and wives are not told to "obey"— or *are* they?

4.) If Paul ever had an opportunity to condemn slavery as being immoral and intolerable, it would be in 3:22—4:1. Instead, he regulated the conduct of Christian slaves and Christian masters. Does this mean that human slavery is good and acceptable? Or does it mean that God permitted slavery without endorsing it? Or ... what do you think?

SECTION FOUR:
FINAL REMARKS AND SALUTATIONS
(4:2–18)

Lesson Twelve:
What Is Expected of Believers
(Col. 4:2–6)

Instructions on Prayer (4:2–4): In this brief but potent section, Paul provides practical application of our holy union with God through Christ. This instruction is for all believers, regardless of earthly relationships or statuses. "Devote yourselves to prayer … " (4:2)—i.e., persevere in this; be earnestly committed to it. There is a difference between those who say prayers and those devoted to prayer. One person uses prayer as a means of appeasing his guilty conscience, or to "get things" that he does not have. Another person uses prayer as a means of holy and intimate communication with his Father—a communication that is as rewarding as it is necessary. "Keeping alert in it" implies a sense of diligent vigilance, or a sense of keen awareness to the need for continual communication with the Lord. This is the case not only when God grants prayerful petitions, but also when He denies them. Thus, the "attitude of thanksgiving" is not to be present only when God says "yes," but also when He says "no" or "wait."

Paul adds a personal addendum to this instruction: "praying at the same time for us as well" (4:3–4)—"us" meaning (at least) himself and Timothy (recall 1:1). Paul is still in Roman imprisonment at the time of this writing, limiting his opportunity to teach the gospel. Nonetheless, he still exerts a great amount of influence and provide apostolic direction despite his circumstances; "I suffer hardship even to imprisonment as a criminal; but the word of God is not imprisoned" (2 Tim. 2:9). Even though an inspired apostle, Paul consistently relies upon the prayers of fellow believers for courage, opportunity, and success (Rom. 15:30, Eph. 6:18, etc.). In this case, Paul seeks an open "door" to teaching the word of God and the "mystery of Christ" (which elsewhere refers to the universal offering of salvation to all men).

God's response to Paul's request is unknown to us, yet his dependence upon *prayer* as a means of accomplishing it is remarkable. Thus, we are not only to ask, seek, and knock (in prayer) for ourselves, but also for others who fulfill the cause of Christ (Mat. 7:7–8). Instead of relying on his own talents or personal knowledge, Paul asks for divine help through the petitions of fellow believers (4:4; compare 1 Cor. 2:1–5). The words "make it clear" indicates a twofold request: first, that Paul would be clear in his communication of the message; second, that the message would be clearly understood by those who received it.

Expected Christian Conduct and Speech (4:5–6): "Conduct yourselves with wisdom" (4:5)—this general instruction is covered in Eph. 5:15–17, yet here it has a more specific purpose: "toward outsiders." These "outsiders" are undoubtedly those outside of the body of Christ— those not yet redeemed by the blood of Christ (recall 1:13–14). The believer is to exercise wisdom, discretion, and maturity in how he behaves in the company of unbelievers, and especially when he shares the gospel with them. His objective is not only to survive this life with his faith intact, but also to *live* his faith as a godly influence to others (Mat. 5:16) and to *share* his faith in hopes that others might hear and repent (see 2 Tim. 2:24–26).

"[M]aking the most of the opportunity" means taking advantage of the moment and realizing the importance of the message that needs to be communicated. Such "opportunity" may not always be comfortable or convenient, but one must seize it when it arises—and in many cases, we must vigilantly *seek* opportunity rather than waiting for it to present itself obviously to us. The Greek text is translated as "redeeming the time," which (consistent with the act of redemption) involves buying back a "time" that could have been lost or used for some lesser purpose (as in Eph. 5:16). (It also implies being productive *with* our time, but the "redemption" idea is often lost on us.)

In conjunction with our proper conduct before outsiders, we must watch what we say—and how we say it (4:6). A person's words reflect what is in his heart or indicate what drives his thinking (Mat. 15:17–20, 1 Peter 4:11). A Christian's words ought to reflect the influence and guidance of the Holy Spirit, to be full of grace. "Grace" here cannot mean *saving* grace (since only God can impart this to anyone) but that which is kind, beneficial, and generous (as is God's benevolence toward wicked men). "Salt" is a flavoring agent as well as a preservative. In the Levitical sacrifices, the "covenant of salt" symbolized the preservation of one's relationship with God (Lev. 2:13, Num. 18:19). Likewise, our words are to be a source of inspiration (or flavor) as well as timeless quality (or preservation), especially to "outsiders" who are seeking the truth. Our response to each person should be already prepared in our heart and conditioned by our desire for the salvation of all men (1 Peter 3:15, 1 Tim. 2:3–4).

Questions

1.) Why should Christians make prayerful requests to a God who already knows all things and exactly what we need (4 2; see Mat. 6:8)? On the other hand, what can be said about a Christian who refuses to pray, or who does not believe in prayer (James 1:5–8)?

2.) Someone has said, "The reason many people do not recognize 'opportunity' is because it often comes disguised as 'work.'"

    a.   How might this be true regarding our conduct toward "outsiders," with respect to winning them to the Lord (4:5)?

    b.   When a Christian says, "I have had no opportunity to share my faith," might it be possible that he did not do the *work* necessary to accomplish this?

3.) Salt that lacks flavor is useless; but so is speech that lacks discretion and godly influence (4:6). Against the background of the gutter language of modern society, will not a Christian's good speech and gracious words stand out even more? Please explain.

Lesson Thirteen:
Paul's Personal Circumstances and Salutations
(Col. 4:7–18)

Not everything Paul wants to say—in the way of instruction or as to his personal circumstances—is in this epistle. His loyal assistants, Tychicus and Onesimus, will bring the rest of this information to the Colossians personally (4:7–9). It is believed that Tychicus was the actual bearer of this epistle to Colossae, just as he was the bearer of the epistle to Ephesus (Eph. 6:21–22). He is mentioned several other times in the NT, always in a positive light (Acts 20:4, 2 Tim. 4:12, and Titus 3:12); even here, he is highly praised as a "faithful and beloved brother."

If Onesimus is a native of Colossae (as is commonly believed), he is well familiar with the area. Both men would bring further details of Paul's imprisonment, as well as the progress of his legal affairs, which would be of great interest to the Colossians. In the next verses, six other men are mentioned, some with whom we are familiar elsewhere and others about whom we know nothing else than these brief words (4:10–15).

- **Aristarchus:** A Macedonian from Thessalonica (Acts 20:4), this man has had a colorful history with Paul so far. He is Paul's fellow worker (Phile. 1:24) as well as his fellow prisoner. He was arrested along with Gaius in Ephesus (Acts 19:23ff); he was with Paul on his ill-fated voyage to Rome (Acts 27:2); and it appears that he is literally imprisoned at the same time as Paul.
- **Mark:** This is John Mark, Barnabas' cousin, the author of the gospel called by his name. Early in Paul's missionary endeavors, Mark had abandoned him, leaving a sour taste in Paul's mouth regarding his reliability (compare Acts 13:13 and 15:36–40). Later, however, it seems Mark has matured in his faith and thus has become very useful to Paul (2 Tim. 4:11, Phile. 1:24).
- **"Jesus, who is called Justus":** Nothing else is known of this man, save that he is willing to minister to the Gentiles. "Jesus" is his

Hebrew name; "Justus" is his Latinized (Roman) name. Aristarchus, Mark, and Justus are "from the circumcision" (i.e., are pure-blooded Jews who have become Christians), and have served as a source of encouragement for Paul. Many other Jews have abandoned Paul.

- ❏ **Epaphras:** This man is considered the founder of the church in Colossae (recall 1:7); thus, he is "one of your number." At the time of writing, he is with Paul in Rome, and possibly serves as a fellow inmate with him at times (Phile. 1:23). Epaphras shows great concern for his home church and labors diligently on its behalf, wanting to see the Christians there come to maturity and completion (recall 1:28–29). Laodicea and Hierapolis are nearby sister cities to Colossae, and Epaphras may have also founded churches there.

- ❏ **"Luke, the beloved physician":** A Gentile who became one of the greatest historians of the early church, Luke has provided an invaluable service to Paul's ministry. He is the author of the gospel account by his name, it being the result of great research and investigation on his part (Luke 1:1–4). Though not mentioned by name in *Acts*, he is nonetheless the author of that work as well as a participant in its narrative (in the infamous "we" sections— Acts 16:10, 20:6, 27:1, etc.). Luke is a dear and loyal friend of Paul's, having accompanied him on his voyage to Rome and his imprisonment there. He will also be with Paul in his final imprisonment (2 Tim. 4:11).

- ❏ **Demas:** Here (and in Phile. 1:24), Demas is identified as one of Paul's fellow workers. In 2 Tim. 4:10, however, we find that he will abandon Paul, "having loved this present world." We know nothing else about this man, and yet it appears that he finds greater gratification in "this present world" than he does in serving alongside one of the greatest men in Christ's church.

"[T]he brethren who are in Laodicea" and "the church that is in [Nympha's] house" (4:15) clearly refer to two groups. Likely, one is the main (or larger) congregation within the city; the other is a smaller group meeting in someone's home. The Greek wording in this sentence is irregular, giving rise to various interpretations, but the conclusion offered here seems to be the most natural and straightforward. It is impossible without any further information, however, to determine from the Greek whether "Nympha" is feminine or masculine. Thus, all we know about her (or him) and the church at her (or his) home is what Paul wrote here.

"The letter {that is coming} from Laodicea" (4:16) appears to be a circular letter (or general epistle) that is to be read in several churches, just as *Colossians* was to be read to more than just the Colossians themselves. It has been suggested that the Laodicean letter is what we call *Ephesians*, but there is no conclusive evidence for this. "Say to Archippus … " (4:17)—Paul singles this man out for special encouragement, like what we find in Phil. 4:2–3. He is mentioned in Phile. 1:2 only as a "fellow soldier"; otherwise, we know nothing else about him or his circumstances other than what is written here.

"I, Paul, write … hand"—though Paul did not personally pen this entire letter, this signature closure indicates that he is nonetheless its author (4:18; see 1 Cor. 16:21, Gal. 6:11, and 2 Thess. 3:17). It was common for him to dictate his letters to an *amanuensis*, what we would call a scribe or secretary today. "Remember my imprisonment"—something that Christians ought to do for all fellow brothers or sisters imprisoned for their faith (Heb. 13:3). "This last reminder would again bring them to consider how he had struggled for them even while in chains and written an epistle to liberate them from erring theology and point them back to Christ as supreme."[119] "Grace be with you"—in essence, "May God continue to impart His grace to you, as those who are called by Him."

Questions

1.) Notice how commendably Paul speaks of those who minister alongside of him (4:7ff). What did these men do to deserve such commendations?

    a.   What would Paul say of us (or of you) if he were writing to someone else about us?

    b.   Sometimes we may not think that our prayers for and support of preachers amounts to much, but Paul's words paint a far different picture. What do you learn from what he has written?

2.) Though in prison, Paul surrounded himself with able Christians who provided a steady source of personal encouragement to him (and vice versa). What does this say about the power—and pleasure—of Christian fellowship, even amid adverse situations?

Sources Used for *Colossians*

Barnes, Albert. *Barnes' Notes*, vol. 12. Grand Rapids: Baker Book House, no date.

Boren, Henry C. *Roman Society*, 2nd ed. Lexington, MA: Heath and Co., 1992.

Coffman, James Burton. *Commentary on Galatians, Ephesians, Philippians, Colossians.* Austin, TX: Firm Foundation, 1977.

Cogdill, Roy E. *The New Testament: Book by Book.* Marion, IN: Cogdill Foundation Publications, 1975.

Geisler, Norman L. *Christian Apologetics.* Grand Rapids: Baker Book House, 1976.

Hendriksen, William. *New Testament Commentary: Galatians, Ephesians, Philippians, Colossians and Philemon.* Grand Rapids: Baker Books, 1995.

International Standard Bible Encyclopedia, electronic edition. © 1979 by Wm. B. Eerdmans Publishing Co.; database © 2013 by WORDsearch Corp.

Jamieson, Robert, Andrew Fausset and David Brown. *Jamieson, Fausset, and Brown Commentary: Commentary Critical and Explanatory on the Whole Bible (1871)*, electronic edition. Database © 2012 by WORDsearch Corp.

Lenski, R. C. H. *Commentary on the New Testament, vol. 9: The Interpretation of St. Paul's Epistles to the Colossians, to the Thessalonians, to Timothy, to Titus, and to Philemon.* Peabody, MA: Hendrickson Publishers, 1998.

Lipscomb, David. *A Commentary on the New Testament Epistles, volume IV: Ephesians, Philippians and Colossians.* J. W. Shepherd, ed. Nashville: Gospel Advocate Co., 1976.

Robertson, Archibald T. *Word Pictures in the New Testament*, vol. 4. Grand Rapids: Baker Books, 1931.

Strong, James. *Strong's Talking Greek-Hebrew Dictionary*, electronic edition. Database © WORDsearch Corp.

Sychtysz, Chad. *The Holy Spirit of God: A Biblical Perspective.* Waynesville, OH: Spiritbuilding Publishers, 2010.

Thayer, Joseph. *Thayer's Greek-English Lexicon,* electronic edition. Database © 2014 by WORDsearch Corp.

Vincent, Marvin. *Word Studies,* electronic edition. Database © 2014 by WORDsearch Corp.

~ **End of *Colossians* Personal Workbook** ~

Endnotes

1 H. I. Hester, *The Heart of the New Testament* (Liberty, MO: Quality Press, Inc., 1963), 282; bracketed word is mine.

2 R. C. H. Lenski, *The Interpretation of Paul's Epistles to the Philippians, Colossians, etc.* (Peabody, MA: Hendrickson Publishers, 1998), 698; bracketed word is mine.

3 "It is rather significant that in a number of such instances in the New Testament, the Apostles, who could have miraculously healed, did not do so in such cases, and these instances emphasize that the Divine powers which God had given them to confirm the gospel never were used for personal, private or selfish reasons" (Roy E. Cogdill, *The New Testament: Book by Book* [Marion, IN: Cogdill Foundation, 1975], 80).

4 William Hendriksen, *New Testament Commentary: Galatians, Ephesians, etc.* (Grand Rapids: Baker Books, 1995), 38.

5 Albert Barnes, *Barnes' Notes* (Grand Rapids: Baker Book House, no date), "Introduction," cxl.

6 "The day of Christ Jesus" and "the day of the Lord" in NT epistles consistently refers to the Second Coming; see 1 Thess. 5:2, 2 Thess. 2:1–2, and 2 Peter 3:10, for example.

7 For further exposition on this point, see comments in this workbook on Col. 1:9–10.

8 "There were originally ten thousand of these picked soldiers, concentrated in Rome by [Emperor] Tiberius. They had double pay and special privileges and became so powerful that emperors had to court their favour. Paul had contact with one after another of these soldiers" (A. T. Robertson, *Word Pictures in the New Testament,* vol. 4 [Grand Rapids: Baker Book House, no date; orig. published 1931], 438; bracketed word is mine).

9 Robert Jamieson, Andrew Fausset, and David Brown, *Jamieson, Fausset, and Brown Commentary: Commentary Critical and Explanatory on the Whole Bible* (1871), electronic edition (database © 2012 by WORDsearch Corp.), on 1:13.

10 David Lipscomb, *A Commentary on the New Testament Epistles, volume IV: Ephesians, Philippians and Colossians,* J. W. Shepherd, ed. (Nashville: Gospel Advocate Co., 1976), 162.

11   J. W. Shepherd (in Lipscomb's commentary) offers another view: "It is very likely … that the Christians at Rome were without a strong leadership before Paul's coming, and that some of their leaders, jealous of his influence, became personal enemies" (*Commentary*, 163). While this seems plausible enough, it is also without substantiation. Given Paul's repeated tangles with Christian Jews (Judaizers) in other places of the NT, the first scenario seems to be more natural. Nonetheless, each Bible student is allowed his own opinion here.

12   Paul did vindicate himself, to the extent that was necessary, in the Second Epistle to the Corinthians. For a full discussion on his defense, and why he chose to engage in it, see *2 Corinthians Commentary* (Spiritbuilding Publishers); go to www.spiritbuilding.com/chad.

13   "Apparently the content of these sermons was similar to Paul's preaching and did not contain such false teaching as Judaizers were bringing to Galatia (Gal. 1:6–8). Their basic error was in motive and not in doctrine" (JFB, *Commentary* [electronic], on 1:18).

14   For an in-depth study of the Holy Spirit, I recommend my book, *The Holy Spirit of God: A Biblical Perspective* (Spiritbuilding Publishers, 2010); go to www.spiritbuilding.com/chad.

15   Joseph Thayer, *Thayer's Greek-English Lexicon,* electronic edition (database © 2014 by WORDsearch Corp.), G603.

16   "Paul is not flattering himself as though his readers still need him. He says only that he is confident they do, and he describes in what respect he thinks they do. He was in a correct position to know, and we know that he judged correctly, that the Lord did let him remain on for a few years. Then came his second and fatal imprisonment, during which he wrote in an entirely different way (II Tim. 4:6–8)" (Lenski, *Interpretation*, 749).

17   This passage (2:1–5) is perhaps one of the most succinct descriptions of the attitude that all Christians ought to demonstrate toward one another. This is an excellent passage to be read before any congregational meeting, business meeting, or any difficult confrontation that Christians must face in dealing with problems in the brotherhood. If every Christian adopts this mindset, then whatever difficulties will arise among brethren will be dealt with quickly, properly, and lovingly.

18 My words are not meant to imply that "one spirit" in this passage literally refers to the Holy Spirit, but that the context of brotherly unity is spiritual in nature, and that this unity can only be accomplished by abiding in God through the written revelation and guidance of His Spirit (John 4:24).

19 This addresses the facetious scenario posed by Hendriksen, "How can a man who knows that he is industrious regard the rather lazy fellow-member as being better than himself?" (*NTC*, 100). Lenski responds: "Paul is not asking the impossible or the untrue, namely that I am to think that every other Christian, just because he is a Christian, has more brains, more ability, more everything than I have. Nor does Paul ask that we merely 'consider' one another [as being] above [us] although we know that the facts are quite to the contrary, that a large number are far beneath us" (*Interpretation*, 767; bracketed words are mine). Paul speaks of the order of the giving of attention—"This other person first, and then myself"—not the comparative value or worth of the one to whom the attention is given.

20 The word "grasped" can be translated "robbery," leading to the awkward KJV translation: " … thought it not robbery to be equal with God." What this passage does mean is "that Jesus did not need to snatch at equality with God, because he had it as a right" (William Barclay, quoted in James Coffman, *Commentary on Galatians, Ephesians, Philippians, Colossians* (Austin, TX: Firm Foundation, 1977), 281).

21 Lenski, Interpretation, 780.

22 "Emptied Himself" cannot mean "He ceased to be God," whether partially or fully. "Of what did Christ empty himself? Not of his divine nature. That was impossible. He continued to be the Son of God. … Undoubtedly Christ gave up his environment of glory. He took upon himself limitations of place (space) and of knowledge and of power, though still on earth retaining more than any mere man" (Robertson, *Word Pictures*, 444). See also Hendriksen, *NTC*, 107–109.

23 "The text cannot mean that 'he exchanged the form of God for the form of a servant,' as is so often asserted. He took the form of servant while he retained the form of God!" (Hendriksen, *NTC*, 109). In my understanding, Paul does not describe an exchange (one for the other),

but a contrast of the two natures: "the form of God" contrasted with "the form of a bond-servant." In becoming—and not merely pretending to be—a bond-servant, however, Jesus also chose not to exercise His divine privileges as God. There is no question that one nature had to be voluntarily subdued for the other nature to exist. As Lenski says, "Christ laid aside, emptied himself of the constant and plenary [complete—MY WORD] use of all that had been bestowed upon his human nature. If he had not done this he could not have wrought out our salvation. If he had come to earth only as his three disciples saw him on the Mount of Transfiguration, his redemptive obedience in his life, suffering, death, and resurrection, as the Gospels record it, would have been impossible" (*Interpretation*, 781).

24 This was the great scandal (or, offense) that made it so difficult for many Jews to see Jesus as Messiah: to be hanged upon a tree is to be cursed of God (Deut. 21:23, Gal. 3:13). Yet it was necessary that Jesus come in the likeness of human flesh and die in likeness of one cursed of God to satisfy (or propitiate) the wrath of God that is otherwise directed toward us (Rom. 3:23–25, 5:9, and 8:3).

25 Hendriksen, *NTC*, 120.

26 "Crooked" comes from the Greek *skolios*, from which the word "scoliosis" is derived (i.e., a crookedness of the spine). "Perverse" [Greek, *diastrepho*] means to turn aside from the right path, or to corrupt or distort the truth (Thayer, *Lexicon* [electronic], G4646 and G1294).

27 Coffman, *Commentary*, 290.

28 James Strong, *Strong's Talking Greek-Hebrew Dictionary*, electronic edition (database © by WORDsearch Corp.), G2473.

29 The word "messenger" literally means "apostle" [Greek, *apostolos*], but clearly this word is used in a generic sense (as in Acts 14:4 [Barnabas and Paul] and 2 Cor. 8:23) rather than referring to the Christ-appointed apostolic office.

30 Once again, it is interesting to note that, while Paul had the power to heal, he did not use this power on his own fellow ministers. Thus, he did not heal Epaphroditus, and he left Trophimus sick in Miletus (2 Tim. 4:20). Our conclusion is: just as Jesus did not use His divine power for

Himself (Mat. 4:1–4), so Paul did not use (or was not permitted to use) his miraculous healing for what might be considered selfish reasons.

31 JFB, *Commentary* (electronic), on 2:30. Compare this with Rom. 12:1–2, where every Christian's service to God is characterized as a priestly ministry offering up gifts and sacrifices.

32 The word [Greek, *katatome*] translated "false circumcision" means "concision" or "mutilation"; it is not the typical word used for ritual circumcision (Thayer, *Lexicon* [electronic], G2699). "Concision refers to flesh-cutting rituals, which carried connotations of disgrace and disapproval. Though necessary for all people under the old covenant, circumcision became more and more associated in the apostle's experience with the open hostility of the NT Jews and with the warped teachings of the false brethren" (JFB, *Commentary* [electronic], on 3:2).

33 Lenski, *Interpretation*, 834.

34 "He has not, indeed, informed us of the exact extent of his loss in becoming a Christian. It is by no means improbable that he had been excommunicated by the Jews; and that he had been disowned by his own family" (Barnes, *Barnes' Notes*, 195).

35 JFB, *Commentary* (electronic), on 3:9.

36 Barnes, *Barnes' Notes*, 201.

37 Lipscomb, *Commentary*, 209.

38 On this subject, I strongly recommend my book, *The New Testament Pattern: God's Plan for Christians and Their Churches* (Spiritbuilding Publishers, 2023); go to www.spiritbuilding.com/chad.

39 Lipscomb, *Commentary*, 214.

40 Hendriksen, *NTC*, 185; emphasis is his, bracketed word is mine.

41 "True companion" [NASB] or "true yokefellow" [KJV] comes from the Greek *suzugos* and is thought by some commentators to refer to an actual person ("loyal Syzygus"); others believe it refers to Timothy, Silas, or an elder of that church. It is difficult to draw any firm conclusions from the text, and we may never know the actual meaning of the reference.

42 Robertson, *Word Pictures*, 459.

43 The doctrine of "realized eschatology" maintains that Jesus "appeared" in AD 70 in a "spiritual" sense, and that the resurrection (of "old covenant believers") has already taken place. Yet the NT simply

does not teach this. It is true that Jesus came in judgment against Jerusalem (Israel) in AD 70; there is no contesting this. Yet, the NT speaks of three different "comings" of Christ: His judgment against Israel (as just mentioned); His judgment against the Roman Empire, which will include individual churches that refuse to repent (as in the letters to the seven churches in Rev. 2 – 3); and His judgment against the world, before which He will rescue His faithful and bring them into glory. All these comings share overlapping features, but they are hardly interchangeable, and those who lump them all into one "coming" do great harm to Christians' understanding of this important subject.

44 Strong, *Dictionary* (electronic), G4586.

45 *Ibid.*, G4375.

46 Robertson, *Word Pictures,* 460.

47 Thayer, *Lexicon* (electronic), G3049.

48 Lipscomb, *Commentary*, 226.

49 Robertson, *Word Pictures,* 460.

50 Thayer, *Lexicon* (electronic), G842.

51 For a further exposition on this situation, I recommend my *2 Corinthians Commentary* (Spiritbuilding Publishers); go to www.spiritbuilding.com/chad.

52 Strong, *Dictionary* (electronic), G782.

53 Robertson, *Word Pictures,* 463.

54 Hendriksen, *NTC*, 14.

55 JFB, *Commentary* (electronic), "Introduction to Colossians."

56 *Ibid.*, "Introduction."

57 Hendriksen (*NTC*, 9), based upon the research of the eminent William Ramsay, argues that while Paul may not have been familiar with the specific members of that church, it is more than likely that Paul did pass through the city itself. The only suitable ancient land route between Antioch of Syria and Ephesus would take the traveler through Colossae, following the Meander River valley rather than a mountainous route that some commentators assume Paul took to keep him out of the city.

58 What this means is: we cannot define Jesus' pre-incarnate existence apart from His eternal existence as a Personage of the Godhead. There was never a time when Jesus did not exist as God; He was not "born" into existence as God, but only as the incarnate Son of God in His earthly role as our Mediator.

59   It is speculated that Paul met (and converted?) Epaphras during his lengthy stay in nearby Ephesus (JFB, *Commentary* [electronic], on 1:7). In Phile. 1:23, Paul refers to him as "my fellow prisoner," although we cannot determine conclusively whether Paul meant that literally or figuratively, or whether Epaphras was in the same prison as Paul (which seems unlikely) or was in prison elsewhere at the same time as him (which is far more plausible).

60   Hendriksen, *NTC*, 58.

61   Lenski, *Interpretation*, 35.

62   For a full discussion on this subject, I recommend my book, *The Holy Spirit of God: A Biblical Perspective* (Spiritbuilding Publishing, 2010); go to www.spiritbuilding.com/chad.

63   For a deeper study of Satan's influence, "the darkness," and the predatory nature of this darkness, I strongly recommend my book, *This World Is Not Your Home* (Spiritbuilding Publishers, 2021); go to www.spiritbuilding.com/chad.

64   The logic of this construction is inescapable. Yet, the modern Theory of Evolution claims that the material universe did create itself (into what it is presently), and did so apart from any outside (i.e., supernatural) intervention.

65   "There can be no doubt that the apostle here has reference to the usual distinctions and honours conferred upon the first-born, and means to say that, among all the creatures of God, Christ occupied a pre-eminence similar to that. He does not say that, in all respects, he resembled the first-born in a family; nor does he say that he himself was a creature, for the point of his comparison does not turn on these things, and what he proceeds to affirm respecting him is inconsistent with the idea of his being a created being himself" (Barnes, *Barnes' Notes*, 247).

66   We know Satan is well-organized and has rulers who serve under him (Eph. 6:12), but our information is scarce and shadowy. We also know that among God's angels there are different classes or levels of authority, but this information is also very limited.

67   See, for example, Isa. 66:2a, where God explicitly says that "My hand made all these things" (i.e., the heavens and earth). There is no contradiction here, however. Whatever Christ did as the Creator was certainly by the "hand" or authority of His Father, just as Moses is

credited with building a tabernacle that he did not literally assemble, and Solomon is credited with a building a temple that he did not literally construct. Regardless of what conclusion we reach concerning the Creation, we must never separate entirely the work of Christ from the work of His Father, as though the two Divine Persons worked independently of each other.

68 "Christ is 'firstborn' in the sense of being the unique (not created) Son of God. Christ is first over creation, not first in it. Likewise, Christ is subordinate to God the Father (1 Cor. 15:28) as his 'head' (1 Cor. 11:3) not in nature but in office or function as Son" (Norman L. Geisler, *Christian Apologetics* [Grand Rapids: Baker Book House, 1976], 338).

69 JFB, *Commentary* (electronic), on 1:17.

70 Our English word "reconciliation" is a Latin compound world that literally means "to be made friends with again" (1:20). The Greek word for "reconcile" means essentially the same: "to bring back to a former state of harmony" (Thayer, *Lexicon* [electronic], G604.

71 Catholicism and Calvinism, for example, have long taught that people are born sinful creatures. Their position is that the entire human race has been pre-corrupted through the sin of Adam (based upon misinterpretations of Psalm 51:5, Rom. 5:12, and other passages). Given this premise, all babies are immediately sinful creatures, and must be purified either through (infant) baptism or some other means. Yet, the very concept of "reconciliation" demands that we once were friends of God, and that something has interrupted this friendship and must be addressed. This interruption is our personal sin against God. Notice that in every reference dealing with atonement in the gospel, we are told that we are cleansed of our sins, not someone else's (such as Adam's).

72 For an exposition on the "ministry of reconciliation," I recommend my *2 Corinthians Commentary* (Spiritbuilding Publishers) on the passage cited; go to www.spiritbuilding.com/chad.

73 Strong, *Dictionary* (electronic), G526.

74 It is true that even wicked people can perform incidental good deeds that appear to conform to the "fruit of the Spirit," but it is impossible for such people to achieve friendship with God through such works. A few good deeds do not make one a Christian, cannot cleanse the human conscience of its guilt, and cannot remove the divine condemnation

upon one's soul. Only the blood of Christ can do these things (Heb. 9:11–14), and no one can receive the blood of Christ without obedience to the word of God and submission to the Spirit of God.

75 The same can be said of Christ's resurrection: " … if Christ has not been raised, your faith is worthless; you are still in your sins" (1 Cor. 15:17). Thus, it is not enough that Christ died, if indeed He has not been resurrected; on the other hand, He could not have been literally resurrected unless He had in fact died. The two actions either stand or fall together, and we cannot preach the one without the other (1 Cor. 15:3–4).

76 "Pliny, not many years subsequent to the writing of this epistle, wrote to the Emperor Trajan (B. X. Ep. 97) saying, 'Many of every age, rank, and sex are being brought to trial. For the contagion of that superstition [i.e., Christianity] has spread over not only cities, but villages and the country'" (JFB, *Commentary* [electronic], on 1:23; bracketed word is mine).

77 "Minister" comes from the Greek *diakonos*, the same word that is translated elsewhere as "servant" (Rom. 16:1) or "deacon" (1 Tim. 3:8). In a sense, Paul is a specialized deacon in the church, and all ministers of the gospel today are to imitate his servitude (though they have not been given his authority).

78 For a fuller study on the Holy Spirit, I strongly recommend my book, *The Holy Spirit of God: A Biblical Perspective* (Spiritbuilding Publishers, 2010); go to www.spiritbuilding.com/chad.

79 "Striving" is from the Greek word *agonizomai*, from which we get our English word "agonize"; see Luke 13:24 and 1 Cor. 9:25, where the same Greek word is used.

80 JFB, *Commentary* (electronic), on 2:4. "Theosophy" refers to the (alleged) doctrine of God that is based upon mystical insight or specially revealed revelation.

81 Thayer, *Lexicon* (electronic), G3862.

82 "The false teachers boasted of a higher wisdom in theory, transmitted by tradition among the initiated; in practice they enjoined asceticism, as though matter and the body were the sources of evil. Phrygia (in which was Colosse) had a propensity for the mystical and magical, which appeared in their worship of Cybele and subsequent

Montanism [Neander]" (JFB, *Commentary* [electronic], on 2:8).

83 This is the actual reference Peter uses for this same word in 2 Peter 3:10, 12. In that passage, Peter refers to the reduction of the earth (i.e., the entire physical system) to its initial, primary, most basic elements through the application of intense heat.

84 Robertson, *Word Pictures*, 491.

85 Literally, "the Godhead," from *theotes* (Strong, *Dictionary* [electronic], G2320), used only here in the NT. Deity is separated from the Creation: whatever is not Deity (the Father, Son, and Holy Spirit) is a creation of Deity, and whatever is Deity cannot be created but has a self-generated, ever-present, and eternal existence. Paul's point speaks to the great paradox of Christ's incarnation: the time when Deity became one with the Creation through the human person of Jesus Christ. "The fullness of the Godhead [dwelt] in Him in a bodily way, clothed the body. This means that it [dwelt] in Him as one having a human body. This could not be true of His preincarnate state, when He was 'in the form of God,' for the human body was taken on by Him in the fullness of time, when 'He became in the likeness of men' (Phil. 2 7), when the Word became flesh. The fullness of the Godhead dwelt in His person from His birth to His ascension" (Marvin Vincent, *Vincent's Word Studies,* electronic edition [database © 2014 by WORDsearch Corp.], on 2:9; bracketed words are mine).

86 JFB, *Commentary* (electronic), on 2:9.

87 See Acts 15:1–11 for the historical perspective of this subject. I also recommend my *Galatians and Ephesians Commentary* (Spiritbuilding Publishing) for a detailed explanation of this; go to www.spiritbuilding. com/chad.

88 According to the Law of Moses, a male child was circumcised on the eighth day of his life (Lev. 12:3). For the first seven days, he belonged solely to his mother and father; after this, however, he was made a citizen of the nation of Israel and a recipient of God's promises to that nation. In other words, circumcision—with its cutting of the flesh (i.e., removal of the foreskin of the penis), shedding of blood, and permanent (and irreversible) change—represented that child's new beginning with God. This new beginning is also indicated by the "eighth day" in which it occurs: the number eight in Scripture often is used to symbolize a new

life, new power, new dynasty, or new beginning. For all these reasons, circumcision becomes an ideal illustration by which to define the new life of the believer "in Christ."

89 This is parallel to what Jesus said to Nicodemus in John 3:3–5: the believer is "born again" through an act of faith (his baptism—the "water" in that passage) and an act of God (summed up as "the Spirit"), not one or the other. No one is "born again" only through baptism, nor is one "born again" only through God acting on his heart apart from his God-ordained demonstration of faith.

90 There are other signs as well, such as obedience, repentance, confession, etc., but Paul only focuses on baptism here. In Rom. 10:9–10, for example, he only focuses on belief and confession, but this does not nullify the need for other demonstrations of faith that are prescribed elsewhere. There is no single passage in the NT that details for the believer all that he must do to be "in Christ." "The sum of Your word is truth" (Psalm 119:160), not the dissected parts of it.

91 Many have assumed that this "certificate" was the Law of Moses itself that was "nailed to the cross." Yet, there is no reason to assume this, much less prove it. The Law only pertained to Jews (Israelites), not to Gentiles. Paul is not explaining what happened on behalf of Jews, but what Jesus did for everyone who was "dead" in their sins and "the uncircumcision of your flesh" (2:13)—i.e., specifically, Gentiles. If Jesus died for the whole world (John 3:16, 1 John 2:2), then His death was equally advantageous for Jews as well as Gentiles. Besides this, Jesus spoke of fulfilling the Law, not nailing it to His cross (or, putting it to death). Christ was put to death, not the Law; likewise, when we "die" with Christ, we are put to death, not sin itself (nor the laws that condemn us of sin). Through His death, the Law was fulfilled, and atonement was made possible for every sinner. Thus, what is actually "nailed to the cross" is God's condemnation against us for having trespassed His laws; Paul characterizes this condemnation as a written document.

92 Robertson, *Word Pictures,* 493.

93 "Festival" probably refers to one of the three yearly observances required by the Law (Passover, Pentecost, and Feast of Booths). "New moon" refers to the monthly observance of the new moon, which was accompanied by sacrifices (Num. 10:10, 28:11–15). "Sabbath" refers to

the weekly observance of the seventh day of the week, the completion of a full cycle of days (Exod. 20:8–11). Thus, Paul cites yearly, monthly, and weekly observances.

94 "No longer necessary" means that they are no longer binding, not that they are entirely useless to us. All that has been written and preserved in the OT serves to bring us to a better understanding of Christ and His redemptive work, as well as provide moral lessons concerning man's relationship to God (Rom. 15:4, 1 Cor. 10:11, etc.). Those who practically disregard the OT because it is "ancient history" or because it has been superseded by the gospel simply do not understand the wealth of knowledge and perspective that is contained in that sacred record.

95 This is at least what Christ meant in John 5:46: Moses "wrote about" Him in the details of the Law that prefigured the redemptive work of the world's Redeemer.

96 The Epistle to the Hebrews is one grand sermon underscoring this point. I recommend my *Hebrews Commentary* (Spiritbuilding Publishers) for a much deeper study on this point; go to www. spiritbuilding.com/chad.

97 "This practice continued for some time in Phrygia, so that in AD 360 the Council of Laodicea specifically spoke against angel-worshipers in its 35th canon. Even as late as Theodoret's time there were oratories to Michael the archangel, and the modern Greeks have a legend of Michael opening a chasm to save the Colossians from a threatening flood. Scripture clearly opposes the idea of 'patrons' or 'intercessors' (1 Tim. 2:5–6). True Christian humility comes from realizing that our only worth is due to Christ's intervention on our behalf" (JFB, *Commentary* [electronic], on 2:18). See similar thoughts in Coffman (*Commentary*, 388, 390–1) and Hendriksen (*NTC*, 126). Lenski, on the other hand, sees the phrase "worship of the angels" as not being one person's worship of an angel, but imitating the kind of solemn and reverent worship that angels give to God (*Interpretation*, 132). This, however, begs the question: what other kind of worship attitude ought we to have? If angels teach us anything, it is how to conduct ourselves in God's presence; certainly, Paul would not have dissuaded us from learning this lesson. Thus, the first interpretation seems to be the most accurate because it is the most natural and relevant.

98 Concerning the word "elementary" [Greek *stoicheion*], see notes on 2:8.

99 Hendriksen, *NTC*, 133.

100 Incidentally, the phrase "born-again Christian" is redundant. No one is a Christian who has not been "born again"; likewise, all who are "born again" are also known as Christians. There is no other kind of Christian than one who has undergone this born-again process.

101 "The 'body' is here viewed as the instrument by which all the sins of the heart become realities in the outward life. The 'body' itself is the seat of the lower appetites and is called 'mortal.' Paul probably uses this term to remind us of how unsuitable this reign of sin is in those who are 'alive from the dead'" (JFB, *Commentary* [electronic], on Rom. 6:12).

102 For an exposition on these words, see my *Galatians and Ephesians Commentary* (Spiritbuilding Publishers) on Gal. 5:19–21 and Eph. 5:3–5; go to www.spiritbuilding.com/chad.

103 "John Calvin may be on the right track when he states that these vices are called members 'since they adhere so closely to us'" (Hendriksen, *NTC*, 145). This seems also to be Jesus' meaning in Mat. 5:29–30.

104 Lipscomb, *Commentary*, 292.

105 Being conditioned by a politically correct society that puts far more weight on feelings and personal offenses than on divine authority and moral righteousness, such talk of the "wrath of God" sounds jarring and inappropriate. Many believe that God is only about love, tolerance, acceptance, and non-judgment; a "God" that deals out wrath and punishment is inconsistent with their version of the God of the NT. (This immediately overlooks all that God did in the Old Testament.) Yet it is God Himself, through His revealed word, who repeatedly informs us of His wrath toward sin and those who practice it, not modern sentiments about God. We must be careful not to embrace the world's soft-pedaled depiction of God. Rather, we are to accept whatever God says about Himself, whether we or others are comfortable with this or not.

106 For an exposition on these words, see my *Galatians and Ephesians Commentary* on Eph. 4:29–31.

107 "Barbarian" refers to a person who is not born into or taught according to a Greek-influenced society. In other words, it is one who is regarded as an uncivilized or uncultured person. "Scythian" refers to those regarded as savages who lived north of the Black Sea and Caucasus Mountains; they are directly related to the Parthians of warring fame. According to the Greek historian Herodotus, they were nomadic, filthy, drank the blood of their enemies, and made bowls from the skulls of those whom they had killed (H. Porter, "Scythians," *International Standard Bible Encyclopedia,* electronic edition [© 1979 by Wm. B. Eerdmans Publishing Co.; database © 2013 by WORDsearch Corp.]). How much of this is true and how much of this is the result of myths, legends, and folklore will never be known for certain. However, it is true that these people became a scourge against the Roman Empire for many years. Paul's point is not to single out these people, but to use them as an example: if (even) a Scythian is in Christ, then he is no less a Christian than anyone else in Christ.

108 Paul's use of "chosen" or "predestined" indicates a collective or corporate sense, not an individual one. In other words, the church has been predestined to be the recipient of God's divine blessings; but no single person has been so predestined against his own will, as Calvinism teaches. Whether one becomes a part of this chosen group of people is dependent upon (or, conditioned by) his personal faith in Christ; regardless, the church remains a chosen group with or without each person's choice to identify with it. We cannot confuse one's choice to be saved with the power that is required to save him. No one is saved only because of his choice; however, anyone who deliberately calls upon the name of the Lord will be saved by Him (Rom. 10:11–17).

109 For an exposition on these words, see my Galatians and Ephesians Commentary on Gal. 5:22–23 and Eph. 4:1–3.

110 For a deeper study of "forgiveness," I strongly recommend my book, *The Gospel of Forgiveness* (Spiritbuilding Publishers, 2016); go to www.spiritbuilding.com/chad.

111 Lipscomb, *Commentary,* 296.

112 This point necessarily implies that the conditions for forgiveness have been met. We cannot forgive someone who will not take

responsibility for and repent of his sins; yet if these conditions are met, we have no good reason to withhold forgiveness. For a far deeper study on this subject, I recommend my book, *The Gospel of Forgiveness* (Spiritbuilding Publishers, 2011); go to www.spiritbuilding.com/chad.

113 For comments regarding a capella singing versus the use of musical instruments, see my *Galatians and Ephesians Study Workbook* on Eph. 5:19.

114 See my *Galatians and Ephesians Commentary* (Spiritbuilding Publishers) on Eph. 5:22 – 6:9 for a much fuller exposition than is found here; go to www.spiritbuilding.com/chad.

115 Robertson, *Word Pictures,* 506.

116 Some slave occupations were domestic (cooks, waiters, maids, seamstresses, costumers, bath attendants, etc.) Others were craftsmen (cobblers, blacksmiths, silversmiths, plumbers, masons, builders, etc.). Still others were trained as accountants, educators, physicians, midwives, or managers. Some slaves even owned property, ran schools, ran their own businesses, and had slaves of their own. Production slavery, however, had the worst of conditions. Slaves who worked in mines, quarries, farming, and other intensely laborious contexts not only endured daily physical exhaustion but were given barely enough food to eat and clothing to stay warm. Not surprisingly, these slaves had short lifespans and had to be regularly replaced (Henry C. Boren, *Roman Society,* 2nd ed. [Lexington, MA: Heath and Co., 1992], 222–5).

117 See 1 Peter 2:18–20, where the Greek word for "unreasonable" [*skolios*] literally means crooked or morally perverse (Strong, *Dictionary* [electronic], G4646).

118 *Ibid.,* G5590.

119 JFB, *Commentary* (electronic), on 4:18.

www.ingramcontent.com/pod-product-compliance
Lightning Source LLC
LaVergne TN
LVHW010318070426
835508LV00033B/3492

Honoring Our Past, Embracing Our Future:

A Collection of Sermons in Celebration of Saint David's Centennial

By Harvey Hill
Priest at St David's since 2011

Burning Bulb
PUBLISHING

Honoring Our Past, Embracing Our Future:
A Collection of Sermons in Celebration of Saint David's Centennial
By **Harvey Hill**

Burning Bulb Publishing
P.O. Box 4721
Bridgeport, WV 26330-4721
United States of America

Paperback Edition ISBN: 978-1-964172-41-5

Dedicated to the people of Saint David's, past, present, and future, with gratitude for your faithfulness and love. And to Carrie Baker, my partner through it all.

Table of Contents

Introduction

Our parish celebrated its first service on Christmas Eve in 1925. Since then, we have built a building and lost it to fire, built another, expanded it, and then moved down the street to our current location at 699 Springfield Street in Feeding Hills. Priests have come and gone. But through the last century, the people of Saint David's have continued to come together for worship, formation, and service, all in God's name.

I arrived at Saint David's as priest-in-charge for my first service on September 11, 2011. I had turned forty-six four days earlier but had only been a priest for two years. I didn't plan to stay at Saint David's long—my initial contract was for just eight months. Fourteen years later, I am the third longest serving priest in our history, and I can't imagine leaving.

I offer the sermons in this book as a contribution to the celebration of our centennial as well as of our fourteen years (and counting!) together.

At this point, the patient congregants of our parish have heard roughly seven hundred sermons from me. My initial thought for this book was a kind of greatest hits. But choosing was daunting. I was not eager to reread all those sermons! And a first pass through one year's worth wasn't encouraging—few stuck out to me as obvious inclusions or exclusions.

I ultimately decided to choose sermons from particular moments in our history. Three seemed especially important: my first year at Saint David's; the year of the COVID pandemic, which was surely our strangest to date and among our most challenging; and this, our centennial year.

For the first part, 2011-2012, I included every sermon I preached at Saint David's from my arrival through my first Annual Meeting the following January. In the second part, I picked up at the Annual Meeting of 2020, shortly before COVID hit us, and included all of my sermons into the Easter season and the closure of our building. From there, I included a few sermons from significant Sundays. Between the two parts, this book covers the Church year, Advent through Christ the King Sunday. In the third and shortest part, I was more selective, choosing only those sermons that had a more or less direct connection to our centennial celebrations. Altogether there are forty sermons, an appropriately biblical number.

Part Three includes one sermon that I haven't preached yet(!). In 2025, the new Christian year begins on November 30 with the first Sunday of Advent. Our task as Christians during Advent is to prepare ourselves to celebrate the good news of Christ's birth as Immanuel, God with us. But the Gospel reading for that day is a prediction of Christ's Second Coming to establish the Kingdom of God in all its power and glory. I am always struck by that combination of looking back to remember what God has done in the past, and also of looking forward in hope to what God will do in the future.

I wanted to include my sermon for that day since it is exactly the theme of our year-long centennial celebrations: Honoring Our Past, Embracing Our Future. We operate on a much smaller scale than the totality of salvation history! But we are spending this year looking back at what God has done among us in the last century. And we are also embracing our future, looking forward in hope to what

God will do among us in the century to come. It also brings the book full circle since that was the explicit theme of my very first sermon at Saint David's.

Of course, who knows what will happen in the weeks leading up to November 30? The sermon I actually deliver that day may not much resemble what I have written. Still, including what I anticipate saying seemed an appropriate way to conclude this book celebrating our centennial.

This is not the place to lay out an elaborate theory of preaching. But I want to comment on two ways in which my preaching has changed during my time at Saint David's.

When I arrived in 2011, I preached from a manuscript. I wrote out my sermon word for word and then read it to the congregation on Sunday morning. There are good reasons for preaching that way. It allows the preacher to choose words carefully, to structure the sermon coherently, and to preach the desired amount of time. I will always remember a sermon preached by one of my mentors without a manuscript. She told us that she had three points. She made the first point. She made the second point. She paused for a slightly uncomfortable length of time, then said, "Amen." I didn't want that to happen to me!

Because we now mail out my sermons each week (a practice we began during COVID), and also post them on our webpage, I still write my sermons out word for word. As a consequence, I still have sermons for Part Three of this book. But after preaching for a few years at Saint David's, I decided to try preaching without a manuscript. Right away, I loved it. Preaching without a manuscript is a little more chaotic, but also tends to be more lively. I was more able to interact with people, by eye contact and sometimes more directly. I could make slight adjustments as I went along. And I had learned a lesson from my mentor—I never announce how many points I will make!

That change is not visible in my written sermons. But a second one is. The single most common structure for sermons in the Episcopal Church, as best I can tell, is to begin with a personal story of some sort and to use that story as a way into the biblical reading for the day. At some point, I reversed that order. In recent years, I tend to begin with a question or challenge that one of the biblical readings raises, and then explore that issue, usually bringing in a personal story to illustrate the problem or the lesson I draw from it.

No preacher is perfectly consistent on this kind of thing, and people wouldn't want preachers to be—it would get boring. But you may notice that the sermons in the first part of this book tend to follow what I take to be the typical structure, while the sermons in the third part tend to reverse it, to begin with the biblical passage and move to a more contemporary story.

Two final thoughts. Earlier this year, Deacon Terry and I led a session for the Diocese intended to help laypeople lead services of Morning Prayer on Sunday mornings in the absence of a priest or deacon. The Diocese offered a separate workshop on preaching in which I was not involved. But the topic of preaching came up at our session, too. Initially I encouraged people to give a sermon of sorts if they felt comfortable doing that. People expressed anxiety, which I minimized. But I quickly realized that they were wiser than I was.

The opportunity to preach is a serious responsibility. Preachers are charged with proclaiming the word of God to God's people. As such, it differs in important ways from other forms of public speaking. The opportunity to offer spiritual healing and the possibility of doing spiritual harm are both great. As I ponder that fact, I am humbled by the opportunity and the responsibility that I have had for the last fourteen years.

Preaching can also be a great joy. Every once in a while, the Holy Spirit starts to swirl around, and I find myself surprised and moved by what comes out of my own mouth, and I feel a spiritual connection to the people in the congregation, and magic happens. That certainly isn't true every week! But when it is, it's special. And even when it isn't, we do our best to hear God's word together, and we share the Eucharist, and we are formed, united together as the body of Christ in a particular time and place. I am grateful to the people of Saint David's for that experience week after week for the last fourteen years.

With that, I offer this collection of sermons as my small contribution to our centennial celebration. It gives little snapshots of our history and also, I hope, invites us to continue moving forward, following Christ who always goes on ahead of us, and who leads us deeper and deeper into the love of God.

Part 1: First Months at Saint David's
2011-2012, Lectionary Year A, B

When I arrived at Saint David's, I was still a relatively new priest, having been ordained just two years before. I was still teaching fulltime—now at Mount Holyoke College—and acclimating to Massachusetts as my new permanent home. My family and I had lived in western Massachusetts temporarily between 2007 and 2009, so not everything was new. But it felt very much like a new beginning for me.

Saint David's was also ready for a new beginning, after a rough couple of decades. We had been one of the largest parishes in the diocese as recently as 2000, but had suffered a couple of waves of decline. Things seemed dire enough by 2011 that the Diocese intervened, strongly suggesting that we enter the "Canon Sixteen" process. That meant putting together a team from Saint David's to meet with people from other parishes and charged with coming up with a plan for our future.

One result of being in Canon Sixteen was an unusual hiring process. Normally parishes and prospective priests get to know each other over a period of a few months in an effort at mutual discernment. In my case, the Bishop nominated me to the Saint David's vestry, and warned them that he didn't have any other candidates for them. They knew virtually nothing about me, and I knew virtually nothing about them. We agreed on an initial contract for eight months at one-third time. That made me the first part-time priest at Saint David's in many years.

I was thrilled to have a parish, but assumed I wouldn't stay much beyond the term of my initial contract. My teaching position didn't allow me to work more than one-third time, but that position was temporary. I assumed that I would shift at some point to a parish that could afford a fulltime priest.

To my surprise, and I suspect the even greater surprise of our vestry, we turned out to be an excellent match. It took a few years before we made it official, and I became the Rector of Saint David's. (I started as Priest-in-Charge.)

In the sermons that follow, you can see me trying to find my way at Saint David's. My goal in many of them was to acknowledge the challenges facing the parish and to encourage people to live into God's future with confidence and hope. They run from my first sermon at Saint David's on September 11, 2011 through my first Annual Meeting on Sunday, January 29, 2012.

(Year A)

1. Following the Pillar of Fire

13th Sunday after Pentecost; September 11, 2011; Year A
Ex 14:19-31; Ex 15:1b-11, 20-21;
Romans 14:1-12; Matt 18:21-35

For our nation, this September 11 is a time to look back and to reflect on the terrorist attacks that happened exactly ten years ago. Today is a day for remembrance. It is important that we remember our past, even when it hurts.

But today is also a time for new beginnings.

Across the diocese, today begins a new program year. Here at Saint David's we have returned to two services and to worship out of the Book of Common Prayer.

And, of course, today begins my time as the priest-in-charge at Saint David's. I cannot tell you how excited I am to be here.

This is also the beginning of the new school year. It is an especially big time in my family, since we only recently moved to Massachusetts. That means both of my children have just started brand new schools.

My elder son Benjamin started high school a little over a week ago. My younger son Nicholas had his first day of seventh grade in his new school on Friday.

Not only that, my wife Carrie Baker taught her first classes of the year at Smith College also on Friday. I taught my first classes at Mount Holyoke College last Wednesday.

Today is our first time to worship here at Saint David's. It has been a big week for new beginnings in my house!

So I find myself looking backwards, at where we have been, and also looking forward at where we are going.

As luck would have it, our readings for this morning speak of just such a time of looking backwards and also looking forwards.

For the last few weeks we have been hearing from the book of Exodus about the escape of the Hebrew people from slavery in Egypt. We just heard the climax of that story.

Pharaoh has finally let the Hebrew people go. The people leave Egypt and march to the shore of the Red Sea, where they camp. But then Pharaoh changes his mind, and he and his army pursue the defenseless Hebrews.

It is a famous story, and we just heard it, so we know what happens next. God miraculously parts the Red Sea, and the Hebrews escape. Then God allows the waters to come back together to destroy the pursuing army.

At last, the Hebrews can celebrate their deliverance with the song that we just recited. All ends well, at least for now.

But to really appreciate the power of this story, we have to pause before we get to the happy ending. We have to sit with the Hebrews for a few minutes, while the Egyptian army is still coming and the Sea has not yet parted.

In that moment, the Hebrews have two problems.

The first is obvious. The Egyptian army is coming, with all that it represents from their past: powerlessness, slavery, domination, violence.

Their second problem is just as important. It is a problem of vision. The Hebrews cannot see a way forward.

The Hebrews are trapped by their past. They are trapped in their present. They have no visible future.

We know something about how the Hebrews must have felt in that moment because we have felt that way too. The details are different. But we have all had times when we feel imprisoned by our past, when things are not going our way, when we cannot see a bright future ahead.

The attack on our country ten years ago made many of us feel vulnerable in a way we had not felt before.

As we look around us today, we can see plenty of problems, from national debt, to persistent unemployment, to political partisanship and opportunism.

But it is not just the national issues. Saint David's has faced its own difficult challenges over the last few years and faces some difficult challenges right now.

And of course, individuals and families have their challenges, like illness or addiction or simple unhappiness.

We all have our moments on the shore of the Red Sea with the Egyptians coming after us, and some of us are there right now.

So, we can all know something about what the Israelites must have been feeling, standing there caught between the Egyptian army and the Red Sea.

The good news is, this is a story of deliverance. The good news is, they do not stay caught.

Deliverance for the Hebrews comes in two parts.

The first comes in the very first verse. "The angel of God who was going before the Israelite army moved and went behind them; and the pillar of cloud moved from in front of them and took its place behind them. It came between the army of Egypt and the army of Israel."

God came between the people and the threat from their own past. God would not let the Egyptian army continue to dominate and terrify the Hebrews.

What was true for them then can be true for us now.

God comes between us and the problems that beset us. God frees us from our own past, from our own difficult circumstances that can sometimes pursue us like a hostile army.

God does not make the past simply go away. The Hebrews still have to live with the legacy of having been slaves in Egypt. But God offers them freedom.

They did not, and we do not, have to be imprisoned by our past, defined by our past. We can be free as long as we can see God standing between us and our problems. That is powerful good news for every one of us. We can be free, with God's help.

But shielding the Hebrews from the Egyptians is not yet enough. The people also need a way forward, and they are blocked. So God makes a way even where there is no way. "The Lord drove the sea back . . . The Israelites went into the sea on dry ground . . ."

That is our hope. That is our faith.

When we look around and it seems like we are stuck, stuck as individuals or as a Church or as a nation, when we look around and it seems like we are stuck, then especially do we proclaim our faith in the one who IS the way.

When we seem stuck, we remember again that God in Christ offers us a way forward, even in the most difficult situations, if only we can see it.

God does not promise us a life without pain and hardship.

After the Hebrew people go through the Red Sea, they still have to contend with forty years in the desert. Jesus warns us that we who follow him will have to take up our own crosses. Faithful living is not always easy or safe.

But the good news is that Jesus makes it possible for us to see new life on the other side of the cross, just as God enables the Hebrews to see new life in the wilderness on the other side of the Red Sea.

That gift of vision, that vision of new life, is the heart of the good news. The good news is that we can have new life even when we are surrounded by death and despair. The good news is that God leads us on. And it might be scary. And it might be hard. But God is always leading us into new life.

Our task is to follow God into that new life. May we here at Saint David's be faithful to that calling. Amen.

2. Our Baptismal Covenant
14th Sunday after Pentecost; September 18, 2011
Ex 16:2-15; Psalm 105:1-6, 37-45; Phil 1:21-30; Matt 20:1-16

Today at the 10:00 service, we will baptize Madelyn Catherine Vosburgh, the granddaughter of Virgina Ventulett.

It will be a big day for Madelyn.

This morning, Madelyn will renounce Satan and all the spiritual forces of wickedness that rebel against God. Madelyn will renounce the evil powers of this world which corrupt and destroy the creatures of God. Madelyn will renounce all sinful desires that draw her from the love of God. That is a lot of renouncing!

But that is not all Madelyn will do. Madelyn will then turn to Jesus Christ and accept him as her savior. Madelyn will put her whole trust in Christ's grace and love. Madelyn will promise to follow and obey Christ as her Lord. Those are some big promises.

But perhaps the most amazing thing of all, if you stop to think about it, is that Madelyn will do all that renouncing and promising when she is only three months old. Baptism this morning may be the biggest event of Madelyn's life that she will never remember.

I suspect the same is true for a lot of us here. I certainly do not remember my baptism. My children do not remember being baptized.

As I told Madelyn's parents and godparents last week, my eldest son literally fell asleep at the very moment of baptism, just as the priest was pouring water on his head.

Afterwards the priest told us that he had never seen that before. I joked that nothing was left in poor Benjamin after we drove out Satan. Carrie, always more charitable than I, insisted that there was no Satan in baby Benjamin to begin with. Maybe not, but that makes his adolescence a little hard to understand.

I am kidding of course. And, for the record, I made sure Benjamin did not mind me telling that story, which is true.

But it does raise a serious question. What happened when we baptized Benjamin? What will happen when we baptize Madelyn?

If we define religious experience strictly in terms of how we feel, then the answer is nothing. Benjamin was asleep. Lots of babies cry. We will see what Madelyn does. Madelyn can do whatever she wants, because it is her day, although I am hoping Allison will stay close, just in case.

Whatever Madelyn does, we can be pretty sure that she will not feel anything particularly religious when we baptize her. She is too young for that.

But we claim that something does happen at baptism. Something big.

When we pray the thanksgiving over the water of baptism, here is what we say: In the water of baptism, "we are buried with Christ in his death. By [the water of baptism] we share in [Christ's] resurrection. Through [the water of baptism] we are reborn by the Holy Spirit."

Later this morning, Madelyn will be buried with Christ in his death. Madelyn will share in Christ's resurrection. Madelyn will be reborn by the Holy Spirit.

That is what will happen at Madelyn's baptism. That is what happened at our baptisms. This morning, Madelyn will become a member of the body of Christ, just like we did when we were baptized.

But, again like many of us, Madelyn will not know what is happening today. So we have to teach Madelyn, just like people had to teach us.

Madelyn's parents and godparents bear the primary responsibility for teaching her. They will promise to see "that the child [they] present is brought up in the Christian faith and life." They will promise to "help [Madelyn] to grow into the full stature of Christ."

I am going to say that again. Madelyn's parents and godparents are committing themselves to help Madelyn grow into the full stature of Christ.

That is an enormous commitment. That is an enormous responsibility.

And they cannot handle that commitment, that responsibility, by themselves. None of us can. So we all have to help them help Madelyn.

As of today, Madelyn is officially part of the life of Saint David's, and we all have to do what we can to help Madelyn know what that means, so that she can live faithfully as one who has been buried with Christ in his death, who shares in Christ's resurrection, and who has been reborn by the Holy Spirit.

But of course we do not have all the answers for Madelyn. Who among us can honestly claim to have grown into the full stature of Christ?

The Christian life is an ongoing journey, and we are all on that journey with each other and now with Madelyn. We may have died and risen with Christ at our baptism, just like Madelyn will at hers. But we, all of us, still have plenty of room to grow before we reach the full stature of Christ.

Part of what it means to be Christian brothers and sisters is that we help each other along the way. We help each other grow into the full stature of Christ, as we each try to be faithful to our own baptismal covenants.

11

We all fail sometimes. We all lose focus sometimes. Sometimes we all get distracted by spiritual forces of wickedness or by evil powers of this world or by sinful desires that draw us from the love of God.

But God is faithful. God is gracious. God calls us back to our baptisms. God calls us back into the process of growing into the full stature of Christ. God calls us back to Jesus Christ, our savior. God reminds us to put our whole trust in Christ's grace and love. God helps us to follow and obey Christ as our Lord. God helps us honor our own baptismal covenants.

Today Madelyn's parents and godparents make big promises on her behalf. The rest of us support them in those promises, and we share with them the responsibility to help Madelyn be faithful to those promises.

But Madelyn's parents and godparents are not the only ones to makes promises this morning. In a few minutes, we will all renew our baptismal covenants. That makes today a day of renewal, a day of new grace. Grace and renewal for Madelyn. Grace and renewal for the rest of us. Grace and renewal for Saints David's Church. Thanks be to God. Amen.

3. Pressing On

16th Sunday after Pentecost; October 2, 2011
Ex 20:1-4, 7-9, 12-20; Psalm 19; Phil 3:4b-14; Matt 21:33-46

I love history. One of the first things I do when I come to a new Church is try to learn the Church's history, which is to say the Church's stories. I am learning about Saint David's history now, and it has been great.

Of course I have lots more to learn. That is one reason why I hope many of you will come to the potluck meal on Monday, October 17. I want to hear your stories about Saint David's. (I also want to get to know you better and to have some fun with you. But that is not as relevant to this sermon.)

Sharing our stories, and teaching the stories to newcomers like me, helps to define our identity. Those stories are a big part of what makes us who we are.

And of course our particular stories are part of the much larger story of God's work in the world. We are one small chapter in the long history of the Church going back two thousand years and more.

Every week, we hear some part of that story when we listen to the Bible readings. Every week, we re-enact the central event of that entire history when we eat and drink in remembrance of what Christ has done for us. And every week we add a little bit to that grand narrative.

As Christians, we are formed by our memories. We are defined by our shared stories.

I say all of that because I want to be very clear that I really enjoy and value learning about the past.

But, and this is an important but, history is not *all* that defines who we are. We are not limited by who we have been. God is always calling us forward, into new life in

Christ. And that is Paul's big point in our reading for this morning.

Paul says, "This one thing I do: forgetting what lies behind and straining forward to what lies ahead, I press on toward the goal for the prize of the heavenly call of God in Christ Jesus."

That is an amazing sentence. "This one thing I do: forgetting what lies behind and straining forward to what lies ahead, I press on toward the goal for the prize of the heavenly call of God in Christ Jesus."

Paul forgets what lies behind him. And a lot of what Paul had to forget would seem, at first, to be the kind of thing you would want to remember. Paul had it all. "Circumcised on the eighth day, a member of the people of Israel, of the tribe of Benjamin, a Hebrew born of Hebrews…as to righteousness under the law, blameless."

That's pretty good. Paul was doing God's work, as he understood it, and everything was going his way.

We can put ourselves in that place. Most of us can look back to a time when everything was going right, or at least it seemed that way.

Not too many years ago, I was a big man on campus at the school where I taught. I felt like every bit of business that effected the faculty had to go through me. It is not clear that the rest of the faculty shared my view. But for a few months, I could have said a modern version of, "if anyone else has reason to be confident in the flesh, I have more." Those are good memories for me.

I am still learning Saint David's story, but the same is true here, as I understand it.

Not so many years ago, this Church was full on Sunday mornings, kids were all around, we had plenty of money. Life was good. And as best I can tell, it really was good.

14

We should treasure the stories that come from that period of success. Those stories are our stories. They are part of who we are, and we should thank God for them.

But Paul teaches us that we have to be willing to let them go. We have to move on. "Whatever gains I had, these I have come to regard as loss because of the surpassing value of knowing Christ Jesus."

Paul refuses to dwell on the good old days if they keep him from moving forward. That is an important lesson for every Christian.

I would not have been faithful to God's call if I had tried to hold on to my brief period of glory, such as it was. It was a good time for me, but if I had tried to hold on to that time, I would not be here now, and that would be my loss.

Letting go of the good times can be hard. But it may be letting go of the bad times is even harder, if for different reasons. And Paul did that too.

Paul may have been a member of the people of Israel, of the tribe of Benjamin, a Hebrew born of Hebrews. But Paul was also a persecutor of the Church, as he admits in our passage.

Paul had to live with the ugly things he had done as well as the good. Paul had to live with his failures. Paul had to live with his own gross misunderstanding of God's will. Paul had to live with the time that he thought following God meant killing Christians. And he had to do that alongside some of the very people he had tried to kill. Looking back on those times must have been a mighty big burden for Paul.

And that, too, many of us can identify with.

I imagine most of us have times in our past that we would like to forget, times when we did something that makes us ashamed, times when we failed, times when things did not go our way.

That is true for me, and I know that is true at Saint David's. The last few years have had good times, but there have been tough times too.

Paul tells us that we can give those times over to God. Paul regards everything, good and bad, *everything* as loss because of the surpassing value of knowing Christ Jesus our Lord. We can too.

Paul gives the good over to God. And then Paul gives everything else over to God, the bad as well as the good. Paul acknowledges who he has been, for good and for ill. And then Paul forgets everything that lies behind him so that he can strain forward to what lies ahead, so that he can press on toward the goal for the prize of the heavenly call of God in Christ Jesus.

And we can do the same, as individuals and as a Church.

We should tell our stories, all of them, the good ones and the bad. And then we can give all those stories over to God so that we, like Paul, can press on toward the goal of the heavenly call of God in Christ Jesus.

That is part of our gospel freedom. Christ sets us free from the burdens of our past so that we can ask God what God is calling us to do in this place right now. And then we listen. And then we press on toward the goal of the heavenly call of God in Christ Jesus.

So we ask God to speak to us. We ask God for the ears to listen. And we ask God for the courage to answer and to follow. Amen.

4. Rejoice Always

17th Sunday after Pentecost; October 9, 2011
Ex 32:1-14; Psalm 106:1-6, 19-23; Phil 4:1-9; Matt 22:1-14

Philippians is one of my favorite books in the Bible, and the 2 passages in Philippians that really stand out for me come from our reading for last week and our reading for this morning. They go together beautifully.

Last week I preached on chapter 3, verses 13 and 14. In those verses, Paul says, "Forgetting what lies behind and straining forward to what lies ahead, I press on toward the goal for the prize of the heavenly call of God in Christ Jesus."

Those verses are a powerful statement of gospel freedom.

We can let go of the burdens of our past and strain forward into our future, in answer to the heavenly call of God who is constantly making us new. That freedom, which we have in Christ, is God's great gift to us.

But with that gift of freedom comes a daunting responsibility. We have been set free. Now we are called to constantly strain forward, pressing on toward a goal that we will never reach in this life.

We can reach provisional goals. We can do God's will in this moment. But then God calls us forward again, to another goal, and then another, and then another.

Ultimately God calls us to be perfect in love. And as much as we can grow in love, we will not ever get to perfect love. That goal always beckons us on. That goal always calls us forward. We will always have room to grow.

That is true for all of us. That was true of Paul, who concedes that he had not reached the goal and that he, too, has to continue straining forward.

But if Paul had not reached the goal, if Paul had not done enough, what chance do we have? Because Paul did a whole lot.

When Paul wrote his letter to the Philippians, he was in prison for preaching the gospel, and he thought that he might die for his faith. That is already a pretty high standard. But it is much worse than that. In another letter, Paul lists some of the hardships he experienced as he travelled the world proclaiming the good news of God in Christ. "Five times I have received . . . the forty lashes minus one. Three times I was beaten with rods. Once I received a stoning. Three times I was shipwrecked; for a night and a day I was adrift at sea; on frequent journeys, in danger from rivers, danger from bandits, danger from my own people, danger from Gentiles, danger in the city, danger in the wilderness, danger at sea, danger from false brothers and sisters; in toil and hardship, through many a sleepless night, hungry and thirsty, often without food, cold, and naked." (2 Cor 11:24-27)

After all that, still Paul strains forward. Then Paul tells the Philippians to keep on doing the things that they learned and received and heard and saw in him.

Paul's example is surely inspiring. But just thinking about all that endless work is also tiring. I already work hard. I already feel pressed for time. I already have enough stress in my life. We all do. And here Paul is, telling us to keep straining forward.

Sometimes I want to ask Paul, how much would be enough? Is there a point when I can stop straining forward and maybe relax for a little while? Then I ask myself, a little nervously, do I really want to hear Paul's answer to that question?

And it turns out that I do want to hear Paul's answer, and Paul's answer is in our reading for this morning, and Paul's answer is great news.

After telling us to keep straining forward, Paul tells us that the "Lord is near." Paul tells us not to worry about anything. Paul tells us that the peace of God, which passes all understanding, will guard our hearts and minds in Christ Jesus.

God does call us forward. But that does not mean God is off in the distance somewhere. That does not mean we have to keep going and going if we ever hope to be with God.

No. God in Christ is near to us right now, right where we are. God is with us. God is helping us even as we strain forward to answer God's heavenly call.

When I read Philippians, I am always struck by these two points: the call to constant straining forward, and the promise that God is near.

And the amazing thing about Philippians is, the two go together.

Not too long ago, my family and I watched the movie "Chariots of Fire." The movie is based on the true story of a British runner named Eric Liddell who competed in the Olympics.

Some of the people in Eric's life did not care for his running. They thought running was a waste of his time. But Eric responded that God gave him the ability to run fast. For Eric, running was a way to celebrate God's gift.

Then the movie illustrates that beautifully. You see Eric running, and he is running hard. He is the picture of a man straining forward. He is running as hard as he can, and I am enough of a runner to know that he must be hurting.

But Eric keeps pressing on. And as Eric keeps going, running hard, his whole body changes. He straightens up, he throws his head back, he opens his mouth wide, and he smiles in a kind of ecstasy while still running hard. While running as hard as he can, Eric feels the presence of God.

It is a powerful image.

And when an opposing coach sees Eric smile that smile, the coach tells his runner, you cannot beat that guy. Straining forward, pressing on, did not beat Eric down. Straining forward enabled Eric to rejoice.

That is what Paul is talking about in Philippians: running hard, and knowing God, and experiencing peace and joy, all at the same time.

That is why Paul, in prison, anticipating possible death, writing to brothers and sisters who may well be persecuted for their faith, that is why Paul, in the midst of all that, can say, "Rejoice in the Lord *always*; again I will say rejoice."

All of our work on behalf of God and God's Church stems ultimately from that joy, the joy of knowing God. And all of our work on behalf of God and God's Church ends in that same joy.

When we get tired, when we get discouraged, when we feel inadequate to the tasks that God has set before us, then especially Paul's letter to the Philippians speaks to us, with its reminder that the Christian life is all about joy before God.

When we get into squabbles inside the Church, like Euodia and Syntyche did, or when we encounter opposition from people outside the Church, like the Christians in Philippi clearly did, then especially we need to hear Paul's message of comfort and hope.

Rejoice in the Lord always; again I will say rejoice... The Lord is near. Do not worry about anything, but in everything by prayer and supplication with thanksgiving let your requests be made known to God. And the peace of God, which surpasses all understanding, will guard your hearts and your minds in Christ Jesus.

Thanks be to God for that promise and for that joy. Amen.

5. What Isn't God's?

18th Sunday after Pentecost; October 16, 2011
Ex 33:12-23; Psalm 99; 1 Thess 1:1-10; Matt 22:15-22

Have you ever woken up in the middle of the night, maybe after a disagreement, and thought of the perfect come-back? You finally realize what you should have said, if only you had thought of it at the time. But the moment is lost. For me, that is a depressingly common feeling.

But as best I can tell, Jesus NEVER had that feeling. Jesus always has a good come-back. People routinely try to trick Jesus into saying something that will make him look bad, and he always thinks of exactly the right thing to say.

Our gospel reading for this morning is a perfect example of what I am talking about. This time the people trying to trap Jesus are Pharisees and Herodians.

The Pharisees were the intellectuals of that day. Pharisees studied the law and interpreted the law and taught other people about the law. Jesus accuses the Pharisees of getting so caught up in their interpretations of the law that they forget the weightier matters of love and justice. But the Pharisees were no dummies.

The Herodians were the political operators of occupied Israel. Herodians were the ones grouped around Herod's family. Ultimately the Herodians worked for the Roman Empire, of which Herod was a client king.

So these students of the law and these political operators decide to get Jesus by asking him a loaded question. "Is it lawful to pay taxes to the emperor?"

These are not people concerned with a ballooning deficit or a bloated bureaucracy. It is a trick question. If

Jesus says yes, it is lawful to pay taxes, then he alienates the crowds, who mostly hated the fact that pagan Rome had authority over the temple of God and the promised land.

But if Jesus says "no, it is not lawful to pay taxes," then the Herodians could accuse Jesus of disloyalty to the Roman Empire. And the Romans knew how to handle tax protesters in the occupied provinces—the Romans crucified them.

So the Pharisees and the Herodians have laid a clever trap, and Jesus, so it would seem, is stuck.

But Jesus refuses to play the game by their rules. Instead Jesus shows the Pharisees and the Herodians a coin and he asks them, whose image is on the coin? They answer Caesar's image. And then Jesus nails them. Give therefore to the emperor the things that are the emperor's and to God the things that are God's.

At first it seems like Jesus is saying, "yes, it is lawful to pay taxes. We owe some things to God. We owe other things to Caesar. Taxes are what we owe to Caesar."

But if Jesus were saying that, then his opponents have won. His opponents could go to the people and say, "see, Jesus supports the Roman Empire. Jesus thinks we owe Caesar taxes. Jesus is not a patriotic Israelite." Then the people would hate Jesus.

But the Pharisees have not won. Instead "they were amazed; and they left him and went away."

Jesus is not saying that we should pay taxes. Jesus has been much cleverer than that. Jesus says to give to Caesar what is Caesar's and to God what is God's. Fair enough.

But we have to start in the right place. Typically we give first to Caesar, and only then do we give to God.

That is backwards. We should first give to God the things that are God's. Then we can give whatever is left to Caesar.

When we look at it that way, we can see just how clever Jesus' answer was. What is left over after we give to God everything that is rightfully God's? What is NOT rightfully God's?

Do you see the cleverness of Jesus' answer? Jesus does not tell us to pay taxes to Caesar. Jesus reminds us that everything belongs to God. Jesus is saying that however we use our money, for taxes or for anything else, we are borrowing from God what is rightfully God's.

The real question is not, should we pay taxes with our money? That is what the Pharisees and Herodians asked, but it is not the right question.

The real question is, how does God want us to use the money God has graciously made available to us?

And that question goes way beyond taxes. That question should inform our decisions about how we spend every bit of money that we spend. Because everything we have is God's gracious gift to us.

We acknowledge that in our offertory each week. Each week, we put a little money in the plate as a symbol of everything that we have. Each week, that money is brought to the altar to be offered to God. And each week at 8:00, I lift that money up to God, as we say, "All things come of thee, oh Lord, and of thine own have we given thee." And at the 10:00 service each week, as that money is brought to the altar, we sing, "Praise God from whom ALL blessings flow."

That is our way of acknowledging exactly what Jesus is teaching in our gospel reading. God has given us everything that we have. We are simply stewards of what rightfully belongs to God.

The good news is that God grants us the things we have so that we can meet our needs and so that we can be happy.

AND God grants us the things we have so that we can meet the needs of others and so that they can be happy.

AND God grants us the things we have with the understanding that we will, in at least some symbolic way, give it back to God.

All three are important, but for the few minutes remaining in this sermon, I want to focus on that last, giving back to God a token of what God has given us, as our way of acknowledging that all that we have and all that we are comes ultimately from God.

We are entering stewardship season, here at Saint David's. There are pledge cards at the back of the Church. In the next few days, you will receive a letter from our senior warden asking you to pledge your support to Saint David's for next year.

Please respond.

The vestry needs your pledges. Without your pledges, the vestry cannot construct a responsible budget.

I hope that you will pledge generously because you are committed to the mission and ministry of Saint David's. I hope you will pledge generously because you are committed to our common life. Certainly our Church needs money.

But there is more to a pledge than that. I hope you will think of your pledge as a part of your spiritual life.

Your pledge is part of your relationship with God. Your pledge is one way of acknowledging that all things really do come of God. When we pledge, it is really of God's own that we have given God.

Your pledge is a public statement of your gratitude to God for the many blessings that God has given you and that God has given us.

Truly God has blessed us richly. And for those blessings, we give thanks to God. Amen.

6. Crossing Over

20th Sunday after Pentecost; October 30, 2011
(Church cancelled due to snow)
Joshua 3:7-17; Psalm 107:1-7, 33-37;
1 Thess 2:9-13; Matt 23:1-12

21st Sunday after Pentecost; November 6, 2011
(sermon delivered)
Joshua 24:1-3a, 14-25; Psalm 78:1-7;
1 Thess 4:13-18; Matt 25:1-13

It is good to see all of you, especially after the week we have had!

At my house, we lost power Saturday night, but I went to bed assuming everything would be fixed by the morning. I was astonished to hear from Virginia the next morning that everything was chaos in Feeding Hills, and over the day to see just how extensive the damage was. To the best of my knowledge, everybody at Saint David's is doing OK, but please let me know if you are aware of anyone in special need.

What you are about to hear is a modified version of the sermon I originally wrote for last Sunday. The basic point struck me as relevant enough that I decided to deliver it this week, even though it is mainly based on the Old Testament reading from last week.

At that time, Diocesan Convention was on my mind. I was struck by the fact that this could be the last Diocesan Convention under Bishop Scruton.

After more than a decade of leadership by a Bishop who, among his other good qualities, has a special relationship with this parish, our diocese is entering into unknown territory.

There are challenges ahead. Some of them we already know. Apparently they include freaky weather. Other challenges will undoubtedly arise. This diocese is going to need the leadership of a good Bishop.

The Old Testament reading we just heard speaks directly to that need.

Moses has died. Moses who led the children of Israel out of bondage in Egypt. Moses who led the Israelites through the Red Sea. Moses who led the Israelites to the mountain of God. Moses who received the law from God and taught it to the Israelites. Moses who led the Israelites for forty years as they wandered through the desert. Moses was dead.

Moses died just when the Israelites had arrived at the Jordan River and were finally ready to enter into the promised land. After decades of leadership, Moses was gone.

Joshua took over after Moses died, and Moses left some mighty big shoes for poor old Joshua to fill.

But Joshua's problem was not just that he had to follow a much-loved predecessor. That would have been hard enough, but there was more to it. Moses had accomplished an enormous amount, but there was still a lot of work to be done.

Once before, the Israelites had arrived at the edge of the promised land, while Moses was still alive. Once before the Israelites had been set to enter into the promised land and take possession of it.

But lots of people already lived in the promised land. They were hostile. And lots of them were really big and scary.

The Israelites took one look at the people they were supposed to conquer in the promised land, and the

Israelites refused to enter. I have some sympathy for those Israelites. It can be hard to follow God into the promised land.

Forty years go by. Now Joshua, Moses' newly appointed successor, wants to lead the Israelites into battle in the promised land.

First they have to get across the Jordan River. Then they have to face the big scary people who still live there: the Canaanites and Hittites and Hivites, and Perizzites, and Girgashites, and Amorites, and Jebusites.

It is not at all obvious that the Israelites can conquer all those big, scary people. Or rather, it is perfectly obvious that the Israelites cannot possibly conquer all those people unless God helps them.

So the question was, would the Israelites have enough faith to trust God this time, and to follow their untested leader into the promised land? They did not have enough faith when they were following Moses. Would they have enough faith this time?

The short answer is yes, they did have enough faith. And our reading for this morning is part of the reason why.

God promises Joshua, God promises the Israelites as a whole, that God will be with Joshua, just as God was with Moses.

We can apply that promise directly to ourselves.

God has been with this diocese under Bishop Scruton's leadership. Under Bishop Scruton, we have accomplished a lot. But there is still a lot to be done. We can trust that God will continue to be with this diocese under our next bishop, whoever that is.

But as applicable as this passage is to us as a diocese right now, it strikes me that the passage is even more applicable to us as a parish.

In some ways, Saint David's has been wandering around in the desert for the last decade.

God was with the people of Israel in the desert. God fed them. God protected them. God led them. In fact, surprisingly, God was more tangibly present to the people of Israel in the desert than at any other time in their history. But they were still in the desert.

As best I can tell, that applies to Saint David's. God has been present here. And we have been wandering around in the desert.

We may have more desert time ahead of us. If we do, my prayer is that we can recognize God's presence among us even in the desert.

But it is at least possible we are coming to the end of our desert time. It is at least possible that we are now standing on the edge of the Jordan River that separates the desert from the promised land. It is at least possible that God is inviting us to cross over the Jordan and enter the promised land.

What is clear is that God is inviting us to keep moving.

It is natural to look back at where we have been, back at Egypt, back at the desert. Tough as Egypt and the desert may have been, that is what we know.

It is just as natural to look forward with anxiety. Standing between us and the promised land is the Jordan River, and it is not at all obvious how we can get across.

Even if we do cross, we can be sure that strong opponents live on the other side of the Jordan in the promised land, opponents who will challenge our right to be there.

Our opponents are not people, like the opponents of the Israelites. Our opponents are the many things that can discourage and demoralize us. Our opponents are the many things that can make it seem like getting to the promised land and living in the promised land is just too hard. Those opponents can seem big and scary.

I wish that our answers could be as clear as Joshua's were.

God will not part the Jordan River for us in quite such an obvious way as God parted the Jordan River for them. God will not destroy our enemies in quite such an obvious way as God destroyed their enemies.

But God does promise us that God will be with us in the future as God has been with us in the past.

We can claim as our own the comfort that Joshua offered to his people: "among you is the living God who without fail will drive out from before you" whatever enemies stand in your way.

Scary as it must have been, Joshua's people trusted God's promise. And with that trust in God, "the people crossed over." They crossed over not knowing exactly what they would find, knowing only that they were following God.

At this time of transition in our diocese and in our parish, as we look ahead at the challenges before us, we too can rely on God's presence among us.

Can we know what the future holds? No. Is the future going to present us with difficult challenges? Yes.

But as long as we can know that we are following God, responding to God's call, then like the Israelites, we can cross over our Jordan. We can enter our promised land. And we can meet whatever challenges we find there.

Thanks be to God. Amen.

7. Christ the King / Thanksgiving/ Stewardship

Last Sunday after Pentecost; November 20, 2011
Ez 34:11-16, 20-24; Psalm 100; Eph 1:15-23; Matt 25:31-46

I want to begin with a frank appeal for sympathy. Today is the last Sunday after Pentecost, which makes this the last Sunday of the Christian year. Not only that, this is Christ the King Sunday. Not only that, this is the Sunday before Thanksgiving. In origin Thanksgiving is a national holiday, not an Episcopal holy day, but we have adopted it. And on top of all that, I have to preach on stewardship. What, I ask you, is a poor preacher to do?

But here is something for which I am thankful. It turns out that thanksgiving—I mean the act of giving thanks, not just the holiday, holds it all together. Talking to people last week helped me to see that.

My lesson began at our potluck last Monday night. Carol Miller had suggested that we share storm stories, and my table did. Pretty quickly, a common theme emerged. We had all lost power. After sharing how difficult that was, people said it really made them thankful for all the blessings they normally enjoyed—things we normally take for granted like a warm house and electric lights at night and showers.

Most days when I wake up, I do not pause to give God thanks for the fact that the lights work and that I am not freezing and that I can take a shower. But not everyone has those things. Now, for a little while at least, I am noticing how lucky I am to have electricity, and I thank God for it.

A couple of days later, I talked to a friend of mine. He is 82 and has recently developed severe back problems. He will have to have surgery in the next few weeks. Not only

32

that, his brother died a couple of weeks ago. But my friend was not bitter. Instead he gave thanks to God for the many years he had with his brother. And he gave thanks to God for the many years of good health that he has enjoyed.

I take those things for granted too. Most days I do not wake up and thank God for the people I love and for the fact that I am in reasonably good health. But not everyone has those blessings. So now, at least for a little while, I am noticing how lucky I am, and I thank God for it.

It is often loss that makes us appreciate what we have had. It is an irony, but loss can fill us with gratitude because when we lose something we can no longer take it for granted.

So, in this Thanksgiving week, let us imagine what would arguably be the greatest loss of all. Ask yourself what your life would like if you took God out of it.

A friend of mine who is preaching at this very moment in a different denomination suggested I ask myself that question. I did, and I did not much like what I saw. Life without God would be pretty bleak. Thinking about that made me thank God for God, which is what my friend is calling her sermon. We should not take God for granted any more than we should take the specific blessings that God has given us for granted. We should all thank God for being in our lives.

Then take it down one notch. What would life be like without this Church? What would your life be like if Saint David's were not part of it?

People have made that choice, of course. Some have doubtless found a new Church home for themselves, and to them I say, go with God's blessing. I do not understand their decision, but I do not need to understand their decision.

Others have left Saint David's without finding a new Church home, and that makes me sad. Because I know that when I think of my life without Church, I do not much like what I see.

Not everybody is like me, I know. But for me Church helps me to be more aware of God's presence in my life. If you take the Church out of my life, you are not taking God out of my life. God is with us all the time, whether we are consciously aware of God or not. But if you took the Church out of my life, I would have a much harder time seeing God at work in my life and feeling God's nurturing presence all around me all the time. God would still be there, even without the Church. But I might not know God was there, and that would be a terrible loss for me. It may not be true for everyone. But I need the Church so that I can know God.

This is what our reading from Ephesians is all about.

Part of what Paul is doing is thanking God for God's presence in his life and in the lives of the Christians at Ephesus. Paul reminds the Ephesians of "the hope to which [God] has called [them]" and "the riches of [God's] glorious inheritance among the saints" and "the immeasurable greatness of [God's] power for us who believe."

Hope. A glorious inheritance among the saints. The immeasurable greatness of God's power. That is what God in Christ offers us. That is what we lose if we take God out of our lives. No hope. No inheritance. No power.

But God is in our lives, and thank God for that. Thanks to God, we can claim as our own the hope, and the inheritance, and the power.

But claiming that hope and that inheritance and that power is harder than it might seem. We all want it. But can we really feel the hope and the inheritance and the power as something that God has truly given us? For most people, the answer is not always. For the Ephesians, the answer was not always.

So, Paul prays for the Ephesians. Paul prays that God will give them a spirit of wisdom and revelation as they come to know God. Paul prays that the eyes of their hearts will be enlightened so that they could come to know the hope, and the inheritance, and the power.

We offer the same prayer for each other, that the eyes of our hearts may be enlightened so that we too can know the hope and the inheritance and the power.

And for most people, Church helps to enlighten the eyes of the heart. For most people, certainly for me, Church is where I am reminded, over and over again, that God offers hope and inheritance and power. Church is where my eyes are opened to God's presence in my life and to God's work in my life.

And so I give thanks for the Church, capital C, and also for this Church, Saint David's Episcopal Church, which has already become an important part of my relationship with God.

But thanksgiving is not enough. There are two moments in the Christian life. In the first, we open our eyes to God and give thanks to God for all that God does for us. Then, in the second moment of the Christian life, we live lives transformed by God's grace.

We look up to God. And then we look around at God's creation.

Our gospel reading is about that second moment. When the Son of Man comes in power and glory, he will separate the sheep and the goats. Those whom he invites into his inheritance have given food to the hungry and drink to the thirsty and welcomed the stranger and clothed the naked and cared for the sick and visited the prisoners.

As we give thanks to God for God's blessings on us, we need also to remember those who do not have the things we have, those who lack the basic necessities of life. Part of thanksgiving is outreach. We show our gratitude to God by helping the least of these who are members of Christ's family. By helping them, we are helping Christ himself.

Now, as we come to the end of the Church year, it is a good time to stop and thank God for all the blessings in our lives, beginning with the greatest blessing of all, God himself.

Now, as we prepare for the new Church year, which begins next Sunday, it is also a good time to stop and think about the second moment of the Christian life, the moment when we look around us and live lives that reflect our gratitude to God for God's many blessings on us.

As we prepare to celebrate the secular New Year, which begins on January one, many of us will make New Year's resolutions. Here is how we do it in my family. We gather around the dinner table and take turns sharing with each other what our resolutions will be. I type them all up, and we post them on the refrigerator.

Periodically one of my irritating children will point out that I am violating my resolution to snack less or to exercise more. And irritating as those moments are, I have to confess that my children are right. I am in violation of one or another of my resolutions. Worse still, I really should thank my children, who are not really irritating at all but are simply holding me accountable to resolutions that I did, after all, make of my own free will.

The new Church year begins next week, which means that now is the time for us to make our Christian resolutions. That is what stewardship is.

We pause first to thank God for God's many blessings on us, including the blessing of Saint David's. Then we reflect prayerfully on how we want our lives to be transformed during the next year.

We may resolve to pray more faithfully or to study the Bible more regularly or to worship more often. We may resolve to share our resources with neighbors near and far who are less fortunate than we are. All of those resolutions are stewardship.

As a part of your stewardship, I hope that you will also make a financial commitment to Saint David's if you have not already done so. Making a financial commitment is one way to thank God for the place of Saint David's in your life. Making a financial commitment is an expression of hope for what Saint David's can be, with God's help. Making a financial commitment is a part of our spiritual journey with God.

But whether or not you choose to make a financial commitment, my prayer is that we all can use this stewardship season, and this Thanksgiving week, to be more conscious of God's place in our lives and more intentional about what that means for how we live day in and day out. Because that helps us to know God better so that, with the eyes of our hearts enlightened, we may know what is the hope to which he has called us, what are the riches of his glorious inheritance among the saints, and what is the immeasurable greatness of his power for us.

Thanks be to God. Amen.

(Year B)

8. Bible Study and Prayer
Advent 1; November 27, 2011
Isaiah 64:1-9; Psalm 80:1-7, 16-18; 1 Cor 1:3-9; Mark 13:24-37

Today is the first Sunday of Advent, which marks the beginning of the new Christian year. So, happy new year!

Today we begin the whole cycle of prayers and readings over again.

Some things will change. We are marking the change in season to Advent from Pentecost, which we finished last week, by changing the Eucharistic prayers. Following the lectionary, we are shifting from Matthew's gospel, which dominated our gospel readings for the last year, to Mark's gospel, our main source for the coming year.

But the fact is, the year we begin today is going to follow pretty much the same pattern as the year we finished last week. Over the year, we will hear the same story one more time. Over the year, we will pray the same prayers one more time. Not all denominations are quite so repetitive, but the Episcopal Church always has been.

Why do we do that? Why is our service so repetitive?

We believe that we can benefit from listening to the same scriptures over and over again. As we hear familiar passages, we catch a nuance we have never noticed before. Or maybe the passage speaks to us in a new way because we are in a new situation. So we listen once again to the familiar story, and we try to dig a little deeper in the conviction that as we do, we grow a little closer to God.

The same is true for our prayers. We say essentially the same words week after week. And over time, those words sink in. Over time, we make that language our own.

Hopefully over time the language of our prayers shapes who we are. We become more thankful as we say prayers of thanksgiving. We become more aware of God's majesty as we say prayers of praise. We become better people as we say prayers of repentance and hear the comforting words of absolution.

We say the same words week after week so that we can live into the deep truth that we pray, so that we can encounter God more intimately, so that we can meet God in more and more powerful ways.

We do that in Church on Sunday mornings.

But as we begin this new Christian year, I encourage all of you to try to go deeper in to the meaning of the Bible and of our prayers on your own as well.

Saint David's offers lots of opportunities for Bible study. The men's group meets every Monday night at 7:00. A group of women meets with me in my office at 1:00 on Fridays, and men are welcome. Beginning this Wednesday evening at 6:00 and lasting through Advent, we will have a special Advent program of Bible study. Of course, you can also read the Bible on your own.

The point is to be intentional about your own engagement with Scripture. Whether you know the Bible well or you feel like you hardly know the Bible at all, spending time with the Word of God is a valuable spiritual discipline that can bring you closer to God.

The same is true for prayer. Here at the beginning of the Christian year, you might resolve to pray a little bit more than you did last year.

People often say that they do not know how to pray. I understand that. I have said that myself.

And in one sense that is true for all of us. No one is such a master of prayer that he or she cannot grow as a person of prayer. That would be like saying that you communicate perfectly with your spouse or your parents or your children. Even people who really are good communicators are not perfect. There is always room for growth.

But we sometimes make prayer harder than it has to be.

I once saw a moving scene in a television program. I came in at the very end, so I do not even know what the program was about. But at the very end of the program, a family gathered around the table after a meal to offer thanks. An older women spoke to God for the whole group. And all she did was tell God what they had just eaten. "God, we enjoyed our turkey and stuffing, a little cranberry sauce and some green beans. And, oh God, the pumpkin pie was great. Thank you, God. Amen."

That woman spoke from her heart to God about what was on her mind, and that is a big part of what prayer is.

Sometimes that is all you need to say. And then sometimes you need to say more. And the Book of Common Prayer can help if you need to say more.

What the Prayerbook calls "The Daily Office" has become a big part of my own prayer life. The Daily Office is a sequence of prayers for morning, noon, evening, and then bedtime.

The best known part of the Daily Office is Morning Prayer. Some of you have probably been to services of Morning Prayer when there was no Eucharist on Sunday morning. You can also say Morning Prayer by yourself at home, and that is what has been so valuable for me. You have to say it a few times to see what works best for you. But it does not take long to get into a routine that feels natural.

Here are three reasons to give Morning Prayer a try, based on my experience with it.

First, it gives me words to pray when I do not necessarily feel like praying. That is really helpful as you try to establish a good prayer discipline, and discipline is important.

Praying is a little bit like exercise. You get better at it if you do it regularly. Like exercise, you do not always feel like doing it. Also like exercise, you usually feel better after you do it even if you were not particularly eager. Morning Prayer is like a prayer exercise routine, and it is good to have a routine.

Second, Morning Prayer takes me through a variety of forms of prayer. It begins with confession of sin. It includes praise of God. There is space for asking God's blessing on our nation and Church and family and people who have asked for our prayers. It has a prayer for mission in the world. It ends with a prayer of thanksgiving.

When I say Morning Prayer, I know that I have covered my prayer bases.

Finally, Morning Prayer includes a regular sequence of readings from the Bible, which are listed in order in the back of the Book of Common Prayer. When you say Morning Prayer, you get in at least a little bit of Bible reading.

If you are interested in saying Morning Prayer, I encourage you just to start in. But if you want some guidance on how you might do it, let me know. I would love to talk about it.

Whether or not you use the particular form of Morning Prayer, the point is to immerse yourself in Scripture and to pray as regularly as you can.

Live into the rhythms of the Bible. Spend time with God in prayer. Go deeper into the old familiar story. Make your own the language of our prayers. That is what we do on Sunday mornings, and that is something you can do every day at home.

Here is the incentive. If you dedicate yourself to Bible study and prayer, you will grow closer to God this year. That is God's promise to us. Thanks be to God. Amen.

9. Active Waiting

Advent 2; December 4, 2011
Isaiah 40:1-11; Psalm 85:1-2, 8-13; 2 Peter 3:8-15a; Mark 1:1-8

Last week was a busy one for me. Among other things, I had a stack of papers my students were anxious to receive back. So on Wednesday morning before I left home, I graded the papers.

I was feeling good when I left home. It was a little later than I liked. I had to hurry. But that was OK.

This story does not have a happy ending.

As I drove off, my car was making a strange noise. That was worrisome. But I was in a hurry. I drove on.

The noise got worse. I could not keep going. It turns out I had a flat tire. I do not mean low on air. I mean flat, like riding on the hub cap flat.

I could not remember ever having had a flat tire. But I am a can-do kind of man, so I figured I would slap on the spare and be on my way.

I asked the department secretary to put a note on my classroom door telling the students that I might be a few minutes late, I rolled up my sleeves, and I opened the trunk, feeling positively manly.

This is one of the unhappy parts of my story.

I could not even get the spare tire out of the trunk, much less on to the wheel. That was a little deflating. Pun intended.

So there I was, by the side of the road, unable to move. Then, miracle of miracles, I noticed that there was a tire shop literally across the street. Time was passing. I was going to be late. But it was possible that I could still make it.

This is another unhappy part of this story.

43

The man in the shop really did try. And despite some real obstacles, he got it done in less than an hour.

But for that hour, as I watched time tick on by, and as I saw any possibility of getting to my class slowly disappear, I was in frenzy of impatience.

The problem is, I HATE waiting.

Many is the time Carrie and I have driven up to a store, and she asks me to wait in the car. I do my best. But after about 15 seconds, I park the car and come in after her. I cannot stand to wait in the car.

One of the restaurants we like has slow service. It seems like that would just be more family time. But I have just about gotten to the point that I cannot eat there any more. I hate to wait for my food.

When I go to my desk to turn on my computer in the morning, I bring a book to read while it boots up. Lines in stores drive me crazy. Traffic lights drive me crazy.

The point is, I HATE waiting. It does not matter why.

I am a little extreme on this point. But I am not unique. Most people I know get impatient when they have to wait. In our culture, we move fast. We keep busy. And not many of us have time to spare for pointless waiting around.

That is probably more true around Christmas than at any other time of year. And because we are so busy, and because most of us hate to wait, we tend to skip Advent altogether, and go straight to Christmas.

The shopping season begins as soon as Thanksgiving is over. Christmas season is here. It is time to be getting ready. There is no time to wait.

And then there is Advent, perhaps the most counter-cultural season of the entire Christian year. In the midst of all our busy-ness, Advent is all about waiting.

Last week, Isaiah told us that God "works for those who wait for him" (40:4). Paul talked about how we "wait for the revealing of our Lord Jesus Christ" (1Cor 7). Jesus said that we cannot know the day or the hour when God will come, so we have to wait patiently and expectantly (Mk 13:32).

This week Peter tells us to live lives of holiness and godliness while we are waiting for the coming of the day of God.

It is all over our Advent readings. God is coming. Our job is to wait.

And I hate that.

And I need that.

I need to be reminded that we wait for God. That God will come in God's own time. That God is in charge, not us.

Our reading from 2nd Peter is all about waiting.

A few verses before our passage, Peter says "scoffers" ask, "Where is the promise of his coming" (3:4)? The scoffers are talking about the Second Coming. Jesus said he was coming back to make all things right. I am looking around, say the scoffers, and it looks like plenty is still wrong with the world. So where is he?

The scoffers lost patience. The scoffers were tired of waiting. I get that.

So Peter tells them, and Peter tells us, "do not ignore this one fact, beloved, that with the Lord one day is like a thousand years, and a thousand years are like one day. The Lord is not slow about his promise, as some think of slowness, but is patient with you."

So we wait. We wait on God, who will come in God's time, not ours. It is an Advent lesson.

But there is a second lesson here too. We are not totally passive while we wait for God.

Peter reminds us that we are waiting for the coming of the day of God. But Peter also tells us, listen to this, Peter tells us that we hasten the coming of the day of God. I am going to say that again. Peter suggests that we can hasten the coming of the day of God. In words that are applied to John the Baptizer in our gospel reading, we have a role in preparing the way of the Lord. That is an astonishing responsibility.

Part of that responsibility involves our work in the world around us. Both Matthew and Luke tell us that John the Baptizer talked about that. But in Mark, the gospel we just heard, the emphasis is on the "baptism of repentance for the forgiveness of sins." As we wait for God, we reflect on our lives, and we acknowledge the many ways we fail to live up to God's will for us.

In a few minutes, we will confess that we have sinned against God in thought, word, and deed, by what we have done, and by what we have left undone. We will confess that we have not loved God with our whole heart, and we have not loved our neighbors as ourselves.

We are not ready for God to come. So we have work to do while we wait.

We do not need to wallow in our own sinfulness. After all, God forgives sin. John's baptism of repentance was for the forgiveness of sins.

But we should acknowledge our sinfulness if only so that we can move beyond our sin. By confessing our sin and hearing the words of absolution, we are strengthened in all goodness.

That is how we get ready for Christ to come while we wait. That is the work of a holy Advent.

May God help us to get ready. Thanks be to God. Amen.

10. The Year of the Lord's Favor
Advent 3; December 11, 2011
Isaiah 61:1-4, 8-11; Canticle 15; 1 Thess 5:16-24;
John 1:6-8, 19-28

God once called a man to leave his home to seek baptism from one of the most famous religious leaders of the day. So off the man went, and he had an amazing experience.

When this man returned, he went to his home Church, where his townspeople invited him to preach. He chose as his passage the one from Isaiah that we just heard.

"The Spirit of the Lord is upon me, because the Lord has anointed me; he has sent me to bring good news to the oppressed, to bind up the broken-hearted, to proclaim liberty to the captives, and release to the prisoners; to proclaim the year of the Lord's favor."

After he read that passage, everyone's eyes were fixed on him, and he preached his first-ever sermon for the home-town crowd. He said, "Today this Scripture has been fulfilled in your hearing." The end.

Now Andy Campbell tells me that a good sermon has an engaging beginning, a strong ending, and not too much in the middle.

Apparently, Jesus agrees because that story comes from the gospel of Luke and it is about Jesus.

The people of Nazareth seem to have agreed too, because Luke tells us, they all spoke well of him. Everybody likes a short sermon. However, I could not get my sermon to be that short, so you might as well settle in for a few minutes!

But I did think a lot about what those people got from Jesus that morning, when he read our passage and claimed that it was fulfilled in their hearing.

There is nothing uniquely messianic about the passage. Jesus was anointed by the spirit of the Lord to bring good news to the oppressed. But that is true for every Christian. We are all anointed by the spirit of God. We are all called to bring good news to the oppressed. We cannot do that with the power of Jesus. But that is my mission; and it is our mission; and it is your mission, each of you individually, just like it was Jesus' mission.

Whatever else Isaiah was saying, and whatever else Jesus was saying when he read from Isaiah, we can be sure at least of this. We are called by God to help those who need help. We are empowered by the Spirit of God so that we can help those who need help. At some level we will be held accountable by God based on whether or not we have helped those who need help.

That is why outreach always needs to be part of what we do as a Church. Outreach is part of our Church's budget. But more importantly, outreach is part of what we do as a community of faith. Things like Operation Christmas Child and the food drive are part of how we fulfill our mission to follow Christ.

But there is more to this passage than a call to outreach, important as outreach is. Isaiah is proclaiming the year of the Lord's favor. Jesus makes that proclamation his own. Jesus says that God anointed him to proclaim the year of the Lord's favor. Today this Scripture is fulfilled in your hearing. The end. It makes me wonder what the year of the Lord's favor looks like.

Here in Advent, we are beginning the new Christian year. What would you hear if I told you that this year is the year of the Lord's favor for us? What would that mean for us?

My own first reaction reflects an embarrassing lack of imagination. What do I want from the next year? What blessings would I like from God for me personally? Well, I would like a little more time, and a little more rest, and a little more money. That is my immediate reaction.

My first answer looks about the same if I think of it as God's favor for Saint David's. I would like more people, more kids, more money. I would like a little more of this or a little less of that.

But God invites us to think much bigger than that. God invites us to use our imaginations. God invites us to dream. God invites us to envision our future. God invites us to transformation.

And anything is possible. Because this is God we are talking about.

Paul can help us to dream. Here is Paul's vision for the Thessalonians. It can be part of our vision too.

Paul says to rejoice always. Paul is not talking about feeling good. Paul is not talking about being in a good mood all the time. Paul is talking about the peace and the joy that pass all understanding. Paul is talking about the joy of knowing that we are children of God, even when life is hard.

Then Paul says to pray without ceasing.

I once read about a man who said the Jesus prayer as he breathed. He would breathe out, "Lord Jesus Christ." He would breathe in, "Son of God." He would breathe out, "Have mercy on me." He would breathe in, "a sinner." Then he would repeat. Eventually for this man, every breath was a prayer. He took Paul's words about praying without ceasing literally.

That is hard. But our whole life can be a prayer. We can live out our praise of God.

Then Paul says to give thanks in all circumstances. In good times it is easy to be thankful, as long as we do not fall into the trap of taking our blessings for granted. It is harder to be thankful when times are tough. But Paul offers us a vision, a possibility, that we can always be thankful, no matter what is happening.

Paul is not telling us to feel guilty if we do not rejoice always, or pray without ceasing, or give thanks in all circumstances. Paul is offering us a vision of what our lives can be like. Our lives can be constant joy, and prayer, and gratitude.

That is not a rule for us to follow. That is a gift God offers us. That is part of what God's favor looks like.

And this could be our year to receive that gift. This could be the year of the Lord's favor for us. This could be the year when we are blessed like we have never been blessed before. This could be the year when we come closer than ever before to constant joy and prayer and gratitude.

This could be the year that Isaiah's words come true for Saint David's. "All who see them shall acknowledge that they are a people whom the Lord has blessed."

Is that too much to ask? Is it too much to hope for?

Maybe so. But this is the season for hope, and for imagination, and for new vision.

Think about what it was like this time two thousand years ago. The first Christmas ever will come in two weeks. Jesus is about to be born. But outside of the holy family, nobody knows that.

Picture yourself, two thousand years ago, right before the very first Christmas, talking to a shepherd.

You say to him, "you know, God is about to come into the world. God is about to do a new thing. God is about to bless you in ways you can hardly imagine."

What do you think the shepherd would have said? My guess is, he would have said it was too much to hope for. But it would have been true. It was true then. It is true now.

God is coming. This will be a year of the Lord's favor. Thanks be to God. Amen.

11. Here Am I

Advent 4; December 18, 2011
2 Samuel 7:1-11, 16; Canticle 15;
Romans 16:25-27; Luke 1:26-38

The Christian life is all about God's call.

Part of our call, each of us, is to share a common life before God. We come from many different places. We arrive here for many different reasons. But we have a common calling to be God's people in this place. We should thank God for calling each of us to be here.

We each have a special call as well. We are each called to share our individual gifts with the larger community of faith. God equips us for a variety of roles. I bring my gifts and talents to Saint David's. So do each of you.

And as the body of Christ in this place, we will thrive only as long as we each answer our own callings in our own ways, but always for the common good.

Here in the final week of Advent, as we prepare ourselves to celebrate the good news that God became incarnate and was born of the Virgin Mary, we should all be thinking about and praying about the shape of our calling to follow God in the coming year.

It may be that it is your turn to serve on the vestry, or to participate in the Caregivers ministry, or to take on an outreach project, or to help with the altar guild, or to become a Eucharistic Minister, or any of the other many opportunities for service that are available to you here.

And those are just opportunities here. There are many, many other possibilities. In fact, the sheer number of possibilities can seem a little overwhelming. In the midst of all that possibility, God's call to us can be hard to hear.

And to help us to think about and to pray about our various callings, we have our gospel reading for this morning, one of the most famous callings in all of Christian history, God's call to Mary to be the mother of Jesus.

Mary's response to her call is a model for how we should respond to our calls.

Mary's emotions in this scene are complicated. Mary starts with perplexity. Mary asks, "How can this be?" But Mary ends with "Here am I." The lesson for us is in that movement from perplexity to willing participation.

The story begins when the angel Gabriel comes to Mary and says, "Greetings, favored one! The Lord is with you." That already is part of the lesson of this passage. God speaks to us.

God does not normally speak to us so dramatically as God spoke to Mary. But if we really knew how to listen, I suspect that we would all hear, in our different ways, God calling us "favored one" and God promising to be with us.

But the part that strikes me is Mary's reaction. Mary "was much perplexed . . . and pondered what sort of greeting this might be."

That is a common reaction as we begin to discern God's call to us. God calls us, but God speaks with a still, small voice, and there is a lot of interference in the world. As a result, our initial reaction is often uncertainty. What does God want from me? Like Mary, we are perplexed and have to ponder.

Mary was still pondering when Gabriel said, "Do not be afraid, Mary." Now you know what comes after "do not be afraid" is going to be mighty scary.

"Do not be afraid, Mary, for you have found favor with God. And now, you will conceive in your womb and bear a son, and you will name him Jesus. He will be great, and will be called the Son of the Most High, and the Lord will give to him the throne of his ancestor David. He will reign over the house of Jacob forever, and of his kingdom there will be no end."

That is big news. That news is scary big. And Mary cannot take it all in.

Her son will be called the Son of God. God will give her son the throne of David, which has been vacant for well over 500 years. Not only that, her son will reign forever, and his kingdom will have no end. That is too big to take in.

But Mary did not get past Gabriel's first sentence, "You will conceive and bear a son." "How can this be," she asks, "since I am a virgin?" Mary is not thinking about the Son of God who will reign forever. Mary has not gotten there yet.

Mary is stuck on the idea of conceiving and giving birth. Mary is just thinking about her part in God's big plan. In that, too, Mary is a model for us.

God has a plan to restore all of creation. Mary had a much bigger role in that plan than any of us have. But we all have some small part to play in God's unfolding plan of salvation. Our worship here this morning is one tiny piece of God's enormous, incomprehensible plan to restore all of creation. God's call to each of us is a tiny piece of God's enormous, incomprehensible plan to redeem all of creation. Your participation in the life of Saint David's is a tiny piece of God's enormous, incomprehensible plan of salvation for us and for all whom God has made.

When you listen for God's call to you, when you try to find your part in God's mission in the world, then you are listening for an angel to say to you, here is your role in spreading God's kingdom. Here is your role in God's enormous, incomprehensible plan.

God's kingdom is too big for us to take in. So the best we can do is to follow Mary's example. We cannot worry about the whole plan.

God's plan is what matters. Our part in God's plan is so tiny as to be virtually invisible. So when we hear the call, it seems like we ought to focus on the plan as a whole, not just on our part. But it is too much.

So like Mary we ask, how can this be? We ask about our small part. We do not ask about our part because it is the only part that matters. We ask about our part because it is the only part we are responsible for. We ask about our part because that is the part we get to play. And our parts, small as they are, are hard enough.

We cannot worry about God's whole plan. None of us individually can even worry about God's overall plan for this Church. Even that would be too much.

Our individual calling is small. But it is still more than we can do. So we ask, not about God's whole plan, but just about our tiny part of God's plan, "how can this be, since I am not the right kind of person?" God, I do not think I can do it. You better find somebody else to do whatever it is you had in mind for me.

Then the angel tells us what we most need to hear. The Holy Spirit will come upon you. The power of the Most High will overshadow you. For nothing will be impossible with God.

What is there left to say? God calls us. God empowers us. So we say, with Mary, "Here am I, the servant of the Lord; let it be with me according to God's word."

Thanks be to God. Amen.

12. Something About That Baby

Christmas Eve; December 24, 2011
Isaiah 62:6-12; Psalm 97; Titus 3:4-7; Luke 2:1-20

Here we are, at last. Christmas Eve.

After four weeks of getting ready, we can put our preparations behind us, and celebrate the good news of great joy for all people, that to us is born this day in the city of David a Savior, who is the Messiah and the Lord.

Tonight, at last, we can stop preparing and start rejoicing. Christ our savior is born. Thanks be to God.

So we come together this night to celebrate, to experience once again what the shepherds experienced so long ago. We come to hear the angel point us to the child. And we come to the child to adore him.

Use your imaginations for a minute. Picture yourself among the shepherds on that first Christmas. They were ordinary people going about the ordinary business of their lives. But it was no ordinary night.

Suddenly the angel appears, and with the angel the glory of God.

We tend to imagine that angels are cute and sweet. But that's wrong. Angels are terrifying. Whenever angels appear, they always have to begin, "do not be afraid."

This is no exception. The shepherds are terrified, and the angel begins by reassuring them. Don't worry. I won't hurt you. I bring you good news. Relax. Just listen for a minute. To you is born this day in the city of David a Savior. I'm just here to tell you about him.

Imagine the shepherds' relief. The angel comes in peace. The angel brings good tidings of great joy.

But the shepherds aren't really thinking about the good tidings just yet. The shepherds are too overwhelmed by the

57

angel who brings the good tidings. The angel still seems a little scary. And the night has just begun.

Suddenly the one angel, who was terrifying enough, is joined by a multitude of the heavenly host. The shepherds must have collapsed entirely.

Think about what those shepherds must have been feeling: terror, of course. But also awe. Wonder. Reverence. Love. Think about what it must be like to see the multitude of the heavenly host and to hear them praising God. And all that massed power and glory that the shepherds see and hear, all of that because of the Savior, the Messiah, the Lord.

After the angels leave, who wouldn't want to go see the cause of so much heavenly joy? He must be truly awesome.

I can imagine the shepherds talking to each other. Their eager anticipation. Them asking each other, what could possibly top everything we have already seen tonight?

I can also imagine the shepherds being puzzled by the sign the angel had given them. "A child wrapped in bands of cloth and lying in a manger." A baby in a diaper in the cheapest motel in town.

That doesn't sound as impressive. It doesn't sound like that would be worth

abandoning the flocks on the hill for. It doesn't sound like that would be worth

walking into town in the middle of the night for. That sounds pretty ordinary. No doubt many of the shepherds had been babies wrapped in swaddling clothes

and living in less than desirable homes.

Maybe some of the shepherds said as much. Maybe some of them said, I'm not sure it is worth it.

But if so, other shepherds prevailed on them. After all, they might have said, if the child is good enough for those angels, the child is good enough for me. So the shepherds went, and they went with haste, to see the great sight.

And they found just what the angel has said: Mary and Joseph and the baby lying in the manger. The shepherds found a poor family, miles from their home, exhausted from travel and from anxiety and from childbirth. The holy family must have looked very ordinary, or maybe not even that good.

But there was something.

Somehow the shepherds could see something. Maybe the angels gave the shepherds the gift of sight. Maybe the shepherds always had it. But the shepherds could see something extraordinary in that very ordinary scene.

And so those shepherds were not disappointed by that baby lying in the manger wrapped in swaddling clothes. When the shepherds finally left the little family, they returned to their sheep, glorifying and praising God for all they had heard and seen, as it had been told to them. The shepherds glorified and praised God for their meeting with the holy family and with the Christ child, just as the angels had said they would.

There was something about that baby that eclipsed even the angels of God.

And now, two thousand years later, here we are. It's Christmas Eve once again. It's our time to encounter the Christ child. It's our time to see something extraordinary in an apparently ordinary baby.

We have done everything we can to prepare ourselves to see. The Church is decorated in our fanciest white linens, with greens everywhere. The altar is surrounded by poinsettias. We have dressed up in our Christmas best.

All of that is supposed to draw our attention to the child around whom this holy night revolves. All of that finery is supposed to help us see that God is here, among us, tonight.

God's presence here among us makes this an extraordinary moment, if only we have the gift of sight, like the shepherds did that night so long ago.

And so we celebrate this night. We praise God. We give thanks.

And in exultation, we cry, "The Lord is King; let the earth rejoice; let the multitude of the isles be glad...The heavens declare his righteousness, and all the peoples see his glory...Light has sprung up for the righteous, and joyful gladness for those who are truehearted. Rejoice in the Lord, you righteous, and give thanks to his holy Name.

Let us add our voices to that song of creation and to the multitude of the heavenly host, praising God and saying, "Glory to God in the highest heaven, and on earth peace among those he favors."

Thanks be to God. Alleluia. Alleluia. Amen!

13. Baptized by the Spirit

Epiphany 1: The Baptism of Our Lord; January 8, 2012
Genesis 1:1-5; Psalm 29; Acts 19:1-7; Mark 1:4-11

This morning marks a change of seasons for us. For twelve days, we celebrated Christmas. The Christmas season ended Friday, two days ago, with Epiphany, the day dedicated to the wise men who followed the star to Jesus.

Today, the first Sunday after Epiphany, we focus on the baptism of Jesus and the beginning of Jesus' adult ministry.

From Christmas Eve until today, the baptism of Jesus, we decorate the Church in white. Then tomorrow we return to green to mark the Sundays between Epiphany and Lent.

So this Sunday we move from white to green. We move from the baby Jesus to the adult Jesus. We go from the joy and adoration of Christmas to the greater challenge of Jesus' ministry, which leads inevitably to the cross.

The question for us, on this Sunday of transition, is, are we ready?

Are we ready to follow Jesus as he wanders through Galilee teaching and healing? Are we ready to follow Jesus, when we know he is leading us to the cross?

If we were left on our own, if we had to do it all by ourselves, the answer is clear. We are not ready.

Thankfully we are not left on our own. That is the good news of this Sunday commemorating the baptism of our Lord. God helps us.

We can start with a question. Why does Jesus allow himself to be baptized?

The traditional answer makes good sense to me. The traditional answer is that Jesus was not baptized because he needed baptism. Jesus was baptized to set an example for us. Jesus was baptized because we need baptism.

That means the gospel story for this morning is not just about what happened to Jesus there on the banks of the Jordan River two thousand years ago.

The gospel story is about that, of course.

But the gospel story is not *just* about that. The gospel story is also about our own baptisms, when we, who do need baptism, follow the example of Jesus, who did not but who set an example for us.

The story of Jesus' baptism is a lesson for us about what happens when we are baptized.

John's baptism, the baptism Jesus received, was all about sin and confession and repentance and forgiveness. Jesus submitted to John's baptism. That reminds us, in case we had forgotten, that we all have sins that need to be forgiven. We should never entirely lose sight of John's baptism of repentance. It was, after all, good enough for Jesus.

But Jesus' baptism goes well beyond John's. Jesus' baptism is not ultimately about sin, like John's was. We can see that in the reading from Acts.

According to Acts, Paul found believers in Ephesus who were baptized into John's baptism for the repentance of sins. But John's baptism of repentance, taken alone, was not good enough. These baptized believers had never even heard of the Holy Spirit. So Paul re-baptized them in the name of the Lord Jesus. Paul laid hands on them. And the Holy Spirit came upon them.

We might need to start with repentance, but repentance is not enough. We need to receive the Holy Spirit.

And that is what happens to Jesus in his baptism. Jesus starts with John's baptism, but then he experiences much more. When Jesus is baptized, the Holy Spirit descends like a dove. And a voice comes from heaven, saying, "You are my Son, the Beloved; with you I am well pleased."

That is going well beyond what John did. That is an amazing scene.

I have seen a lot of baptisms. But I have never seen the heavens torn apart and the Spirit descending like a dove. And yet that is what we claim happens in baptism. It is less dramatic for us than for Jesus. But less drama does not make the experience less real.

In baptism, we pray that God will fill the baptized person with God's holy and life-giving Spirit. We thank God that through baptism we are reborn by the Holy Spirit. At the end of the baptism itself, the newly baptized person is anointed with holy oil, with the words, "you are sealed by the Holy Spirit in baptism and marked as Christ's own forever."

The Holy Spirit is most definitely at work in our baptism even if we do not see the heavens torn apart and the Spirit descending like a dove.

I have also never heard a voice from heaven telling me that I am a beloved child of God with whom God is well-pleased. But that, too, happens in baptism, if again less dramatically for us than for Jesus.

Baptism can conclude with this prayer: "All praise and thanks to you, most merciful Father, for adopting us as your own children, for incorporating us into your holy Church, and for making us worthy to share in the inheritance of the saints in light; through Jesus Christ your Son our Lord, who lives and reigns with you and the Holy Spirit, one God, forever and ever. Amen."

In baptism, we are adopted by God as God's children. That is our version of "You are my son. You are my daughter." In baptism we are made worthy to share in the inheritance of the saints in light. With that God is well pleased.

Now it would be nice if the story ended there, with God calling us beloved children who please God.

But this is just the first Sunday after Epiphany. We are still in chapter one of Mark's gospel. The story has hardly begun. The Spirit is nowhere near finished yet. It is a long way to the cross, and we have to walk there.

So, we cannot simply kick back and enjoy being God's beloved children with whom God is well pleased, at least not indefinitely.

Here is what happens to Jesus in the next verse after his baptism: "And the Spirit immediately drove [Jesus] out into the wilderness." The same Spirit who anointed Jesus, the Spirit of the God who proclaimed Jesus a beloved Son, that same Spirit drove Jesus into the wilderness to do battle with Satan.

And that too is true of us. Would that it were not so, but experiencing the wilderness is part of what it means to be filled with the Spirit.

We all know that.

Some of us have spent a lot of time in the wilderness. Some of us are in the wilderness right now. Even those of us who have not been in the wilderness for a while know that wilderness is part of the deal.

Liturgically, as a Church, Lent is our time in the wilderness. Starting next week, liturgically, we will be in the space between baptism, which we celebrate today, and the wilderness of Lent, which begins in something like seven weeks.

64

But for today, for now, even knowing about the wilderness in front of us and the crucifixion that comes at the end of it, today we take comfort in the promises of our baptism, which is based on the experience of Jesus in his.

Today we celebrate the gift of the Spirit. Today we celebrate the good news that we are beloved children of God.

And when the wilderness time comes, we can rejoice at least that we are not alone. Baptism has prepared us, and the Spirit goes with us. Thanks be to God. Amen.

14. Being Church

Epiphany 2; January 15, 2012
1 Sam 3:1-20; Psalm 139:1-5, 12-17;
1 Cor 6:12-20; John 1:43-51

Each summer for the last several years, I have gone hiking on the Appalachian Trail.

Conversation with people you meet on the Trail tends to be pretty simple. Mostly we talk about what we have to eat and how much our feet hurt. On the Trail, it is generally considered bad form to talk about how you spend your time when you are not hiking.

As a result, I may spend hours with someone before we get to talking about work. But eventually the question comes up. Somebody asks me about my job. Normally I mumble something about teaching, but that never works. Sooner or later, I confess that I am a priest.

Then comes the awkward pause.

My conversation partner does a quick mental inventory, asking himself, "Have I been cussing to a priest?" Then, because the answer is almost always yes, he apologizes.

But what comes next is the part that is most interesting to me.

Often, not always but often, the person tells me that he is not really "religious." He prefers to think of himself as "spiritual." I hear that distinction between religion and spirituality a lot, especially from young people.

For these young people, religion, which they do not like, means the Church. These young people experience, or at least they claim to have experienced, the Church as an obstacle to their relationship with God.

The hikers I meet on the Trail who call themselves "spiritual" say they can more easily meet God when they are alone in the woods than when they are with other people in a building on Sunday morning.

Now of course, I have a professional interest in the Church.

But a part of me agrees with those hikers who call themselves spiritual but not religious. God invites all of us to a personal relationship with Him, and cultivating that relationship takes time alone with God.

For a lot of people, including me, the best times alone with God seem to happen outside. Some of the real high points in my own relationship with God have come when I have been alone in the woods.

That is what I think many of these young people are saying when they claim to be "spiritual" but not "religious," and they are on to something worth taking seriously.

We who are the Church, we who represent "religion," also need to take seriously the criticisms of those who say that they are not religious. There are things about the Church that can be off-putting to one seeking God. We can get so attached to our building or to our traditions or to our hierarchy—I say this as a priest in that hierarchy—we can get so attached to our building or our traditions or our hierarchy that we forget that all that stuff is only a means to the end of a deeper relationship with God.

"Religion," the institutional Church and all its trappings, is ultimately at the service of spiritual growth. Religion is valuable only to the degree that it promotes spiritual growth.

We might even say that Jesus was "spiritual" but not particularly "religious," if you mean by "religious," committed to the religious institutions of his day. Jesus did not build any buildings. Jesus was not from the priestly line. Jesus was critical of the religious traditions of his day.

So why should we be "religious" as well as spiritual? What is the value of the Church for us, who do come here on Sunday mornings, who pay for the building and pay for a priest and follow our traditions?

What might I say, as one who is religious in that sense of the term, to my hiking companions who are spiritual but not religious? What can you say to the people you meet who claim to be spiritual but who do not belong to any Church?

Well, there is a lot that we might say. Here is just one thing.

Church is important because we need each other, and Church is where we meet.

Our gospel reading reminds us that we need each other. Jesus commands Philip to follow him. And what is the first thing Philip does? Philip goes to find Nathanael.

Philip follows Jesus. But Philip does not follow alone. Right away, Philip seeks a companion for the journey. Because we need each other.

Let us put ourselves in this story. Let us be Nathanael for a minute. Think back to a time when you did not know Jesus. You may have to go all the way back to when you were a baby. But there was a time. That means you need Philip.

Sometime somebody was Philip to us. Sometime somebody came to us and said "We have found him about whom Moses in the law and also the prophets wrote, Jesus son of Joseph from Nazareth." Sometime, somebody introduced us to Jesus.

It might have been so long ago that you cannot even remember who it was or when it happened. That is basically the case for me. It might have been more recent.

But sometime somebody introduced you and me to Jesus. If you remember who was Philip for you, you should say a little prayer of thanksgiving for that person every once in a while.

Or put yourself in the place of Samuel in our Old Testament reading. Samuel was living with Eli the priest and serving at the ark of the covenant itself. God calls Samuel by name. God says, "Samuel, Samuel." It seems like Samuel has everything he needs.

But Samuel still needed Eli. Samuel did not know what was happening. Samuel keeps going to Eli until finally "Eli perceived that the Lord was calling the boy."

We can be a lot like Samuel. God calls us all the time. "Harvey, Harvey," God's voice is constantly calling.

Sometimes we get it. But a lot of times we need someone to be Eli for us. We need someone to tell us that it is God's voice we are hearing, and so we better listen.

We need each other. We need someone to bring us to Jesus.

And even after we meet Jesus, we still need each other because we need someone to help us to listen for God's voice and to hear what God is saying to us in this moment.

We need people to be Philip and to be Eli for us. That means we need the Church, where we find our Philips and our Elis.

Then turn it around. This time, put yourself in Eli's position.

Who are the Samuels in your life who need to be told, "That is God's voice you hear. Listen carefully." We need to be Eli for our Christian brothers and sisters. We need to help our brothers and sisters hear God's call to them.

Or else put yourself in Philip's position. Jesus has called you. Jesus commands you to follow Him. Who do you tell?

Who are the Nathanaels in your life who need to hear that you have found the one about whom Moses in the law and also the prophets wrote, Jesus son of Joseph from Nazareth? Who are the skeptics in your life who think nothing good can come from Nazareth?

To the Nathanaels in our lives, we say, "come and see." God can take it from there.

If people come to Jesus, if people really see Jesus, then they will say, with Nathanael that first-century skeptic, "Rabbi, you are the Son of God! You are the King of Israel!" And they will follow.

When we do our part, when we seek out the Samuels and the Nathanaels in our lives, when we are Eli and Philip for the people in our lives, then we are religious and spiritual both.

That is when we are Church in the best sense of that term.

Thanks be to God. Amen.

15. Promiscuous Love

Epiphany 3; January 22, 2012
Jonah 3:1-5, 10; Psalm 62:6-14; 1 Cor 7:29-31; Mark 1:14-20

As you have already heard this morning, next week is our annual meeting.

Among other things, our annual meeting is a chance for us to think together about how we are Church in this time and this place. I hope that you will all be there as we look back over the last year, and as we look forward into our future.

Our readings for the last few weeks have been good preparation for our annual meeting because they are all about how Jesus formed his Church at the start of his public ministry.

Two weeks ago, we heard about Jesus' baptism, which is the model for our baptisms. In baptism we are empowered by the Holy Spirit and brought into a community of faith. Then we spend the rest of our lives living out our baptismal covenant as part of God's holy Church.

Last week we heard Jesus calling some of his earliest disciples to follow him, and I preached about how much we need each other as we try to answer his call to us.

This week we hear Jesus calling more disciples. But Mark, the gospel we just heard, is so short that we need to turn to Jonah to appreciate exactly what Jesus is doing when he calls Simon Peter and Andrew and James and John.

Now kids who know anything at all about the Bible are likely to know that Jonah was swallowed by a whale. And let us just pause to note that being swallowed by a whale,

71

and living to tell about it, is a very cool thing, although maybe a little gross.

But the whale is not the point of Jonah. So let me run you through the whole story.

In the first couple of verses, God appears to Jonah, and God commands Jonah to cry out against the people of Nineveh because their wickedness is very great.

Now Jonah had no doubt what the Lord wanted him to do. But Jonah did not want to do it, so Jonah decided to run away. That was a bad idea. Jonah boarded ship, a storm came up, Jonah went overboard, and a whale got him. It took three days and three nights, but Jonah finally gave in, so God had the whale spew Jonah out onto dry land.

This is where our reading picks up.

God says to Jonah a second time, "Jonah, I would like you to deliver a message to the people of Nineveh." This time, Jonah goes.

But we are left with the question, why did Jonah resist God's will in the first place?

So far we have not been told. We only know that the prophet of God did resist God and that the prophet went to real trouble and danger to do so. Hold that thought.

As we heard in the reading, Jonah walks through Nineveh crying out "Forty days more and Nineveh shall be overthrown."

And an amazing thing happens. The people of Nineveh listen to Jonah, and they fast, and they repent. And "when God saw what they did, how they turned from their evil ways, God changed his mind about the calamity that he had said he would bring upon them; and he did not do it." God forgave the Ninevites.

That itself is worth thinking about, but it is not the end of the story.

Here are the next couple of verses.

"This was very displeasing to Jonah, and he became angry. He prayed to the Lord and said, "O Lord! Is not this what I said while I was still in my own country? That is why I fled . . . at the beginning; for I knew that you are a gracious God and merciful, slow to anger and abounding in steadfast love, and ready to relent from punishing. And now, O Lord, please take my life from me, for it is better for me to die than to live.""

Jonah is angry, Jonah is really angry, that God is merciful, and loving, and forgiving. Jonah knew from the beginning that if he delivered God's message to the people of Nineveh, they might repent, and God might forgive them. And Jonah did not want that to happen. Jonah wanted to see those people die.

The historical context helps to explain why.

Nineveh was the capital of Assyria, and Assyria was the mightiest empire of the day. In another generation or so, the Assyrians would conquer Israel and treat them brutally. You did not have to be a prophet to see that coming. The Assyrians were like the Nazis of the time. Their program of global domination was clear to anyone paying attention.

So everybody in Israel feared and hated the Assyrians.

And everyone in Israel had to be praying that God would judge the Assyrians and that God would punish the Assyrians.

So when God sends Jonah to the people of Nineveh, when Jonah realizes that God is calling him to be an agent of forgiveness to the people of Nineveh, Jonah does what any Israelite of his day would have done: he runs in the opposite direction.

Now fast forward 800 years. Jesus calls Peter and Andrew and James and John. And Jesus tells them, "Follow me and I will make you fish for people."

Jesus does not explain what he means by "fish for people." But we know. Jesus is calling these first followers to go and make disciples of all nations, even folks like the hated Roman empire.

If Jesus had said that right up front, some of his disciples might have run the other way, just like Jonah did.

But Jesus gave his disciples time to learn how to love, so when Jesus did finally send them out, they were ready to go.

Now fast forward another two thousand years. We are the ones who are supposed to follow Jesus in this time and this place. We are the ones fishing for people today. We are the ones sent to Nineveh or to Rome.

So, who do you hate? Do not actually answer that question! But think about it. Who would you prefer never to see walking through that door?

I can think of a couple of people I would just as soon not see. Thankfully they live a thousand miles away, so I am pretty safe.

But in a way, that is too bad. Because that means I am not forced to practice loving those whom I do not particularly like. And the fact of the matter is, God does love them. And God commands me to love them too.

That is the shocking thing about Jesus' call to be fishers of people and the shocking lesson of Jonah.

God loves everybody, even the people who seem most unlovable.

The good news is, that includes us even when we do not feel particularly worthy.

But the challenge is, that includes everybody else too.

We are called to love others just like God loves us and God loves them. We are called to think of even the people we most dislike as potential brothers and sisters in Christ.

That kind of promiscuous love, love for everybody no matter who they are, defines God's Church. As Jesus says, by this everyone will know that you are my disciples, if you have love" (John 13:35).

God help us to love like that. Amen.

16. Priest's Report/ Annual Meeting[1]

Epiphany 4; January 29, 2012
Deuteronomy 18:15-20; Psalm 111; 1 Cor 8:1-13; Mark 1:21-28

For the last couple of weeks, our gospel readings have been setting up Jesus' public ministry. This morning Jesus' public ministry actually begins. For the first time, Jesus teaches a crowd. For the first time, Jesus works a miracle. Today is where it all really gets going.

On a Sabbath, Jesus enters the synagogue. What happened at synagogues most mornings would not have been so very different from what we are doing at this very minute. The people would listen to a reading from Scripture, and then someone would offer an interpretation of it.

That morning when Jesus began his public ministry presumably started out more or less as normal. But this was not a normal morning, because Jesus was not a normal preacher.

As we look back at what happened in the synagogue that morning two thousand years ago, we need to pay careful attention to what Mark tells us and also to what Mark leaves out.

Let's start with what Mark leaves out. This is Jesus' first sermon, and people are astounded at it. So, what does Jesus say in this first truly public speech? We do not know. Mark leaves it out. Apparently, Mark did not want to emphasize the content of Jesus' preaching on this first morning of Jesus' public ministry since Mark does not tell us anything about it.

---

[1] This sermon was my report at my first Annual Meeting at Saint David's, which seemed an appropriate way to wrap up the first part of this book.

So, what does Mark tell us? What is Mark emphasizing?

Mark tells us the people who heard Jesus were astounded because Jesus taught them as one having authority. The amazing thing about Jesus' sermon that morning was not so much in what he said as in how he said it, with an authority like nothing the people had ever heard before.

But Jesus' authority is only the first surprise for the people that day. Suddenly a man possessed by an unclean spirit calls out. And Jesus rebukes the unclean spirit and drives that spirit out of the man.

Now the people in the synagogue have two things to talk about.

They are still amazed at how much authority Jesus has when he teaches. Mark repeats that for us in case we have forgotten. And they are also amazed that Jesus commands even the unclean spirits and they obey him.

Jesus preaches with authority, and Jesus acts with power.

Our services are not likely to be quite so dramatic. But Jesus is a model for us in this, as in all things.

We are called to a common Christian life that is characterized by authority and by power.

This is not just about sermons. In our lives and our daily interactions, we are all called to proclaim the gospel of God with authority and conviction. We are all called to act with the power of the Spirit of God.

It is easy to be afraid. The pressures of life, the very real challenges that we face, can eat away at our authority and our power. We can lose sight of the promises of God. We can grow deaf to the call of God. We can turn away because it seems too scary or too hard.

But God gives us authority, and God calls us to use that authority to proclaim God's gospel. God gives us power, and God calls us to use that power to do God's work. That is heady stuff. And not a little daunting.

Today is our annual meeting. Today is a time for us to look back over the last year and forward into the next. So, how have we done? Have we spoken with authority? Have we acted with power?

Well, we are not Jesus.

There is definitely room for improvement. But, as I wrote in my report for the annual meeting, you all have reason to be proud.

You began the year without a priest and without a senior warden. The vestry was incomplete. The budget looked grim. Under those circumstances, the standard of faithfulness is the courage to persevere, and you did that.

More, you rose to the challenge.

You continued to hear and to proclaim the gospel with authority. You continued to care for each other and to reach out to the world with power.

I was only at Saint David's for the last four months of the year, so the credit is yours. But I can still say that I am proud to be part of this Church because God is at work here.

Looking ahead to the coming year, the question for us is, how to amplify the authority and the power that God has given us? How can we proclaim the gospel to each other and to the world with the astonishing authority that Christ makes available to us? How can we do God's work with the astonishing power of the Holy Spirit? How can we open ourselves to God and become agents of God's reconciliation and love in the world?

It has to begin with God. If we try to do it on our own, if we rely on our own authority and power to take on the problems of the world or even the problems of this Church, we will fail.

Our work begins with prayer and worship and study of God's word. True spiritual power comes from an ever-deepening relationship with God. Everything we attempt, everything we accomplish, has to come from God.

So first, we look in, or maybe up. First, we look to God. When we are tired, or discouraged, or alienated, or afraid, we look to God. God is the only source of true authority and power for us as Christian people and as a Christian community.

Then, second, we look out.

We look out to each other for fellowship and mutual support. We look out to the world, where we can find additional fellowship and support, but where we also find opportunities for ministry.

Who knows exactly what shape our ministries in the world will take this year? Not I, though I have some ideas. That is a question for all of us. All of us have the task of looking for opportunities for ministry, of listening for God's call, of discerning where God is leading us.

As we engage in this ongoing task of discernment during the next year, we need to be careful to avoid two common pitfalls, both of which could keep us from doing God's work with authority and power. I suspect that both have sometimes held us back in the past.

The most dangerous pitfall of all is to get too focused on our own needs. Churches die when they shift away from doing God's work and to survival mode. It is a strange paradox, but the more we think about the needs of others, the more our own needs will be met.

A second pitfall is to think that our work does not make a difference. We are a small Church. We cannot solve all the problems of the world. But if we are faithful, we can change lives.

Jesus started with twelve, and his twelve were not initially very impressive. We have ten times that number. We can accomplish great things with God's help.

So here is my hope. I hope that we can all be proud of our Church. I hope that we will all want to tell our friends and neighbors and co-workers, "you know, you really should check out Saint David's."

And here is my prayer. I pray that this time next year, when we are looking back at 2012, we can see God's authority and God's power at work among us and through us in the world. May it be so. Amen.

Part 2: Preaching Through COVID 2020, Lectionary Year A

Heading into 2020, I was proud of how Saint David's was doing and optimistic about our future. I had officially become Rector several years earlier, which represented a long-term commitment between me and the parish. In 2019, I was tired and a little burned out, but I had three-month sabbatical, which re-energized me for ministry.

As our Annual Meeting for 2020 approached, I remember thinking we were in a little golden age at the parish. Everyone was getting along, new ministries were emerging, our numbers were growing. I anticipated a great year. The sermons in this section pick up at that Annual Meeting.

By that time, COVID was already on the horizon, but we at Saint David's remained oblivious. I was shocked when people began to seriously discuss closing Church buildings. During Lent, the Diocese told us that we could have in-person services the following Sunday, but had to close our building after that (March 22, I believe). I still assumed the closure would last no more than a couple of weeks. I expected to be back in person by Palm Sunday (April 5 that year). In fact, our building remained closed until All Saints Day, November 1.

I am proud of how quickly we pivoted, particularly for a parish without a lot of tech-savvy people. By the first Sunday our building was closed, we were able to livestream the service. We had also moved all our meetings online to Zoom. When the infection numbers improved in the summer, we shifted to drive-in services in our parking lot, beginning on June 7. Those carried us through October.

Adjusting to preaching during a pandemic was sometimes challenging. Pretty quickly, we gathered a skeleton crew to run the services: other than me and

Deacon Terry, we just had a lay reader, the choir, and a streamer. My task was to preach to a largely empty room as if people were present. Moving outside in June helped. At least I was obviously talking to people. But I mostly couldn't see them in their cars. And, of course, the elements became relevant. One day there was an earthquake during my sermon! Sadly, I didn't even notice it.

As noted, these sermons begin at our Annual Meeting. They are consecutive through Easter. After that, I have included sermons at the transition points in our responses to the pandemic, e.g. when we shifted to drive-in services, and when we came back inside. My goal in these sermons was to offer encouragement, to emphasize that we were still connected to each other, and to help people find God in new ways despite the trying times.

17. The Kingdom Has Come Near: An Annual Meeting Message[2]

3 Epiphany; January 26, 2020
Isaiah 9:1-4; Psalm 27:1, 5-13; 1 Corinthians 1:10-18; Matthew 4:12-23

If you think our gospel reading for this morning sounds familiar, you are right. Last week we heard John's version of Jesus calling the first disciples. This week we have Matthew's version of the same events.

The two versions are pretty similar, of course. But what sets Matthew's version apart is the context he provides.

Immediately before our reading, Jesus has been baptized in the Jordan River and then tempted in the wilderness. Now, in our passage, Jesus is beginning his public ministry. This is his first sermon. This is his introduction to the world as a preacher, teacher, and healer. (Think Deacon Terry in his first sermon with us just last week.) As Jesus' very first sermon, this one deserves careful attention. It sets the stage for everything that is to follow.

What comes next, just a couple of verses after our passage, is the Sermon on the Mount, Jesus' longest and greatest sermon, three full chapters. That is quite a contrast with the sermon we get this morning. The sermon for this morning is just one sentence. That is another reason we should pay careful attention to it.

---

[2] Ironically, given what happened a few weeks later, I disavowed any interest in a television ministry in this sermon. On the other hand, I acknowledged that we might need to embrace technology as a tool for evangelism. Little did I know how much technology we would be embracing in just two months!

So here is Jesus' first sermon, in full: "Repent, for the kingdom of heaven has come near." That's it. You might wish I could learn something from Jesus' brevity! Unfortunately for you, I am more of a Sermon on the Mount kind of preacher! But it does help to work through Jesus' single sentence slowly.

What does it mean to say that the kingdom of heaven has come near?

When we think about the kingdom of heaven, many of us think first about where we want to go after we die. That is looking ahead to the kingdom we hope to experience. Or maybe we think about the end of history, when Jesus returns in power and great glory. That is looking even farther ahead, to the kingdom that will come.

But Jesus is not talking about where we go when we die, or what he will establish at the end of time. Jesus is talking about God's kingdom in the present tense, as something his hearers are experiencing at that very moment. That is striking!

Now, we who know the story, can go farther than Jesus' hearers could have gone on that day. The good news is that Jesus came to live as God with us even now. The good news is that Jesus himself brings the kingdom, that where Jesus is, there is God's kingdom.

On that day in Capernaum, Jesus' hearers were experiencing the kingdom of heaven because Jesus was with them. On this day, here in Agawam, we are experiencing the kingdom of heaven because Jesus is with us.

We still look forward to a deeper and fuller experience of the kingdom of heaven, both when we die and when Christ returns. But the good news of Jesus' first sermon is that the kingdom of heaven begins with Him right then.

That is what Jesus does for us. Jesus also tells us what we should do in response: "repent."

And here again we have to go slowly. For some of us, the command to repent can sound like a command to think about what wretches we are. We sometimes do wretched things, and we should repent of them. But that is not what Jesus is talking about here.

The root word that is translated "repent" just means to turn around, to face in a different direction.

It is easy to get so wrapped up in worldly concerns that we begin to act as if this world were all there is, so wrapped up in worldly concerns that we forget about God. And so Jesus says, "Repent. Turn around. Pay attention. I am here with you. The kingdom has come near. Don't miss it because you are too focused on other things."

And then, as our passage goes on, Jesus says it again. Jesus invites Peter and Andrew to follow him. Jesus calls James and John. Jesus says, over and over again, in all sorts of different ways, pay attention to the good news of great joy that God loves you enough to enter your lives and invite you into intimate relationship with Him.

That is our calling, too. The kingdom of heaven is at hand. Jesus invites us to repent and enter in.

Peter and Andrew, James and John, accept Jesus' invitation. And as they travel with Jesus, Jesus shows them what kingdom living looks like, what it means to repent since the kingdom of heaven is at hand.

Clearly a lot happens. But what we get is a summary of kingdom living in another single, pregnant sentence. It turns out kingdom living boils down to three things: "teaching in their synagogues"; "proclaiming the good news of the kingdom"; and "curing every disease and every sickness among the people."

For the first, we substitute Church for synagogue. But we continue to come together for Christian formation. We gather for worship and prayer and study. And in the process we are touched by grace. We are gradually shaped into something closer to what God created us to be. We are united with Christ and with each other so completely that we become the very body of Christ.

The second, proclaiming the good news of the kingdom, is the task of evangelism.

I don't want to stand on street corners shouting at people, and I don't want to create a television ministry, and I don't want to travel to some faraway land to share the gospel. My guess is, most of you feel the same. But we are called to "proclaim by word and example the good news of God in Christ." Each of us, in our own ways, is called to share the good news of God's love with a world that needs to hear that good news.

Finally, kingdom living means doing what we can to help hurting people: to heal the sick and feed the hungry and clothe the naked and visit the prisoners and so on. We call that outreach.

In a few minutes, we will have our annual meeting and we will talk about our common life in Christ. In the booklet of annual reports you can read a great deal more about our common life. All of it is important.

But our gospel reading offers a helpful structure for reflecting on our ongoing task of responding to Christ's call to live as his disciples in the world. We need to think in terms of Christian formation, evangelism, and outreach.

All three are moving targets. Christian formation today needs to look different than Christian formation a few decades or a few centuries ago. So does evangelism and outreach. We have different challenges and different opportunities today.

We might ask, for example, if we are using technology effectively in our efforts at formation and evangelism. We have ways of broadcasting our message that earlier times could never have dreamed about. But we also face stiffer competition for people's time and attention than anything our predecessors faced.

The same is true for outreach. There too we face issues that our predecessors never considered, things like climate change, opioid addiction, or the lack of affordable housing.

It can feel overwhelming. But we always return to the good news with which Christ began his ministry. Truly the kingdom of heaven is at hand. Christ is with us. And with Christ's help, we can heed his call to be effective disciples in this time and place. Certainly, that is my prayer for us. In Christ's name. Amen.

18. Fasting

Ash Wednesday; February 26, 2020
Joel 2:1-2, 12-17; Psalm 103; 2 Corinthians 5:20b-6:10;
Matthew 6:1-6, 16-21

The Apostle Paul perfectly captures the paradox that stands at the heart of Christian life in a single sentence from his letter to the Philippians. "Work out your own salvation with fear and trembling; for it is God who is at work in you, enabling you both to will and to work for his good pleasure" (2:12).

The most important part of that sentence comes at the end. God is at work in us, shaping both our will—that is to say, the choices we make—and our work, meaning the things that we do.

Ultimately Paul is reminding us that everything comes to us as a gift from God, including most importantly, our relationship with God.

We couldn't get to God on our own, so God came to us in the person of Jesus Christ. We were trapped in sin and death, so Christ freed us by submitting to death on the cross and then rising again. Even now, the Holy Spirit is within us, inspiring us, empowering us, helping us to take the next step in our journey with God.

All of it is God's grace. The most we can hope for on our own, and even here grace is at work, is to respond in gratitude and faith to what God has done and is doing for us.

That is the Christian good news. And that is one part of the paradox that Paul identifies.

But with that good news of God's grace comes a responsibility, which is the other side of the paradox. Our choices, our actions, matter. God is at work in us. AND

Paul tells us to work out our own salvation. There is mystery here. But both God's action and our action are necessary.

Now, we always celebrate the first part of the paradox, the good news of God's grace and love. But two seasons of the Christian year, Christmas and Easter, particularly focus on God's gracious actions on our behalf. If it weren't Lent, I might add an "alleluia" here!

The main season of the entire Christian year focusing on the second half of the Christian paradox, focusing on our actions, begins today: Lent.

Lent is the season for us to work at our relationship with God. In Lent, we are invited, in the name of the Church, to take on a whole series of practices that are part of working out our salvation. Self-examination and repentance. Prayer, fasting, and self-denial. Reading and meditating on God's holy Word.

I encourage you to take that invitation seriously, to commit today to some form of Christian discipline, and to stick with it through Lent.

Here at Saint David's, we offer lots of options.

Say Morning Prayer or another set of daily prayers from the Prayerbook. There are forms on the table at the back. Take a Prayer Partner, or use one of our prayer cycles.

Join us in reading a chapter of the New Testament each day, or attend one of our Bible studies. Maybe our Sunday Lenten Study on the Apostle Paul. Use a Lenten devotional. There are some of those at the back, too.

Participate in Lent Madness, and learn a little something about the saints of our tradition.

Walk the Stations of the Cross with us on Friday mornings. That's a really powerful way to engage with the story of what Christ went through for us.

And those are just things that we are sponsoring. There is a LOT you might do this Lent to work out your salvation, or at least to work on your relationship with God. Please take advantage of the opportunity this season presents.

But there is an obvious problem, or at least an obvious obstacle. A lot of us are busy. The prospect of taking on one more thing can feel burdensome.

In a book I just finished, Thomas Kelly says that "our lives… grow too complicated and overcrowded. Even the necessary obligations which we feel we must meet grow overnight, like Jack's beanstalk, and before we know it we are bowed down with burdens, crushed under committees, strained, breathless, and hurried, panting through a never-ending program of appointments" (89).[3]

Kelly goes on to say that we tend to blame the problem of our busyness on the complexity of the demands on us and on technologies that "give us more stimulation per square hour than used to be given per square day to our grandmothers" (90).

None of that is exactly news. The startling thing is that Kelly wrote those words in 1941. Think what he might say today!

So here is the Lenten dilemma. On one hand, Lent is a season for us to work, for extra prayer and worship and Bible study and works of love. On the other hand, the real task of Lent is to grow closer to God. And for those who feel over-committed, harried, and exhausted, growing

---

[3] *A Testament of Devotion*, 1941.

closer to God requires us to reduce our commitments, to do less.

This is, in part, a practical problem. If we are already busy and we want to take on something new, we need to give something up in order to create space for the new thing.

So, with heaviness of heart, I will, once again, give up Sudoku. In flagrant disregard for Jesus' instructions in our Gospel reading, I will look dismal and complain about that a lot! But I recognize that dropping something is necessary if I want to spend more time with God without making myself even crazier.

But Kelly's goal is more radical than simply balancing our responsibilities better. Kelly insists that "religion isn't something to be added to our other duties, and thus make our lives yet more complex" (97). Religion, our relationship with God, is supposed to be the center around which other responsibilities revolve. Our relationship with God should be part of everything we do, not one task among others.

It might seem like that would be easy for a priest. My job description includes God. God floats around the edges of most of what happens at Church.

And yet I forget. As I work on the tasks of my day, I often have little or no thought of God. I assume the same is true for most contemporary Christians.

So how can we integrate God into our lives so that our every act becomes a prayer, an offering to God?

For most of us, becoming conscious of God during the ordinary course of our lives requires times of intentional practice. And that is what Lent is for. But giving things up, if only temporarily, may be more important than taking things on.

So, take a few minutes, in these first days of Lent, to think about what most distracts you from God. Think about what you need to give up in order to make time each day to truly focus on God. Think about what you can let go, at least for a few weeks.

Call it your "fast," your fast from distractions that draw you from the love of God.

Come Easter, we may well stop our "fasting." I will certainly return to Sudoku! But hopefully a season of fasting can help us to become more conscious of God, who is always with us. Hopefully our regular lives will reflect God's presence a little more clearly. Hopefully our regular lives will become a little more of a prayer and offering to God. If that happens, we will truly have benefitted from a holy Lent.

That is my prayer for us: that we can open ourselves up to God's presence and God's gracious work in us. In Jesus' name. Amen.

19. Doing the Little Things

1 Lent; March 1, 2020
Genesis 2:15-17; 3:1-7; Psalm 32; Romans 5:12-19; Matthew
4:1-11

Today we commemorate our patron, Saint David. This is my ninth Saint David's day since coming to Saint David's, but only the second time David's day has fallen on a Sunday. That makes today a preaching treat. It's also the first Sunday of Lent, and the Sunday before many of us go to the polls, so a lot is going on.

As it happens, David speaks to all of that.

First, a bit of David's story. During David's lifetime, in the sixth century, Christianity was in crisis in the British Isles. We think of Anglo-Saxons as the native people of England, but in the sixth century the Angles and the Saxons were pagan invaders from what is now Germany. David represented the Celtic Christians who were being invaded.

At David's death, around 544 AD, Christianity was in significant retreat, paganism was on the rise, and it was unclear whether the Celtic Christianity of which David was a part would survive.

David himself seems to have been active in support of the Celtic resistance to the invading Angles and Saxons. But that is not what David is mostly remembered for. Mostly David ran his own monastery, and he established other monasteries. Despite living at a very dramatic time, David's life was not particularly dramatic. At his death, his final advice to his monks was, "Do the little things."

Hold that thought. We'll get back to it.

Our Presiding Bishop Michael Curry is one of an ecumenical "group of elders" from across the political spectrum who recently issued a statement, "Lent 2020: A Call to Prayer, Fasting, and Repentance Leading to Action."[4]

Their call begins, "The United States is in the midst of a struggle for its very soul. Are we merely collections of self-interest and partisan identities or are we 'one nation under God, indivisible, with liberty and justice for all?'"

Now, our problems today are not nearly so bad as what David faced all those centuries ago. But I believe Michael Curry and the other elders are right that the bitterness in America today has created "a moment of spiritual peril and decision. Nothing less than the soul of our nation is at stake."

To their credit, the elders acknowledge that they "are not fully sure what to do in the growing national crisis in which we now find ourselves." They don't have an easy answer. They don't propose a dramatic action to reclaim and restore the soul of America. Instead, they call all Christians to prayer, fasting, and repentance.

It's a Saint David strategy. In a time of peril, when there is no obvious way forward, when there is no obvious solution to our problems, we can at least "do the little things."

Our Gospel reading for this first Sunday of Lent makes the same point.

Jesus has just been baptized. Jesus is about to begin his public ministry. Jesus' task, remember, is the salvation of the world. It doesn't get more pressing than that! But before Jesus acts, Jesus prepares. Jesus undertakes a forty day fast in the wilderness.

---

[4] ReclaimingJesus.org

In Lent, which is modelled on Jesus' fast, we, too, we are invited to spiritual practices that should inform our action in the world. Just as the elders suggest, we are invited in Lent to take time for repentance, prayer, and fasting, in the hope that, when we act, we can act in God's name and in God's way.

There is more Lent lesson to our Gospel reading. Our reading is all about facing temptation. In Lent, we pause to acknowledge the temptations we face, and also, here unlike Jesus, our failures, the times when temptation overcomes us and we fall into sin.

Our failures take many forms. But the one the elders emphasize is our complicity in the divisions besetting our nation. I have preached on this before, and I will surely preach on it again. It is so tempting to demonize people with whom we disagree. It is so tempting to assert our own wisdom and righteousness by pointing out the folly and the wickedness of the other side.

That is true when we are talking about other Americans who presumably are trying to do the right thing, even if we disagree with them about what the right thing is. So think about how easy it would have been for Jesus, faced with the devil, and when he is really hungry.

I had never paused to think about the range of options open to Jesus in this moment. But the early Christian commentators spend a lot of time on Jesus' options. They point out that the devil can't make Jesus do anything. Jesus doesn't have to go with the devil to the pinnacle of the temple or the high mountain. Jesus doesn't have to talk to the devil at all. Jesus could have dismissed the devil right from the beginning, as he does at the end. Jesus could even flex a little divine muscle and wipe the devil out altogether. Would that he had!

But what does Jesus do? Jesus talks to the devil. Courteously! Jesus doesn't agree with the devil. Jesus challenges the devil. Jesus proves the devil wrong. What Jesus does NOT do is call the devil names. Jesus doesn't insult the devil. The devil!

Being God and all, Jesus has an unfair advantage. We are not likely to do as well. But if Jesus can disagree with the devil without getting personal, surely, I should at least try to do the same with good people who happen disagree with me.

Notice as well how Jesus resists the devil. Jesus goes to Scripture. The devil does, too. The Bible is often misused. But Jesus finds in Scripture the wisdom that guides his actions. That's a good lesson for us.

But the early Christian commentators helped me to see something else here. The first thing Jesus says in this passage, responding to the first temptation by the devil, is, "One does not live by bread alone, but by every word that comes from the mouth of God." Jesus is quoting the Bible, and Jesus is talking about the Bible as the word of God.

But more even than the Bible, Jesus himself is the Word of God, the Word who was in the beginning, who was with God, who was God. It is Christ himself who gives us life, who helps us to resist temptation, and who reconciles us to God when we fail.

I fail in lots of ways and most of them have nothing to do with politics or the divisions in our country. But I am certainly not immune to the temptation of political divisiveness that is one of the great problems facing America today. And in Lent, I, we, are called to name that temptation for what it is, to resist it as best we can, and to repent when we fail to resist it.

It is just a little thing. But it is exactly the kind of thing our patron saint encourages us to do. And it is exactly the kind of thing our nation needs right now.

So, I invite us to do our best, with Christ's help, to resist the temptation to demonize people who are different. I invite us to do our best, following Christ's example and with Christ's help, to treat even the worst of our opponents with civility. I invite us, with Christ's help, to try to love even those people who are hardest to love.

That would be a great blessing for us as individual Christians, for our parish, and for our nation. I pray that we can be so blessed. In Christ's name. Amen.

20. The Living Water[5]
3 Lent; March 15, 2020
Exodus 17:1-7; Psalm 95; Romans 5:1-11; John 4:5-42

In our Gospel reading for last Sunday, Jesus and a Pharisee named Nicodemus had a long conversation about being "born again." As you may recall, Nicodemus wondered how adults could possibly crawl back into their mothers' wombs. I picture Jesus shaking his head as he gently explained that he meant a spiritual rebirth, not a literal one.

We see something similar this week in Jesus' conversation with the Samaritan woman at the well.

Jesus offers the woman living water. Like Nicodemus, she takes him literally. First she points out that Jesus doesn't have a bucket to draw water. Then, when Jesus explains that people who drink his water will never be thirsty again, she is thrilled at the prospect of not having to come to the well any more. Here, too, I picture Jesus shaking his head.

Jesus changes topic. Jesus asks the woman about her husband. She says she is not married, which is not news to Jesus. Jesus tells her he knows about her previous husbands and about her current relationship.

At that point the woman realizes Jesus is a prophet. Soon thereafter she speculates that Jesus could even be the long-awaited messiah. That's quite a reaction!

So, what is going on here? Let's go back through our story, following the progression from water, to husbands, to Jesus.

---

[5] This sermon includes my first sermon reference to COVID.

The story starts with physical needs. The Gospel writer points out that Jesus is worn out and in need of refreshment. Jesus' request for water was surely genuine. He wanted something to drink. The woman did, too. That's why she was coming to the well in the first place, and that is why she was initially so happy at the prospect of receiving living water from Jesus.

After her conversation with Jesus, in her hurry to tell others about Jesus, the woman forgot her water jar. Her enthusiasm is endearing. But the fact is, she is going to have to come back for more water. Our physical needs are inescapable.

But, and this is the point, satisfying our physical needs is not enough. We need literal water. But we also need the living water that is Christ.

The woman wasn't getting it, so Jesus shifts to her marital history. She is struck by his knowledge of her past, but that is not particularly impressive. Anyone who had met one of her gossipy neighbors could know that. More is going on here.

I think Jesus is saying to this woman, you are looking for intimacy. You long to love and be loved. And so you have gone from man to man, but none of your men have met your deep need for relationship. That is not their fault. No human being can satisfy the deepest longing of your soul.

Relationships with other people are important, of course. We all need people just like we all need water. But even when our relationships are loving and good, we are left with a longing for more. To meet that deepest longing, says Christ, you need me, your heavenly bridegroom.

At that point, the Samaritan woman still has a little way to go. But she glimpses the truth of what Jesus is saying to her. It is as if she has sipped a bit of living water.

Now let's bring the lesson Jesus teaches the Samaritan woman up to today.

We are in an anxious time, the most anxious time I can remember. Carrie pointed out to me that the Covid-19 virus did not exist 90 days ago. Now it is reshaping life for virtually all of us. At some point, the worst of the virus will have passed, and we will return to normal. But now we are all scrambling to figure out what we should be doing, and not doing, in a situation that seems to change and to get more threatening virtually every day.

Based on our Gospel reading, what might Jesus say to us today, if we were the ones to meet him at the well?

The one who recognized the Samaritan woman's need for water would, I think, first acknowledge our physical vulnerability in the midst of this emerging epidemic. He would encourage us to take proper precautions to avoid infection. That's because our health and well-being really are at risk.

But Jesus surely wouldn't stop there. Jesus wouldn't stop there because our souls long for more than practical guidelines about how to avoid infection. The one who spoke to the Samaritan woman's marital history would go on to remind us that we are connected to each other, that we need each other, that we need to look out for each other, that we need to be particularly sensitive to our most vulnerable brothers and sisters, the people who are most isolated and have most reason for fear. That is because God calls us into relationship with each other.

But Jesus wouldn't stop there either. Jesus wouldn't stop there because our souls long for more love, for deeper relationship, than any other human being can provide. And so Jesus invites us, as he invited the Samaritan woman, to drink deeply of the living water, to grow in our relationship with Him who is our heavenly bridegroom.

Jesus does not promise to protect us from sickness or death. But Jesus promises to accompany us always, no matter what happens. Jesus promises to love and strengthen us as we face this crisis together. And, in the end, Jesus promises us victory, victory over sin and death, the ultimate victory of new and unending life with God.

That is good news. That is good news on which we can rely.

And it helps. Last week I received an email from a friend of mine in Georgia who has to travel in the next couple of weeks. He told me, the prospect of getting on a plane right now terrifies him. Making matters worse, he feels isolated, like he doesn't have anyone to talk to.

My friend went on to say that he knew Christ was with him.

And he ended his message by saying he felt better.

In the midst of his fear and loneliness, my friend took a sip of living water. And externally nothing changed. But he was different. And that made all the difference.

So what can we do to drink a little more deeply of the living water, especially in those times when we need strength?

It's not rocket science. This is a time when the spiritual practices of our tradition matter more than ever before.

As we all rightly pull back from our various commitments, as we cancel plans to avoid crowds, as we increasingly isolate ourselves from each other, as we face relentless, widespread anxiety that can easily spiral out of control, we need to get really focused on our relationship with God. We need to spend time in things like prayer and meditation, in reading and meditating on God's holy Word.

If you are not already doing so, I strongly encourage you to adopt a daily prayer practice. It will help you feel connected to God.

We all need to do what we can to be safe. And we all need to manage our anxiety. But most of all, we all need to drink of the living water.

And that is my prayer for us, that we can drink from the living water of Christ. And I pray that we can share the living water with the people around us who so desperately need a drink.

In Christ's name. Amen.

21. Revealing God's Works

4 Lent; March 22, 2020
1 Samuel 16:1-3; Psalm 23; Ephesians 5:8-14; John 9:1-41

That was a LONG Gospel reading! Thankfully, it is a really wonderful story, straight through to the end. But as it happens, I want to preach on just the first three sentences.

Our story begins when Jesus and his disciples meet a man who was born blind. The disciples are troubled by this blind man, and they ask Jesus the great question, the question that has plagued people for centuries. "Why?" Why was this man born blind?

When they ask that question, the disciples are assuming that virtually everything that happens must have an explanation. If a bad thing happens, someone must have done something bad to deserve it.

So how about this man who was born blind? Did he sin? Of course, it is hard to see how he could have, since he was born blind. So maybe his parents sinned. Maybe his blindness is their punishment. But that doesn't seem quite fair either....

We'll get to Jesus' answer in a minute. But first let's think about how the attitude of the disciples would play today.

We are in the midst of a public health crisis. Lots of people around the world have gotten sick. A growing number of people close to home are getting sick. The economy is suffering. All of us are affected.

So, the disciples might ask, whose fault is it? The Chinese? The Trump administration? The people who spread the illness, however unintentionally? The victims themselves? Somebody must be to blame. Otherwise it wouldn't be happening. The question is, who can we blame?

Now, mistakes have no doubt been made. Hopefully we will learn from our mistakes so that we will be better prepared if and when something like this happens again.

But in the meantime, while we are in crisis mode, the question of whose fault it is is not very helpful. This is a time for uniting in a common effort to slow the spread of the virus, to figure out effective ways to treat and to prevent it, and to get our lives back to normal.

But the problem with the disciples' question about blame goes deeper than just being unhelpful during a crisis. The disciples are also making a major assumption about how God acts.

Behind the disciples' question about sin stands the assumption that not only must someone be to blame, but also that God struck the man with blindness as punishment for the sin, whoever it was that committed it.

It as if God sits up in heaven watching us, judging us, waiting for us to make a mistake, and then zapping us.

The disciples probably would not have put it quite like that. Not many of us would put it quite like that. But that is the implication of their question.

And that is the implication every time we ask, why is God doing this, that, or the other bad thing. The question itself presumes that God is a more or less mean-spirited score-keeper who happily punishes us for reasons that we often cannot fathom.

But is that the God we worship? Is that the God we meet in Jesus Christ?

Certainly, Jesus doesn't think so. Jesus flatly rejects the disciples' way of framing the question. "Neither this man nor his parents sinned." That is not the right way to think about human suffering.

No, says Jesus, this man "was born blind so that God's works might be revealed in him." And then, to reveal God at work, Jesus heals the man of his blindness.

This is really important, especially right now.

God did not strike this man blind as a punishment for sin. Jesus is perfectly clear about that. God didn't strike the man blind at all. God's will for this man was not blindness. God's will for this man was sight. It was only when Jesus healed the man that God's work in this poor man was finally revealed.

We are now at the heart of the Christian gospel. We are now at the most important lesson in the Bible, and one that we need to hear over and over again.

When Jesus heals the blind man, he is showing, once again, that "God so loved the world that God gave His only Son, so that everyone who believes in Him may not perish but may have eternal life. Indeed, God did not send the Son into the world to condemn the world, but in order that the world might be saved through Him" (John 3:16-17).

The disciples were totally wrong in their assumption about God.

God does not float somewhere above creation ready to punish us whenever we get out of line. God enters into creation, above all in the life, death, and resurrection of Jesus Christ. God takes flesh and walks among us, teaching and healing and forgiving and feeding and suffering, all for us. God takes flesh and walks among us in order to reveal His love by working in us for good.

So, where is God today?

Start with where God is not. God is NOT somewhere out there watching us struggle with covid-19.

Where God is, is right here with us, in the midst of the messiness, the struggle, the pain. God is especially with the people who are sick or scared or lonely or hopeless.

And what is God doing? Well, God is NOT striking us with this virus because somebody sinned.

What I know from my own experience, what I am guessing lots of people know from their own experiences over the last couple of weeks, is that God is sustaining us as we do our best to get by in a profoundly disorienting time. And thank God for that!

I suspect that God is also working miracles of protection and healing. But God is not likely simply to make the coronavirus go away. For whatever reason, God doesn't seem to work like that.

Instead, God delegates that work to us. God invites us to join Jesus Himself in revealing God's love in our works right now, by how we live with the reality of the covid-19 virus.

For some of us, the works that we are called to do are heroic. I think particularly about nurses and others on the front lines of the battle with the virus.

But God's love is being revealed in lots of ways. At the Parish Cupboard, Martha continues to offer groceries to needy families. We can help with that by continuing to make food donations. That's a great way of revealing God's works.

People are reaching out to each other in all kinds of ways. Several members of the vestry agreed to contact folks just to see how they are doing. Others have agreed to go shopping for people who can't get out. That's a way of revealing God's works.

Lots of us have been trying to use technology to stay connected, to worship and pray and study together. This service is an example of that. And, despite technical glitches brought on by my incompetence, God's works are revealed.

Most touching of all to me, young Kaylin has been wondering what lessons she might learn from this crisis. Kaylin speculated that maybe God is encouraging us to spend less time on screens that separate us and more time with our families. If more of us could learn that lesson, surely God's works would be revealed!

So, my prayer for us all, in this time of quarantine, is that we can see God's works being revealed around us. And I pray that we can do our part in helping to reveal God's works. In Christ's name, I pray. Amen.

22. Looking for Resurrection
5 Lent; March 29, 2020
Ezekiel 37:1-14; Psalm 130; Romans 8:6-11; John 11:1-45

At the center of our Gospel reading for this morning stand the three siblings, Martha, Mary, and Lazarus. We don't know very much about them, but they were clearly close friends of Jesus, perhaps Jesus' closest friends other than the disciples themselves.

Shortly before our reading begins, Lazarus became seriously ill. His sisters immediately contacted Jesus and asked him to hurry to Bethany to heal their brother. As we just heard, Jesus is slow to respond, and Lazarus dies. Jesus doesn't arrive for another four days.

Much is striking about this passage. But the part that is most relevant for us right now is Jesus' interaction with Martha. Martha already knows Jesus well. Martha already has great faith. But Martha still has room to grow. In our passage, we can see Jesus working with Martha to help her take the next step in her journey of faith. And what Jesus says to Martha, we can hear as addressed to us, too.

When Martha learns that Jesus is finally close, she hurries out to meet him. And what is the first thing Martha says when they meet? "Lord, if you had been here, my brother would not have died."

We are not told what Martha is thinking to herself as she says that. But that sounds angry to me. I think Martha is fussing at Jesus for having been so slow to arrive. Martha knows that God listens to Jesus, so she can't fuss much. But it sounds a lot like she blames Jesus for her brother's death.

Jesus promises Martha that her brother will rise. Martha knows that; she is a woman of faith. But it is cold comfort. "I know," she says, "that [Lazarus] will rise again in the resurrection at the last day." But that isn't much help. I am grieving now.

That is when Jesus delivers the big line of this passage. "I am the resurrection and the life."

What does that mean?

Well, first, Jesus is explicitly not talking about resurrection in some distant future, as Martha had assumed. Jesus, the man standing right with Martha, is himself resurrection and life in that very moment.

Now, we know how this story ends. Jesus will literally raise Lazarus from the grave in just a few minutes. That is part of what Jesus is telling Martha here.

But let's not go there quite yet. Let's stay with Jesus and Martha in this moment, while Martha is still grieving and Lazarus is still in the tomb.

Jesus is telling Martha that resurrection is not just something that will happen when God's kingdom finally comes in all its power and glory. Resurrection is not limited to what he is about to do for Lazarus either.

Resurrection is something that happens wherever Jesus is present. Resurrection is, in some mysterious way, happening in that very moment, as Jesus and Martha chat and before Lazarus comes out of his grave.

Jesus asks Martha if she believes him, if she believes that He is resurrection and life, if she believes that resurrection is a present reality as well as a future hope. Martha says she does.

But Martha doesn't mean it, as we see a few verses later when she objects to opening the tomb. Martha can't wrap her mind around Jesus' claim that he is resurrection, that resurrection happens wherever and whenever Jesus is present. I don't blame her. That is a hard thing to take in.

Bring this up to today. A lot of us are in the exact same place as Martha was. There is fear and death and grief all around us. So, we do what we do. We pray. We pray for Christ to come, to come protect the well and heal the sick. But Jesus seems to be delayed.

What would happen if Jesus showed up right now, if Jesus were standing here in front of me? Probably I would dissolve into a puddle of fear. But if I had the courage, I might be tempted to say a version of what Martha says. "Jesus, if you had been here, this whole pandemic would have gone away. So where have you been?"

We can keep going with this. If Jesus responded with a promise of eventual resurrection, I would surely thank him for that. But I might also add, if I had the courage, "Resurrection hope sustains me. But I would still prefer for you to fix the problem right now, not to wait until the literal end of time."

And now that we are right where Martha was, we may be able to hear the mind-boggling promise in Jesus' words. "I am resurrection and I am life. Where I am, there is resurrection and life, whether or not you can see it."

Best of all, Jesus says elsewhere, "I am with you always" (Matthew 28:20). Resurrection and life is happening all around us all the time.

So here is the promise that Jesus makes to Martha, the promise that Jesus makes to us, too. Resurrection and life is happening even in the midst of our fear and grief and death. This is an invitation to open our eyes and notice the signs of God's grace all around us.

Let's return to Martha. Martha appears in one other story in the Gospels that helps us to understand her a little better and that helps us to get better at seeing resurrection and life around us.

Sometime before Lazarus' death and resuscitation, Jesus and his disciples visited the two sisters. Martha's sister Mary sat at Jesus' feet with the other disciples listening to him talk and soaking in his beloved presence. Meanwhile, Martha was trying to keep this horde of hungry people fed.

Finally Martha has enough, and she complains to Jesus. Martha wants Jesus to make Mary help her with all the housework. But Jesus tells her, "Martha, Martha, you are worried and distracted by many things; there is need of only one thing. Mary has chosen the better part, which will not be taken away from her" (Luke 10:38-42), which, we might add, is available to Martha, too.

We see here what we can also see in our Gospel reading. Martha is an active, take-care-of-business kind of woman. I like women like that. I am married to a woman like that! I am like that. A lot of us here at Saint David's are like that. We tend to be active, busy people.

But we Martha people are in a Mary moment. We can't do a lot of the things we would normally be doing. Many of the distractions that occupy us in normal times have been taken away. My poor sons are suffering serious sports withdrawal!

But there is an invitation to us, in this terrible time. Like Martha, we tend to be worried and distracted by many things. But in this moment, when those things have been taken away, perhaps we could spend more time sitting at Jesus' feet, attending to Jesus' holy word, soaking in Jesus' beloved presence.

If we use this time of quarantine as an opportunity to sit at Christ's feet, we will get better at seeing Christ's presence in the world around us. We'll get better at spotting moments of resurrection and life even now. That would truly be a great gift.

And that is my prayer for us. I pray that Christ will protect and sustain us in this difficult time. But I also ask Christ to help us sit at his feet, and to open our eyes to resurrection and life all around us. And I pray this in his holy name. Amen.

23. Towards the Cross
Palm Sunday; April 5, 2020
Isaiah 50:4-9a; Psalm 31:9-16; Philippians 2:5-11; Matthew
21:1-11

In the Gospel story that gives this day its name, Jesus enters Jerusalem in apparent triumph. Such a large crowd gathers to greet him that the whole city is in turmoil. They spread cloaks for him, and wave palms at him, and cheer him as the Son of David who comes in the name of the Lord.

More ominously, Luke tells us that offended Pharisees demand Jesus keep his disciples quiet. Jesus refuses, but they will get their revenge in just a few days (Luke 19:39-40).

But that is getting ahead of ourselves. For now, let's stick with the main event we commemorate this morning.

It is interesting to speculate about what might have been going through the minds of the cheering crowd that morning. But we know what the disciples were thinking.

On the way to Jerusalem, Jesus repeatedly warned his disciples about the horrible events that would take place there. But the disciples couldn't absorb what he was saying.

And immediately after one of these warnings, I mean the next verse!, James and John, two of Jesus' closest disciples, ask Jesus if they can "sit, one at [his] right hand and one at [his] left, in [his] glory." James and John are looking forward to glory and triumph, not suffering and death (Mark 10:35-37).

The other disciples don't seem to be any better. They resented James' and John's effort to get the best seats in the coming kingdom (10:41).

We can see the same hopes and resentments after Jesus and the disciples reach Jerusalem, at the Last Supper itself. Jesus tells them his betrayal is imminent. And once again they dispute "as to which one of them was to be regarded as the greatest" (Luke 22:24). Their stupidity would be comic if the situation weren't so tragic.

If that is what the people who knew Jesus best were thinking, the crowds must surely have been thinking something similar. God's agent is coming to make everything right. At last, our kingdom will gain its independence, and the glory of our nation will be restored. That's why they cheer and greet Jesus as the messianic king.

On Palm Sunday, we always reenact this moment of apparent triumph. We process with palms, singing "All glory, laud, and honor to Thee, Redeemer, King! To whom the lips of children made sweet hosannas ring. Thou art the King of Israel, Thou David's royal Son, who in the Lord's Name comest, the King and Blessed One."

Normally, of course, we all process. It is not as glorious as what Jesus experienced on that day. But it is spirited and fun and, in its own way, a little glorious.

Unfortunately, we couldn't do that today. We had a procession of just three, all at a safe distance from each other. And I, for one, was not singing out loud!

But what I am suggesting is that the glory surrounding Jesus' entrance into Jerusalem was false. It was based on a fundamental misunderstanding of what Jesus was coming to do, a misunderstanding that was common to the crowd and to Jesus' disciples, despite Jesus' best efforts to prepare them.

We see that it is false when Jesus is arrested. His disciples scatter in fear and shock, and the crowd that today was hailing Jesus as their king screams for his execution.

So now, let's look not at the crowd and not at the disciples, but at Jesus himself, the one at the center of all the enthusiasm.

As we do, we need to remember that the Romans of the first century knew how to stage impressive processions. Victorious generals would parade through the streets of Rome at the head of their troops, displaying their captives and all the booty they had won. The crowds would cheer. And the whole thing was so overwhelming that Romans took to having a slave stand immediately behind the victorious general, reminding him over and over again that he was just a man, not a god. That's what glory and triumph looked like to Roman citizens at the time Jesus entered Jerusalem.

Jesus does enter Jerusalem as the king foretold by the prophet Zechariah long ago. But, as the prophet said, Jesus comes in humility, not in great pomp. Jesus enters Jerusalem riding on a donkey at the head of a ragtag band of peasants, not on a stallion at the head of an intimidating army.

If Pilate saw Jesus' entry, he might have worried about mob violence. But he certainly would NOT have been impressed by the grandeur of the procession.

That's the point. Jesus' entrance was not grand and glorious. Jesus' entrance was a parody of the grandeur and glory that human power aspires to.

The enthusiastic crowd and even Jesus' disciples seem to have entirely missed the point of Jesus' parody even though it was explicit in the prophecy Jesus was fulfilling.

Ironically, our little procession this morning was closer in spirit to what Jesus was doing on that day than anything his followers were doing, and closer than our own normal way of celebrating Palm Sunday. Our little procession is appropriate homage to the one who entered Jerusalem on a donkey, and who was coming to the city in the full knowledge that he would soon be beaten and killed.

On that first Palm Sunday, the people wanted victory without cost. They wanted to rule without paying the price. They wanted resurrection life without the cross. They wanted Easter without Good Friday.

On that day, Jesus, alone as best we can tell, had a different vision. Jesus entered Jerusalem in humility, despite the cheering crowds. Jesus loved his disciples, knowing that they would fail. Jesus went willingly to his death in order to open our way to real new life, to the true glory of Easter, which only comes after crucifixion.

In our New Testament reading for this morning, the Apostle Paul gives classic expression to the theology of the cross that is the true meaning of Jesus' entrance into Jerusalem and of all the events we commemorate in Holy Week.

"Christ Jesus,… though he was in the form of God, did not regard equality with God as something to be exploited, but emptied himself, taking the form of a slave, being born in human likeness. And being found in human form, he humbled himself and became obedient to the point of death—even death on a cross."

The cheering crowds didn't get the whole emptied-himself, humbled-himself, obedient-to-the-point-of-death-on-a-cross message. But that is exactly what Jesus' journey to Jerusalem was all about.

Bring this up to today. Our situation is grim. People are dying of a pandemic in growing numbers. Even those of us who are healthy are isolated, afraid, and vulnerable in all kinds of ways.

But the suffering of our present time has one benefit. It helps us see through the wrong-headed pretensions of even Jesus' closest followers in the days before the crucifixion. It helps us see Jesus' actions on the day of his entrance into Jerusalem for the parody of human power and glory that it was.

It also prepares us to see still more deeply, to see the victory of the cross, to see the resurrection life that truly does triumph over death.

On this Palm Sunday, I give thanks to God for the humility of our king, who enters the great city on a donkey. I give thanks to God for Jesus' willingness to suffer and die for us. And I give thanks to God for the truly good news of resurrection that ultimately triumphs over suffering and death.

In Jesus' name. Amen.

24. Getting Our Feet Wet

Maundy Thursday; April 9, 2020
Exodus 12:1-14a; Psalm 116:1, 10-17; 1 Corinthians 11:23-26;
John 13:1-17, 31b-35

For the last few weeks, it has been hard to think of anything except the covid virus. Among other things, it prevents us from being in each other's physical presence on one of the holiest days of the year.

But in each of the next few days, I hope we can take a break from covid to commemorate the events around which all of history turns.

Today we remember Jesus' Last Supper. But today's Gospel reading is a little puzzling. The main thing to happen at the Last Supper was the institution of the Eucharist. Jesus broke the bread, and blessed the wine, and gave them to his disciples as his body and blood, and commanded his disciples to continue the ritual in remembrance of him. Matthew, Mark, and Luke all tell that story. So does Paul in the passage we just heard.

But John doesn't tell that story. Now, we can be pretty sure that John's community celebrated the Eucharist virtually every time they came together. But John found meaning in the Last Supper other than the Eucharist. That is good news for us on this Maundy Thursday since we are not in a position to celebrate Holy Communion the way we normally do.

In his version of the Last Supper, John emphasizes foot washing. So what does the foot washing mean? What did it mean when Jesus did it? What does it mean for us today?

Start with how we might feel about a foot washing.

You will perhaps be happy to know that I took a shower this morning, and I washed my feet. Indeed, thinking about

119

this very moment in my sermon, I made a point to wash my feet very thoroughly! That was just a few hours ago. My feet are not particularly nasty right now.

But still, you wouldn't really want to wash my feet even under normal circumstances. You especially wouldn't want to wash my feet now, when we are not allowed to come within six feet of each other.

More to the point, I wouldn't want you to. And I am not just talking about the possibility of spreading infection. Having someone wash my feet would be uncomfortably personal, uncomfortably intimate. Sitting there with my bare feet exposed, I would feel vulnerable and probably a little ashamed.

Foot washing was more common in the first century, so it wouldn't be as weird for them as it would be for me. But foot washing could still be uncomfortably intimate even in the first century.

Once when Jesus was eating at the home of a Pharisee, a sinful woman barged in, in the middle of the party, bathed Jesus' feet with her tears, dried his feet with her hair, kissed his feet over and over again, and then anointed his feet with oil.

Jesus' host was scandalized that Jesus would let such a woman handle him in that way. Clearly his host saw the foot washing as somehow binding Jesus and the woman together. Jesus saw it the same way. Jesus called it an act of great love, and he told the woman that her sins were forgiven (Luke 7:36-39).

The closest parallel to that foot-washing in my life was giving my children baths when they were little. Getting my children clean could be hard work, and it was sometimes gross. But I loved it. I am talking about when they were young enough that they accepted my love as a matter of course, without embarrassment or vulnerability or shame.

That is how Jesus accepted the sinful woman's anointing, as an act of love that concealed nothing and held nothing back. That's what Jesus offered when he washed his disciples' feet.

But love that conceals nothing and holds back nothing is unnerving if you are older than about three.

Other than Peter, we don't know how the disciples experienced Jesus' foot washing. My guess is, most of them shared Peter's reservations about having their lord and master wash their feet.

But I think particularly about Judas. Judas was all set to betray Jesus when the foot washing began, and he actually did the deed only a few minutes afterwards. Judas knows it. Jesus knows it. And there Jesus is, kneeling at Judas' feet. The humble love and forgiveness in Jesus' action is itself a kind of miracle.

But how do you think Judas felt about it? How would you feel as you shared a moment of intimacy with a man you planned to have brutally killed?

My guess is, Judas felt mighty vulnerable and exposed and ashamed. And my guess is, Jesus' love and forgiveness made those feelings worse. For the moment, Judas had to act as if everything was OK. But my guess is, Judas was so uncomfortable that betraying Jesus came as a relief.

Now, this is where it gets really awful. That is our place in this story.

Judas stands for us, for us who betray Christ every time we choose sin, for us who make Christ's sacrifice necessary every time we fall short of perfect love. Jesus died on the cross for our sins. Every time we sin, we team up with Judas to put Jesus on the cross. And the whole time that we are betraying him, Jesus is at our side, loving us, helping us, carrying our burdens, washing our feet.

The question for us is, how do we respond to the loving Lord we are helping to crucify?

For Judas, the burden of guilt and shame proves too heavy to bear. In the end, Judas could not believe in, and could not accept, Christ's forgiveness or Christ's love.

It is not easy for most of us either. Often we try to do what Judas does at the Last Supper. We pretend like everything is OK, and remain in a state of sin and imminent despair.

But it doesn't have to be that way.

In the very act of washing his disciples' feet, Jesus demonstrates his forgiveness and his love even though he knows they will all fail him in the next few hours. Jesus demonstrates his love and forgiveness even more powerfully on the cross itself, where Jesus prays, "Father, forgive them; for they do not know what they are doing" (Luke 23:34).

Jesus offers that same forgiveness to us, knowing all there is to know about our sin and failure.

I think again about having our feet washed, about exposing the dirty parts of ourselves. It is uncomfortable. But it is how we get cleansed.

So now let's pretend we are at the table with Jesus on that night. Jesus has finished with the feet of the disciples, and now he approaches us. Do we hide our feet in shame, as if he doesn't know they are dirty? Do we let Jesus wash our feet and experience the whole thing as a humiliating affront, as Judas did? Or can we accept Jesus' washing as the act of our loving and forgiving God?

I think again about my children at bathtime, filthy but happy, paddling in the water, enjoying my touch, reveling in the experience of their father's love.

That is God's invitation to us who remain God's children even when we are dirty. God knows us straight through, and God loves us as we are. Our task is simply to let go of our foolish pride, acknowledge our sin and our weakness, and receive the forgiveness and love of Christ.

My prayer for us, as we go through these most holy days of the entire year, is that we can do that, with God's help. In Jesus' name. Amen.

25. Keeping the Faith and Looking Ahead
Good Friday; April 10, 2020
Isaiah 52:13-53:12; Psalm 22; Hebrews 10:16-25; John 18:1-
19:42

As I prepared for this service, in this strangest year of my life to date, two things struck me about my experience of this Lent and Holy Week.

In one way, this has been my worst Lent in many years. None of my Lenten disciplines are particularly dramatic. But for the last several years, between a few things taken on and a few things given up, the rhythm of my days has shifted in Lent. As a consequence, no matter what else was going on, I was always pretty well focused on the fact that it was Lent, that it was a season of prayer and fasting and self-denial and so on.

But not this year. I have more or less stuck with my usual disciplines. But this year my routines were so fundamentally altered by the covid-19 virus that the little changes I made to acknowledge Lent seem almost irrelevant. Mostly I have been trying to figure out how to do the basic things I need to do without coming within six feet of other human beings or even touching things that other people have recently touched.

So, in one way, this has been a failed Lent for me. I suspect the same has been true for a lot of people.

But in another way, my experience of Lent this year, what I am guessing has been the experience of many of us this year, has been more faithful to the true spirit of Lent than has ever been the case for me before.

Lent is supposed to be a season for facing our limitations, our failures, and our mortality. At the beginning of Lent, on Ash Wednesday, we are invited, in

124

the name of the Church, to choose different disciplines that help us to do that.

This year, my particular Lenten practices weren't a big help. That itself has been a lesson in my own limitations.

But more importantly, the corona virus and the dramatic measures we have all had to take to slow its spread have forced us all to acknowledge our vulnerability, our anxiety, and our all too obvious mortality. The corona virus has forced us all into a Lenten season of withdrawal, of broken routines, of helplessness, and of grief.

Despite ourselves, even against our will, we have all been prepared over the last few weeks for this day, for Good Friday and the brutal lessons of the long Passion Gospel we just heard.

The Good Friday reading puts us at the foot of the cross where we have to watch helplessly as Jesus dies. It must have been awful even to contemplate for anyone who loved Jesus. It must have been especially hard for the few who were brave enough to be present with Christ in his last agonizing moments. And it must have been worst of all for Jesus' mother who could do nothing to help her beloved son.

I have certainly never experienced a pain so intense as what Mary must have felt that day. But we have all had a little taste of that pain in the last few weeks, as a force beyond our control has ravaged our communities, disrupted our lives, and killed so many.

Most of the time, most of us do our best to carry on, to do what we can to live normally, to fight the sense of helplessness and fear that has been growing in many of us over the last several weeks.

But today we pause to look straight at the horror of the cross, to acknowledge that most inevitable, and usually most ignored, fact of human life: we will all die and there is nothing we can do about it. Today we pause from whatever routines we have been able to establish in order to express our fear and grief, our fear and grief over what happened to Jesus all those centuries ago, and our fear and grief at what is happening around us right now.

Today is a day for lamentation, which is not something we do naturally in contemporary America, but which is something we need to do when we are hurting.

But lamentation is not the full story. In addition to lamenting, we can, if we put ourselves back at the foot of the cross, learn two invaluable lessons for our situation today.

Not even the Virgin Mary can prevent Jesus from suffering and dying. But Mary can prevent Jesus from dying alone. Sometimes standing with people is all we can do. But it is something, and it makes a difference. Ask anyone who has kept vigil at the bedside of someone as they die. It is a holy act. It is a profound act of faithfulness and love. And it matters.

In this time of quarantine, we cannot be physically present with each other in the normal way. But all of us, the sick and the healthy, need companionship, moral support, the comfort of knowing that we are not alone. So we reach out in the ways that we can. It may seem like a small gesture. But we can all do our little part to follow the example of Mary at the cross by staying in contact with each other. That is a first lesson we can learn from our Gospel reading.

The second is just as important. There is life after crucifixion.

In three days, we will celebrate Christ's resurrection, which is the great fact of life after crucifixion. But that is not what I am talking about now.

As Christ dies in agony, as his mother watches in her own agony, Jesus nods at his beloved disciple John, and he says to Mary, "Woman, here is your son." To John, Jesus says, "Here is your mother" (John 19:26-27).

What is going on here? As he says those words, Jesus is not looking ahead to his own resurrection, important though that is, of course. Jesus is reminding Mary and his beloved disciple that the horror of the crucifixion will come to an end, that they have a future, that their lives will go on. Who knows if Mary and John could take in what Jesus was saying in that moment? But Jesus was reminding them that, horrible as things truly were, the horror would end. The pain would linger, of course. But crucifixion was not the end of the story, not for Jesus who would be raised. And not for them either, who had the ongoing responsibility of caring for each other.

As I look ahead today, the end of our current crisis is not in sight. There is more suffering to endure. And for many of us, the pain of these days will linger, perhaps for the rest of our lives.

But the covid virus will pass. There is a future after covid. Even as we endure, we can look ahead in hope to the day when our lives will resume, changed no doubt, but still they will resume.

And so today we grieve. We acknowledge our helplessness and vulnerability. But with Christ's help, we can remain faithful even in these days, both to God and to each other. And with Christ's help, we can look forward to a future life, in this lifetime and for all eternity with God.

And so on this Good Friday, I give thanks to God. In Christ's name. Amen.

26. Seeing the Risen Lord

Easter Sunday; April 12, 2020
Acts 10:34-43; Psalm 118:1-2, 14-24; Colossians 3:1-4; John
20:1-18

Most years, Easter morning is the highlight of the whole year for me. The Church is packed, including lots of kids who make their own joyous noise to the Lord. The music is glorious. Everyone is in a good mood. And we celebrate the good news of great joy that death could not hold Christ, that Christ is risen, that Christ is alive. And to that, we always say, for the first time in weeks, "alleluia, alleluia!"

I look forward to Easter every year, but this year was going to be extra special. My parents were going to join us. They planned to arrive late yesterday, and I was going to see them for the first time since Thanksgiving at this service.

Things have turned out to be quite different than any of us expected when Lent began seven weeks ago.

This Easter is happening in the valley of the shadow of death. Many of us are mourning. Many of us are isolated and afraid. None of us know what the future will hold.

The reality of life in the face of the covid virus is not at all what I associate with Easter. This seems like more of a Good Friday moment.

But that is not so different from how the first Easter began.

What we know, as our Gospel passage begins, is that Christ has in fact already risen. But Jesus' disciples did not know that yet. They were grieving their crucified Lord. They were hiding in fear for their lives. They could not see a way forward.

Mary Magdalene was braver, but otherwise not much better than the others. Mary didn't have any more hope than they did. Mary didn't anticipate resurrection. Mary wasn't looking for her risen Lord. Mary just wanted to grieve as close to Jesus' body as she could get.

On that first Easter morning, Christ was risen. And, as that first Easter morning dawned, Christ's followers didn't feel any resurrection joy.

The big news of that day was Christ's resurrection, of course. But part of the story, the part that speaks to us right now, is the slow process by which Mary comes to recognize her Lord and to experience Easter joy almost despite herself.

As we meditate on Mary's story on that first Easter morning, we can also see it as our story, our invitation to discover Easter joy in our difficult time.

God starts working on Mary right at the beginning. Mary shows up at the grave and sees that the stone blocking the entrance to Jesus' tomb has been miraculously removed.

I never thought much about that stone. But one of the early Christian fathers named Peter Chrysologus pondered why the stone was removed. Not so Jesus could get out, as I had always assumed. Jesus didn't need any help. Jesus could appear wherever he wanted. We'll hear stories about Jesus doing just that over the next few weeks.

No, the stone was not removed for Jesus. So why? Chrysologus answers that the stone was removed for Mary. The stone was removed so Mary could see that the tomb was empty.[6] The stone was removed as an act of grace aimed at restoring hope to a grieving woman.

It is a comfort to think that God removes obstacles to our faith, just as God did for Mary. But we need to keep going. We need to keep going because this first grace moment doesn't work. Stone or no stone, the empty tomb does not reveal anything to Mary. With the empty tomb right in front of her, Mary literally runs in the opposite direction.

Sometimes we do exactly the same thing. God invites us into relationship with the risen Christ. God nudges us along by removing some of the stones strewn in our way. But faced with Christ's resurrection, we all too easily assume it just means someone has stolen the body.

Thankfully God wasn't done with Mary. Something drew Mary back to the tomb. Mary still didn't go in. But Mary had the wisdom to recognize that more was happening than she yet understood.

That, I think, is the first stirring of faith, that sense, however ill-defined, that God is at work even when life seems bleak and hopeless.

So there Mary stood, just outside the tomb, unable to see God, unable to walk away, stuck weeping in a complicated mix of despair and just a little bit of hope.

Finally Mary looks in. Mary turns away. Jesus Himself appears. And still Mary is blind to the presence of her risen Lord.

The story goes on. And on any other Easter, we would go right on with it. But this Easter we need to pause at this most poignant moment in the entire story. Because this is

---

[6] *Ancient Christian Commentary, New Testament 1B: Matthew 14-28*, 2002: 306.

the good news of resurrection that many of us need to hear right now.

Christ didn't rise because his disciples gathered together in great faith and with great joy to celebrate the good news of resurrection in the kind of Easter celebration we have most years.

Christ rose, and his terrified disciples had no idea.

God opened the way for them to enter Christ's tomb, to see that it was empty, to connect what they were seeing with their own eyes to everything Jesus had told them. And they remained blind to the resurrection.

The risen Christ stood right in front of Mary, quite possibly the person who loved him most of all, and Mary could not see him for who he was.

The good news of Mary's encounter with Christ is not so much that she finally recognized him. The good news of Mary' encounter with Christ is that Christ was there, with her, even when she could not yet see.

That is good news we can celebrate this morning. The good news of Easter is that Christ is risen. Christ is alive. Christ is with us. That good news is true no matter how we feel, no matter how blind we may be.

Now, at last, with some relief, we can go on to the end.

Jesus calls Mary by name. Mary sees Jesus for who he is. Mary sees that the person she thought was a gardener was in fact her risen Lord.

There is an Easter invitation to us here. We, too, can learn to see Christ in the person right in front of us, to see Christ in the gardener, or the nurse, or the Post Office worker, or the person delivering groceries or the family member we share space with. Christ is all around us all the time, blessing us often through people in our lives who may not even know that they are acting as Christ's hands and heart in our world.

And having recognized Jesus in a place and person she would never have expected, Mary experiences resurrection joy. And Mary rushes back to the disciples once again, this time to share not her fears, but her restored faith and hope.

Mary's story on that first Easter morning reminds us that Christ's resurrection does not depend on how we feel on any given day. It is the opposite. Christ's resurrection makes it possible for us to find joy even in times when sin and death seem to prevail. Because Christ defeated sin and death, and Christ invites us to share in his victory.

And so on this day, which may seem bleaker than most Easters, I invite you to look around for glimpses of the resurrected Christ. And for Christ's glorious resurrection, we can all give joyful thanks. Alleluia, alleluia! Amen.

27. Blessed Are We Even When We Do Not See

2 Easter Sunday; April 19, 2020
Acts 2:14a, 22-32; Psalm 16; 1 Peter 1:3-9; John 20:19-31

Every year, on this second Sunday of the Easter season, we have this Gospel reading. And virtually every year, I speak a word on behalf of Thomas. Because of this passage, we remember him as Doubting Thomas. And it is easy to criticize him. Thomas refuses to believe that Christ has risen without first seeing Christ and, just to make sure, actually touching Christ's wounds.

Jesus himself implies that Thomas asked too much. Jesus says "those who have not seen and yet have come to believe" are "blessed." By implication, Thomas receives a lesser blessing since he had to see in order to believe.

We could even go one step farther. We have not seen Christ, at least not in bodily form the way the apostles did. And yet we believe. In our Gospel reading, Jesus blesses people like us. Maybe we are justified in criticizing Thomas. We can read this story as highlighting our own superiority to the one who doubts, the one who has to see in order to believe.

But that cannot be right. Jesus is quite clear that we are beloved children of God. But Jesus was not in the habit of stroking people's egos. Over and over again, Jesus had to tell his disciples that they should not be comparing themselves with each other, evaluating each other, asserting their own superiority to their brothers and sisters in Christ.

God knows we often need that message too. No, we can be sure this story is NOT about how much better we are than Thomas. Something else is going on.

So what does this passage mean? What good news does it proclaim? What is the lesson for us here?

Let's go back to that first Easter morning. Mary Magdalene and the other women went to Jesus' tomb so they could grieve and so they could properly care for Jesus' corpse. These women, courageous and loyal though they were, did not yet believe in the resurrection. As we know, the risen Lord appeared to them. And still, Mary could not see Christ for who he was. Only when Jesus called her name was Mary able to see. And only after seeing was Mary able to believe. That was our reading for last Sunday.

Today we keep going. Mary and her companions returned to the apostles to announce the good news of great joy that Christ was risen. And, Luke tells us, "these words seemed to [the apostles] an idle tale, and they did not believe [the women]" (24:11).

Peter and John raced to the tomb to check Mary's story and found it empty, just as Mary had said. But Peter and John didn't see Christ that morning, and Peter and John did not yet believe. So they returned to their hiding place and locked the doors behind them for fear of what might happen next.

Hours go by. That evening, "Jesus came and stood among [his disciples] and said, 'Peace be with you.'" Jesus showed them his wounds. And, at last they believed. John tells us, "they rejoiced [now that] they saw the Lord."

But poor Thomas wasn't there. And Thomas didn't believe the resurrection because, like every other disciple in this story, Thomas needed to see the risen Christ in order to believe.

Thomas was no more a doubter than every other follower of Jesus in the days immediately after Christ's resurrection. Thomas needed what they all needed. Thomas needed a personal encounter with the risen Lord.

But where does that leave us? We can't see Jesus standing right in front of us. We can't touch Jesus' wounds. We can't eat with Jesus, or do any of the other things that the disciples did with Jesus while he was bodily present in the weeks between his resurrection and his ascension.

We have the reports of the apostles. But Mary's report was not enough to convince the other disciples. The apostles' report was not enough to convince Thomas. Their testimony wasn't good enough for each other. And the fact is, their testimony isn't good enough for us either. Fortunately for them, they could see Jesus physically present. We can't. So what helps us believe, even without seeing?

Our reading gives us the answer, and this is really good news that we need to hear over and over again. After greeting the disciples, "[Jesus] breathed on them and said to them, 'Receive the Holy Spirit.'"

In that moment, the disciples received some spiritual gifts which were unique to them. But every Christian, from that first Easter straight through to today, has also received the Holy Spirit.

We can receive the Spirit in lots of ways. But the Spirit is promised to us in baptism.

Here's the language we use at every baptism. Harvey, or Carrie, or Benjamin, or Nicholas, or whoever, "you are sealed by the Holy Spirit in baptism and marked as Christ's own forever."[7]

---

[7] *Book of Common Prayer (BCP)*, 308.

Two thousand years after Christ ascended to heaven, we can't see Christ bodily present except in rare acts of extraordinary grace. But for two thousand years, the Holy Spirit has empowered Christians, who have not seen Christ in that way, still to believe.

If we were perfect saints, that might be enough. We have been redeemed by Christ and touched by the Holy Spirit. What more do we need?

But life is considerably more complicated than that. We struggle with faith sometimes, of course. Doubt is part of the journey of faith for most of us, as it was for Thomas and all the other disciples all those centuries ago.

Thankfully, the Holy Spirit persists. The Holy Spirit nudges us along. And the Holy Spirit brings us together as the household of God.

And an amazing thing happens. We gather, in Christ's name, and Christ is with us. We share the Eucharist. And in some mysterious way, Christ is present in the sacrament of his body and blood. We do see Christ after all.

And the Holy Spirit swirls around. And even as we struggle, our lives are changed, and we become a little more the people that God created us to be. We experience the move we see Thomas make, the move from doubt through sight to adoration.

At least, that is how it normally works. But not now.

Now we can't gather, at least not physically. Now we can't experience the fullness of sacramental grace. Now we can't experience ourselves as the body of Christ, at worship or in mission, at least not as we normally do. I long to gather in worship, to feel a part of the body of Christ, to share Eucharist face to face, to see Christ in the sacrament and in the community. Eventually I will. But right now, I can't.

We do our best. We are gathered now, in a virtual way. We have heard God's word. We will share a virtual Eucharist. We are praying. But it is not the same.

And this brings us to the real good news of our Gospel reading for this moment, good news we have never so needed to hear as now. These are my words. But this is Christ's message.

Blessed are those who cannot see me right now, those who cannot gather, those cannot share Eucharist in the normal way. Blessed are they because, even in this time, the Holy Spirit continues to work on them, individually and collectively. Blessed are they because I am with them. Blessed are they because their faith endures.

And to that I say, thanks be to God. In Christ's name. Amen. Alleluia!

28. Christ With Us On The Road
3 Easter Sunday; April 26, 2020
Acts 2:14a, 36-41; Psalm 116:1-3, 10-17; 1 Peter 1:17-23;
Luke 24:13-35

In our Gospel reading we are, once again, back on that first Easter morning.

That day two Christians heard Mary's astounding report about the empty tomb, the angels, the proclamation that Christ was risen. But like everyone else, Cleopas and his companion couldn't wrap their minds around the good news of resurrection. And these two went farther than the others. They gave up entirely. They left.

Luke doesn't tell us why they left. But it's not hard to guess. Jerusalem was becoming a scary place for anyone associated with Jesus. Better not to be caught hanging out with a bunch of Jesus' followers, just in case the authorities decided they needed to make an example out of a few more Jesus people.

Cleopas and his companion are us. We have no reason to fear police hauling us off to be crucified. But like Cleopas and his companion, we worry that gathering with our Christian brothers and sisters could be dangerous. And so, on a day when we might be together celebrating Christ's resurrection, we, like them, find ourselves separated from each other.

The next bit of this reading is common to all the stories of resurrection in those first days, and it is a familiar bit of good news. But it is certainly worth repeating. Jesus shows up wherever his disciples are. And Jesus does whatever they need him to do.

At the tomb itself, Jesus calls a weeping Mary Magdalene by name. In the midst of a gathering of believers, Jesus shows his wounds to a doubting Thomas and offers to let Thomas touch them. Similarly in our reading for this morning, Jesus takes a walk on the road to Emmaus to teach a fleeing pair of disciples about the truth of resurrection.

Jesus opens the scriptures to Cleopas and his companion, and their hearts burn within them. Jesus takes bread, blesses and breaks it, and gives it to them. And in that Eucharistic moment, their eyes are opened, and they recognize their risen Lord, and they embrace the truth of resurrection.

How about us? Does Jesus show up where we are? Does Jesus do what we need him to do?

So far Jesus has not materialized bodily at my house, and, for the record, I would like that to happen. But the fact is, Jesus has been showing up in all kinds of ways. I have just needed a little help opening my eyes to his presence in the people around me.

Several people from our parish contacted me over the last week to check in and see if I needed anything. What a generous gesture! As I read those messages and received those calls, my heart burned within me just a little bit, and I knew Christ was present in our Church community, separated though we are.

Eight days ago my former boss and wonderful friend Derrick Fetz took his final vows as a Third Order Franciscan. The service was done on Zoom, which at the time I had not seen done before. On Zoom we prayed and we sang. We heard a couple of short homilies on the Franciscan life. Derrick made his vows and received a blessing. And I was reminded that the Church lives, that the Church keeps moving forward even in difficult times, even when we can't be together. And my heart burned a little within me because Christ was with us as we gathered in his name.

Last Wednesday, a former student of mine contacted me to say that she has been approved for ordination in the Episcopal Church. It is scheduled for June. It may happen on Zoom. Or maybe we can gather. Either way, the Jesus movement rolls on.

As it happened, the Gospel reading for Morning Prayer the day she contacted me was the passage she had chosen for her wedding several years ago, at which I preached. I had been thinking of her all day as I meditated on the scriptures, as they opened up for me. And my heart burned when I received her good news.

And here is what I recognized this week, as my eyes began to open to the presence of Christ with me even locked away in my home. I had a great week. I am a little stir crazy. I am a little paranoid about my health. But Christ has been all around me all week, showing up, providing what I needed, just like he did for Cleopas and his companion.

I am even beginning to see a silver lining to this time of quarantine, a bit of resurrection life happening right now.

I have said Morning Prayer virtually every day for years. But many's the time I have just rushed through it without much paying attention to the passages I read or the prayers I said.

Now that I am livestreaming Morning Prayer, I spend time each day thinking about the readings. I spend time reflecting on which prayers go with which passages. Morning Prayer, which has always been a great comfort to me, has become even better. New life in the midst of pandemic quarantine.

I hope something similar has been happening for everyone joining us for this service. Christ is with us even when we cannot be with each other. Prayer and the reading of Scripture can light a little fire in us, can open our eyes, can lead us deeper into the truth of resurrection that we celebrate even in this strangest Easter season ever.

Two more things about our passage strike me as particularly relevant right now.

The climatic moment when the eyes of Cleopas and his companion were opened came at a meal. At one level, this was just an ordinary supper for three weary travelers. And yet Christ was present. Christ took bread, blessed and broke it, and gave it to his companions. Those are Eucharistic actions. Through Christ's presence, an ordinary meal became a Eucharist capable of revealing the truth of Christ's resurrection to a pair of discouraged disciples.

The same came be true for us. Our ordinary meals can become mini-Eucharists if we, too, take our food, and bless it, and serve it, and if possible share it, all in Christ's name. After all, Christ is with us always. And it is Christ's presence that makes the difference, not a Church setting and not a priest. It is a great comfort to know that even when we cannot gather, we are not without benefit of Eucharistic grace.

But that is not quite the end of the story. Right now we are stuck on the road, so to speak, separated from each other. But separation is a necessary evil, not a positive good.

Cleopas and his companion get that. As soon as their eyes were opened, they hurried back to Jerusalem to rejoin their brothers and sisters in celebrating Christ's resurrection.

I long for the day when we can do the same!! I long for the day when we can come back together as a gathered community of faith to worship our Lord, to share the fullness of the sacrament, and once again to experience ourselves as the body of Christ.

In the meantime, I give thanks to Christ for meeting us where we are, for sustaining us in our separate homes, for filling us even now with sacramental grace. And I invite each of you to reflect this week on how Christ is appearing to you, on moments when your heart burns a little bit, on times when, however dimly, you can see Christ's grace at work.

And I make that invitation in Christ's name. Amen.

29. Going "Out"

4 Easter Sunday; May 3, 2020
Acts 2:42-47; Psalm 23; 1 Peter 2:19-25; John 10:1-10

One of the treats of the Easter season every year is hearing readings from the Acts of the Apostles. At the beginning of Acts, Jesus' boneheaded disciples receive the Holy Spirit and are transformed into dynamic heroes of the faith. Miracles happen. Peter proclaims the gospel with great power. Thousands join the movement. It is an exciting time.

In our reading for this morning, we get our earliest description of what can properly be called the Church, the community of Christian believers.

And I am struck with how similar we are in many ways.

We learn that "they devoted themselves to the apostles' teaching and fellowship, to the breaking of bread and the prayers." Check. We do that. Or at least, we commit to doing that every time we renew our baptismal covenant, as we have done twice in just the last few weeks.

We learn that "they had all things in common; they would sell their possessions and goods and distribute the proceeds to all, as any had need." Well, we don't do that one. It turns out, they didn't either, at least not for long. Already in Paul's ministry, which began just a couple of years after this, Christians mostly didn't give away all their property. Instead Paul encouraged them "to put aside [each Sunday] and save whatever extra you earn" to support the mission and ministry of the Church (1 Corinthians 16:2). So we are OK there, too.

But we differ pretty dramatically right now in something I have always taken for granted. Acts tells us that "all who believed were together." Again, "day by

144

day… they spent much time together in the temple." Most years the same would be true for us. But not this year.

Our separation is necessary. But it is also means that we can't be Church right now in one of the obvious, taken-for-granted ways that we have been Church for the past two thousand years.

That is a burden. But, as I have said many times in the last few weeks, there is also gift in this unprecedented moment. We are being forced to turn to Scripture with fresh eyes, to seek guidance on what God would have us do, now that many of our old ways are necessarily on hold.

And as we turn to Scripture with fresh eyes, new things begin to jump out. I notice for the first time that though the early Christians spent much time together in the temple, they also "broke bread at home and ate their food with glad and generous hearts, praising God."

We can do that. We can't break bread together. We can't celebrate Eucharist as we normally would. But we can still share a spiritual communion. And every meal can be a kind of mini-Eucharist as long as we, too, eat with glad and generous hearts, praising God.

But it is our Gospel reading that I find most helpful for this time. And I don't just mean this time of quarantine. I mean guidance for right now, for questions that I have been wrestling with this week.

Jesus uses a parable that is a little confusing at first. But the image is a familiar one. Jesus is the good shepherd. We are Jesus' flock. Right now, we are stuck in the sheepfold. We are stuck in our different versions of quarantine.

But our good shepherd comes to us in our different sheepfolds. Our good shepherd opens the gate. Our good shepherd calls us by name. Our good shepherd leads us out.

145

We need to be careful here. Jesus is NOT leading us out so that we can do exactly the things we used to do. Jesus is NOT inviting us to violate quarantine and put our own health or the health of others at risk. If we come out of quarantine too soon, we will experience more infections and deaths, particularly among our most vulnerable populations. Just last Wednesday, Massachusetts recorded the highest single-day death total so far, along with nearly 2000 newly confirmed cases of COVID-19 infections.[8] We need to continue to do what we can to be safe and to keep others safe.

No, this is a new moment, and it calls for a new kind of discipleship. The question is, what is Jesus calling us to do now, even while we continue to shelter in place?

In my experience, things began to shift this week.

When everything first shut down, my immediate concern was the safety and well-being of our people. We began streaming services, calling each other, and doing whatever we could to support each other and our common life. By now, we have more or less established a "new normal," with something like our regular round of worship and Bible Study, except that it is all online.

We were doing something similar at my house, as I assume everyone was. In our case, Nicholas and Benjamin came home, to Carrie's and my great joy.

Then came the inevitable adjustments. We began creating new routines. Our new routines included a delicate dance around the use of our one shower. Our new routines included a significantly expanded food budget and a good bit of additional time cooking and cleaning.

---

[8] Jacquelyn Voghel, "COVID-19 deaths hit single-day high," *Daily Hampshire Gazette*, page 1, April 30, 2020.

When the quarantine began, Carrie bought what she thought was several weeks' worth of food. But young men can eat. We polished it all off in just a few days.

After a couple of weeks, we had more or less figured it out. Then I got it into my head that I might have the virus. I spent a week living in my home office, which turned out to be not all bad, particularly given how much cooking and cleaning was happening. I couldn't help because I was supposed to stay in my room. Whenever I got hungry, I would text Carrie to bring me some food. When I was done, I put my plate outside my door. Carrie warned me not to get used to it. She told me I would have to come out some day.

That day was last Wednesday. Within an hour, Nicholas was openly longing for me to be back in quarantine. Carrie wasn't far behind him. Long-suffering Benjamin does his best to be sweet, while at the same time ignoring me as much as possible. All in all, life is back to a weird kind of normal.

And I find, for the first time since the shut-down began, that I can think about the world beyond my home and Saint David's. For the first time since the shut-down began, I have begun to hear a quiet call to embrace God's larger mission, to do my part, for us to do our part, to bring good news to the poor and to bind up the broken-hearted.

Many of you have probably been thinking about this for a while. But only now do I find myself asking, what is Christ calling us to do beyond the limits of our own sheepfolds? We can't really be with other people. But surely there are things we can do, things Christ is calling us to do, even now.

Our vestry began wrestling with this question last week. We, or at least I, don't yet know the answer. But asking the question is a first step.

And so I invite everyone hearing me now to prayerfully reflect on what Christ is calling us to do. Share your thoughts with me and with each other. Together we can hear better. And together we can make a difference.

May Christ help us to hear and to follow. In his name. Amen.

30. Constant Prayer, At Least For Now

7 Easter Sunday; May 24, 2020
Acts 1:6-14; Psalm 68:1-10, 33-36;
1 Peter 4:12-14; 5:6-11; John 17:1-11

This pandemic, and the measures we continue to take in order to be safe, have been horrible. But there have been for me a few silver linings to this very dark cloud.

One silver lining of this whole experience has been a new freshness in how I see Scripture. Week after week I have been struck by how directly our readings speak to our current situation. Week after week, things I have never noticed before have popped out at me and helped to make sense of what we are going through and of God's call to us in the midst of it.

That is true once again for this morning's reading from Acts. It is the story of Christ's ascension into heaven, Christ's return to his heavenly Father. Over the years, I have read this story dozens of times. But until this year I never read this story while sheltering in place to avoid a pandemic, and it makes a difference. As Christ and the angels talk to the disciples about Christ's departure, it is like they are talking to us about life in quarantine.

Just before our passage begins, Jesus orders the disciples "not to leave Jerusalem, but to wait there" (Acts 1:4). It's the story of our lives right now. We are not to leave home except when necessary. We are to wait there.

But it's not easy to stay in place and wait, not for us and not for them. By the time our passage begins, the disciples have gotten impatient. They have been through the trauma of crucifixion, and they have come out on the other side. They have met their risen Lord. They want to get on with it. They are ready for action.

So they ask Jesus, Is now the time? "Is this the time when you will restore the kingdom to Israel?"

Our question is a lot like that. We have been through the trauma of a sudden shut-down. Admittedly that is not nearly as bad as witnessing the crucifixion of our Lord! But it has been hard. And now we are coming out on the other side. We are beginning the long process of reopening our economies.

And many of us are ready, indeed impatient, to reopen our Churches. We ask ourselves, we ask each other, some people ask me, we ask our Bishop, we ask God: Is now the time? Is this the time when you will restore our Churches? Is this the time when we can get back to what we love? Is this the time when we can return to doing what we feel called to do?

So far, the answer to us is exactly the same as Jesus' answer to the apostles: Not yet. In our case, not until specific "public health indicators" have been met. We can't know when that will be. Apparently, it is not for us to know the times or the periods, any more than it was for the disciples all those years ago. Like the disciples, our calling at the moment is to wait, as patiently as we can.

Thankfully, especially for those like me who are impatient, Jesus keeps going. Now, Jesus says, is not the time for the disciples to act. But Jesus assures them that the time for action will come. They will receive power from the Holy Spirit, and they will be Christ's witnesses, beginning in Jerusalem, where they were at that moment, and extending all the way to the ends of the earth. That's a lot of action!

For us, too, the Holy Spirit is swirling around. And we, too, will spring into action as soon as we can. There remains plenty of work to be done witnessing to Christ, both here and to the ends of the earth.

In fact, of course, we are still doing what we can. Our building is closed but we, the people of Saint David's, are the Church. And we remain active in worship, prayer, study and service even in this time.

But what we can do is limited. For now, and this is likely to continue for some time, our primary task is not to act as much as it is to wait for the right time, for God's time.

That brings us to the ascension itself. And our passage continues to speak to our situation.

Watching Jesus ascend to heaven must have been startling! Understandably, the disciples just stand there, staring up after him.

But Christ won't come back, at least not in that form, until the literal end of time. So God helps the disciples out. It's a good thing. Otherwise, who knows how long they might have stood there?

God sends a pair of angels to tell the disciples that they can't keep looking for Christ in the form they have always known him. After this moment, their lives with Christ will never again be the same.

Their lives with Christ will continue. They will find Christ in Scripture, and in the breaking of the bread, and in the midst of their gatherings, and in the faces of the people they serve. But they won't see Christ in the way they were used to seeing Christ.

That is probably true for us, too. Our common life will continue to be shaped by the pandemic in one way or another for the next several months at a minimum. And even when the last of the restrictions are finally lifted, things will almost certainly look and feel different. Just as one particular example, I doubt we will ever do the Peace the same way again.

Going forward, Christ will still be with us. Christ will continue to invite us to share in God's mission. We will still be Christ's people. But Christ seems to be calling us— I mean us here at Saint David's but not just our parish; ALL of us—Christ seems to be calling us into a future which will differ from our old, familiar ways.

For me, and I suspect for most of us, the prospect of change is a little sad and a little scary. But it is also a little inspiring. We are not limited by who we have been. We are in the process of being made new by Jesus Christ and the work of the Holy Spirit. That is good news. And that is kind of exciting!

But that is still the future. For now, we wait. We wait for God's time. We wait for God's call. We wait for God's direction.

And while we wait, we can do exactly what the disciples did while they waited, all those centuries ago. They went to the room upstairs where they were staying. And they were constantly devoting themselves to prayer.

For now, we, too, remain in our rooms. And we too can devote ourselves to constant prayer.

Inspired by the example of the disciples in our passage, I invite everyone to make this week between Ascension and Pentecost a special week of prayer. Ask God for patience. Ask God for guidance. Ask God for the gifts of faith, and hope, and love. Ask God to send the Holy Spirit to us in a new and more powerful way.

And when the time does come, when God calls us back together, we will be ready. We better be. Because there will be plenty of work to do in loving service to God and our neighbors.

And so my prayer for us today is that we can wait patiently for now, and then be ready. In Christ's name. Amen.

31. United

Trinity Sunday; June 7, 2020
Genesis 1:1-2:4b; Psalm 8; 2 Corinthians 13:11-13;
Matthew 28:16-20

It is good to be together![9] Not all of us can be here this morning. And those of us who are here can't come face to face. But the fact that we can come together at all, even in this limited way, is an encouraging reminder that the Church remains open and active even when our building is closed. And for that, I give thanks to God.

I will come back to what I think this service represents in just a moment. But first I need to take a little detour.

My poor family members are routinely victims of my tendency to detour. Although none of us much fish, they use a fishing metaphor. They complain that in my detours I cast a long way out. To which I always reply that I will eventually reel it back in. That's my promise this morning.

But I need to cast into some deep theological waters. Today is Trinity Sunday. Today we are invited to reflect on the greatest mystery of our faith, the mystery of one God in three persons, Father, Son, and Holy Spirit, fully equal and perfectly united.

The question on which we meditate every Trinity Sunday is what our faith in a Triune, a Trinitarian God tells us about our own nature as human beings and about the Christian life to which we are called.

We get our first glimpse—just a glimpse—of the mystery of the Trinity in the very first verses of the Bible at the very beginning of creation itself. Our translation

---

[9] This was the first Sunday we worshipped in our parking lot, Drive-In style. We stayed in the parking lot for the next five months.

154

doesn't emphasize the Trinity, so I have changed it slightly to make the Trinitarian significance of the passage a little clearer.

"In the beginning, when the one God created the heavens and the earth, the earth was a formless void and darkness covered the face of the deep. God's Holy Spirit swept over the face of the waters. And God the Father brought forth the divine, creative Word, saying, 'Let there be light.' And there was light."

Creation goes on from there, of course. But that's enough for the moment.

Here's the point. Creation itself is a Trinitarian act. The one God creates all things. But the three persons are visible in the act of creation. All things come from the Father. The Father's Holy Spirit is at work over the face of the waters. And God the Father creates all things through God's Word, the only Son of the Father, who we know incarnate in Jesus Christ. Three persons, in perfect unity, doing God's work. Hold that thought.

God speaks again at the end of the creation story. "God says, 'Let us [Father, Son, and Holy Spirit] make humankind in our image, according to our likeness…So God created humankind in his image, in the image of God he created them; male and female he created them."

We, who are created in the image and likeness of God, are created to reflect God's own nature. Like God, we are separate persons. But also, like God, we are created for unity with each other, unity grounded in love and the Holy Spirit.

At least, that is how it is supposed to be. But sin enters the picture. The first family, Adam and Eve, Cain and Abel, was not united at all. One son kills the other. The image of God in us, that image of separate persons united

155

to each other in love, is badly damaged. And human history is off and running.

Thankfully, Christ comes to repair the damage of our sin. In a new act of creation, Christ restores the image of God in us. And so we are baptized, in the name of the Father, and the Son, and the Holy Spirit. We, who are separate persons and divided by sin, are redeemed by Christ and reunited with each other and with God by the Holy Spirit. We who are many are made one in the body of Christ. As we say at the beginning of our baptismal service, we are formed into "one Body and one Spirit," with "one hope in God's call to us, one Lord, one faith, one baptism, [with] one God and Father of all" (BCP, 299).

I am reeling it in. It is good to be together this morning not just because it is good to see each other, though that is certainly true. It is good to be together on this Trinity Sunday because we are created in the image of one God in three persons who are perfectly united with each other. It is good to be together this morning because we belong together, because coming together in worship is part of what makes us who we are.

I am particularly glad to come together, and I am glad to celebrate Trinity Sunday, and I am glad to be reminded that we are created for each other, and I am glad that we can make our own small statement about Christian unity, at this moment.

Our nation has been divided for a long time. But our divisions are more visible now than ever.

When the pandemic first hit Massachusetts, people responded with inspiring resilience, kindness, and generosity. That still happens among neighbors and friends.

156

But then the temperature of our political discourse started to rise. The challenges are certainly real. But instead of having difficult conversations about the health risks of reopening versus the economic and psychological risks of remaining closed, people began taking sides, as if we weren't all in this together. Our fragile unity began to fray.

Now throw into the mix the murder of George Floyd, which exposed once again long unresolved problems of racism, anger, and pent-up violence.

That is where we are as a nation right now.

But we are here, the people of Saint David's, coming together as best we can. We are here on this Trinity Sunday because we are created in the image and likeness of one God in three persons, perfectly united. We are here as a community of faith because we are many who have been incorporated into the one body of Christ. Our presence here this morning is a witness to Christian unity.

Our presence here this morning, and I include in our "presence" those who join us on Facebook or YouTube, as well as those who are united with us in spirit even if they are not able to join us in worship, our presence here this morning matters, because this is a time for every American to emphasize, each in his or her own way, what unites us.

In our small way, our presence here at Saint David's this morning exemplifies the motto chosen by our founding fathers, and printed on our currency: *e pluribus unum*, out of many, one. Our presence here this morning, physical and virtual, expresses our continuing commitment to the words with which our national Constitution begins: "We the people of the United States" come together "in order to form a more perfect union...."

As Christian people, we are called to join in God's mission, to strive for justice and peace, to respect the dignity of every human being, to be peace-makers, to work at reconciliation, and forgiveness, and love. That is always our calling. But our calling is more important now than ever.

And so I am grateful this morning for the opportunity be with you as we worship our God, and as we proclaim our unity with each other and with all people in God. May the grace of the Lord Jesus Christ, the love of God, and the communion of the Holy Spirit be with all of us and with our nation. In Christ's name. Amen.

32. Laborers in the Vineyard
2 Pentecost; June 14, 2020
Genesis 18:1-15; Psalm 116:1, 10-17; Romans 5:1-8; Matthew 9:35-10:8

It is really good to be worshipping with you again this morning, and this time without the noise of the generator next door! Until last Sunday, I hadn't realized exactly how much I was missing you and our worship together. Simply being together after so much time apart is truly healing.

I suspect most of us need a little healing right now, given the turmoil in our world. Anything that gives us a spiritual boost is a great blessing. Anything that helps us to see good in this moment, and in each other, is truly a sign of God's grace at work.

Our service last week was a first shot of grace for me. I went home in a good mood, and I got another shot of grace. I read our Gospel reading for this morning just to let it begin percolating, and it gave me a much-needed attitude adjustment. It helped me to see this moment a little differently, not simply as a time of troubles, but as a real opportunity for service and a real occasion for hope.

The line that sticks out for me comes near the beginning. "When Jesus saw the crowds, he had compassion for them…Then he said to his disciples, 'The harvest is plentiful, but the laborers are few.'"

There is much work to be done. There was then; there is now. Our world is hurting. The challenges we face are substantial.

But Jesus encourages us to focus on what God is doing, on the glorious harvest being prepared even now. That should give us hope, and purpose, and perseverance.

I look around at our gardens. That's one of the nice things about being outside—we can! If you are joining us online, I encourage you to check them out at some point. All you have to do is drive slowly through the parking lot. Our grounds look great.

And here are two things we can all see as we look at our gardens. First, a LOT of work has gone into our grounds. And second, the results, the "harvest" is totally worth it.

Now that is easy for me to say, since I didn't do any of the actual work. But I suspect that if I were to ask the people who did, they would agree that the results are worth every bit of work they have done. They might even add that the work itself was not all bad, that the work is part of the joy they take in the results.

Not all of us are going to work on the Saint David's gardens. But we are all called to labor for the Lord's harvest. We are all laborers in God's vineyard. We are all called to work, each in our different ways, to do our part to bring in the glorious harvest of God's people. And the work may be hard at times. But the work is also a great joy, and the harvest really is glorious.

So far, so good. But there is an obvious problem. How many of us feel truly competent to do the work, God's work, that needs to be done? After all, our task is to do what we can to transform the world from the nightmare it is for so many into the dream that God has for it. That's a tall order!

But if the task seems too much, just take a look at the first set of laborers: Peter and Andrew, James and John, and the rest. The disciples will emerge as great heroes of the faith. But on this day, when Christ sent them out to labor for God's harvest, their emergence as heroes is still in the future. The disciples only become great after Christ's resurrection and the gift of the Holy Spirit. Our passage comes long before that.

In our passage, the disciples are still a group of clowns. Among several nobodies were bunch of fishermen, at least one tax collector which is not great, Thomas the doubter, and Judas, the traitor who will betray his Lord and all his companions. This is NOT a dream team.

But Jesus sends them out. And Jesus gives them the authority they need to do what they have to do. And even that first effort was a great success. A few years later, they were literally changing the world.

Jesus sent the disciples out, despite their many limitations. And Jesus sends us out despite ours. Jesus gives us the authority we need to join in the blessed work, the apostolic work, of healing the sick, and helping the poor, and proclaiming the good news of God's love. The challenges are certainly real. But that's just because the potential harvest is so great.

Seeing that was the attitude adjustment I needed. I needed to focus a little less on the mountain of problems we face and a little more on the opportunity for real change, real growth, real revival. God is at work, and the potential harvest is plentiful, and we get to be part of it.

It all starts with God. The trick is to get a little better at seeing God, at hearing God's call to us. I got a help on that, too, last Sunday.

The weather was nearly perfect for our service. But the wind was blowing. I experienced the wind as a nuisance. It was flapping the pages of my Prayerbook and at one point nearly blew away my sermon. It was also shaking the canopy enough that ushers had to hold it down.

161

I saw the wind as a problem. But not Jim. After the service, Jim said the wind felt like the Holy Spirit swirling around. Jim saw God at work where I only saw a problem.

Listening to the wind, or rather to the voice of God in the wind, became a theme for my week.

On Monday, I spoke to a Franciscan from Georgia about prayer. He told me that he says a simplified version of Morning Prayer each day, outside, with his four-year-old son. That is already a very sweet picture.

But it gets sweeter. After they finish, he and his son spend a little time in silence, which his son apparently loves. (This man is doing something right!) He and his son listen to the wind. And then they talk about what God seems to be saying to them in the wind, how God is responding to their prayers. Sometimes his son gets a message. Sometimes his son tells him that God has a message for him.

The wind continues to swirl around us. God is on the move. Something is happening in our world right now. And every new birth involves some death, some letting go, some pain. But something new is coming into being. The harvest is prepared. And we are invited to be part of it. That is good news.

This week, I invite you to look around for little shots of God's grace. Listen for God in the wind, or wherever else you think you might hear God. We should be doing that all the time, but especially in this time, which is really hard but also when it is clear that something new and potentially glorious is going on.

And that is my prayer for all of us: that we can see this moment as God's time, this world, with all of its problems, as God's world, that we can hear God's voice in the midst of the confusion, and that we can take our place as laborers in God's harvest.

And I pray in Jesus' name. Amen.

33. Being Like Christ

All Saints, November 1, 2020
Revelation 7:9-17; Psalm 34:1-10, 22; 1 John 3:1-3;
Matthew 5:1-12

Today we are blessed.[10] There are all kinds of reasons to be anxious about our nation and our world, of course. That anxiety is weighing on me, as I am sure it weighs on many of you.

But for this hour, we are in a little oasis of blessedness.

It is good to be back inside, even though it is a little scary and we have to make all kinds of safety adjustments.

Not coincidentally, this is one of the holiest days of the Christian year: All Saints Day, when we remember those who have died.

Best of all, later today we'll do our first baptism since the pandemic began, and, in honor of Vivienne, the about-to-be newly baptized, we'll all renew our own baptismal covenants in a few minutes.

That means in this service we get to experience in a summary way the full cycle of the Christian life, from its beginning in baptism to its end when we enter into the nearer presence of God.

Our second reading for this morning, from First John, is perfect for this day. It is a common reading at funerals, including, most recently for us, at the memorial service for Bob Rendrick Sr. two weeks ago. It is also a good reading for baptism, and a good reminder for all of us of our shared Christian journey.

Start with the first bit, which speaks to the beginning of the Christian life. "See what love the Father has given

---

[10] This was our first day worshiping together in our sanctuary since March.

us, that we should be called children of God; and that is what we are….Beloved, we are God's children now."

"We are God's children now." We know that. But we still need to hear it over and over again. And that is one of the gifts of baptism. After being sprinkled with water in the name of the Father, the Son, and the Holy Spirit, the baptized is anointed with these words: "You are sealed by the Holy Spirit in baptism and marked as Christ's own forever."

For most of us, that happened a long time ago. But the good news of our baptisms remains as true today as it was whenever we were baptized and anointed. We are God's children now, and nothing can ever take that away from us, not even our own sins and weaknesses and failures. God's love endures. Thanks be to God!

But that is not the whole story, not for any of us. As lots of people have said, "God loves you just the way you are… and God loves you too much to let you stay there."[11]

That is part of the baptismal service, too. As part of their own vows, parents and godparents commit to helping their child, who is already deeply loved by God, "to grow into the full stature of Christ." The child is deeply, deeply loved. And the child needs to grow into that love.

Our epistle says the same thing. We are all works in progress. "Beloved," says the elder, "we are God's children now; what we will be has not yet been revealed. What we do know is this: when [Christ] is revealed, we will be like him, for we will see him as he is."

For all of us, the great task of our lives is to grow, to grow more and more Christ-like, to resemble more and

---

[11] I have no idea who is the original source for this quote. The internet attributes variations of it to Anne Lamott and Max Lucado, among others.

more our Lord, to grow closer and closer to the full stature of Christ.

Later today, Vivienne's family and their friends will commit to helping her do that. Every time we renew our own baptismal covenants, as we will do in just a minute, we promise to do our best to do the same, with God's help.

In our Gospel reading, Jesus gives us a verbal picture of what the full stature of Christ looks like.

Some of it is not too surprising, if not necessarily easy to achieve. We should hunger and thirst for righteousness. We should be merciful and pure in heart. We should be peacemakers. Christ was all those things. We should be, too. Clear enough.

Other parts of our Gospel reading are equally familiar, but a little less comfortable if we pause to think about them. As we grow to resemble Christ, we will become poorer in spirit, meeker. We may well mourn. In the worst cases, we may be persecuted. That doesn't sound as good.

I talked with Bishop Scruton this week about these more challenging beatitudes. He focused on "poor in spirit," and suggested a few different ways to think about what that might mean. Jesus might mean, blessed are those who recognize the true poverty of their spirit apart from God. Then they will be open to God's grace.

Or, even more freely, this is the version from The Message, "You're blessed when you're at the end of your rope. With less of you there is more of God and his rule."

I don't know if that is exactly what Jesus meant. But it gets at the paradoxical truth at the heart of our faith. As we mature spiritually, as we grow in our relationship with God, as we come to resemble Christ more and more, Christ gradually fills us up. We find our own truest identity as unique and beloved individuals precisely in surrendering to Christ.

That process of giving ourselves over to Christ more and more begins in baptism, continues throughout our lives, and only comes to an end after we die and enter into the nearer presence of God.

We are all somewhere on that journey. What a gift that today we can celebrate Vivienne's first steps on that journey and also celebrate the memory of those who have now completed their journeys.

Celebrating the newly baptized and remembering the saints who have gone before, I give thanks to Christ for helping us along the way, and I pray that Christ will continue to propel us forward until the day that we see Him as He truly is. In Christ's name. Amen.

34. The Vision

Thanksgiving/ Christ the King, November 22, 2020
Ezekiel 34:11-16, 20-24 4:1-7; Psalm 100; Ephesians 1:15-23;
Matthew 25:31-46

Today is a big day for at least two reasons.[12] First, today begins the week of Thanksgiving, a time when, at least in theory, our entire country pauses to reflect on our many blessings. Today is also Christ the King Sunday, the last Sunday of the Christian year, a time when Christians around the world pause to reflect on God's kingdom, with Christ at its head.

That is two good reasons to celebrate.

But the fact is, we may not feel a lot like celebrating right now. At the urging of our Bishop, our vestry voted this week to keep our building closed through the end of December.

That is the prudent and loving thing to do. But it means giving up a lot of things that I value. No ecumenical Thanksgiving service; no Agawam Christmas Project; no Breakfast with Santa; no Greening the Church. Worst of all, in terms of our parish life, it means no in-person Christmas Eve service and no Christmas carols for us as a group.

The deeper problem, of course, is the pandemic that will not go away, the pandemic that is getting worse and that continues to disrupt our lives and to divide our nation.

So how might we, as Christians, approach Thanksgiving in the midst of the pandemic?

---

[12] Christ the King Sunday is, as the sermon says, the last Sunday of the Christian year, ending what will surely be the strangest and most challenging liturgical year of my priesthood, and one of the most challenging in Saint David's history.

168

I start with a passage from the prophet Habakkuk, which we read as part of Morning Prayer this week.

Habakkuk prophesied at a grim time in Israel's history, just before Israel's brutal conquest by Babylon. Habakkuk could see what was happening—that didn't take a special gift of prophecy. And Habakkuk was understandably distressed by what he saw. And so, Habakkuk begins his book with this prayer: "O Lord, how long shall I cry for help, and you will not listen?" (1:2)

I have been feeling a little like that, and I suspect I am not alone. God, things are a little rough right now. We need some help here. Where are you?

God answers Habakkuk. And God puts the responsibility back on Habakkuk himself. "Write the vision," says God. "Write the vision; make it plain on tablets, so that a runner may read it. For there is still a vision for the appointed time; it speaks of the end, and does not lie. If it seems to tarry, wait for it; it will surely come" (2:2-3).

In that grim time, Hababbuk's prophetic task was to remind his people of God's vision, to assure them that God was at work even in the midst of their trials and tribulations, and to promise them that God would ultimately redeem them.

That vision is what we commemorate on this Christ the King Sunday. Today we celebrate Christ's victory over sin and suffering and death. Today we picture Christ reigning in God's kingdom and making everything right. That is the vision Habakkuk is talking about.

But when people are suffering, it is easy to lose sight of that vision. In the middle of this pandemic, it is easy to lose sight of that vision. Today more than ever, our people need a prophet to write that vision.

And that is our job. In a hard time, we, who are people of faith, we who look forward to Christ's victory, we are called to hold on to God's vision. We are called to share God's vision.

Listen to the Apostle Paul. Paul is talking to the ancient Ephesians. But Paul is also talking to us.

"I pray that the God of our Lord Jesus Christ, the Father of glory, may give you a spirit of wisdom and revelation as you come to know him, so that, with the eyes of your heart enlightened, you may know what is the hope to which he has called you, what are the riches of his glorious inheritance among the saints, and what is the immeasurable greatness of his power for us who believe, according to the working of his great power" (1:17-19).

That is a packed sentence! But it is really great news for us right now, so it is worth spending some time with it.

Paul begins by praying that God will give us the kind of wisdom that will open what he calls "the eyes of our hearts." And with the eyes of our hearts opened, we know hope. We know the inheritance of Christ and all the saints, including us. We know the power of God for us who believe.

In a world that sometimes seems hopeless, among people who are often blind to God's power at work in us and for us, our calling is to be people of hope and faith and love and, this week especially, of gratitude.

And even in this year, which has been kind of a drag(!), we have a lot to be thankful for.

Here are things I am thankful for this morning. I am thankful for the fact that we can worship together. I am thankful for the internet which allows people to join us in worship even when they can't be physically present. I am thankful for the office angels who mail out materials every

170

week to people who can't join us in person or online but are still part of our worshipping community. I am thankful for all the people who help to lead our worship week after week, up front and behind the scenes.

I am thankful because our worship always reminds me, and I need reminding, of Christ's triumph over sin and death and evil, a triumph which began two thousand years ago, and which continues to unfold until the day when it will finally be complete. That vision is a BIG reason to be thankful.

And I give thanks to God for you, who help to keep the vision alive, even in the midst of the pandemic. And I pray that God will help us all to be effective advocates of that vision in the world. In Jesus' name. Amen.

Part 3: Our Centennial Year 2025, Year C

In the first two parts of this book, I generally included all the sermons I preached over a period of time. Between the two parts, the sermons cover a complete Church year.

For the third part of this book, I just publish selected sermons from this, our centennial year. In this section, I have largely limited myself to sermons directly related to our centennial. They formed part of a Centennial Preaching Series, that also featured our Bishop, Doug Fisher, retired Bishop Gordon Scruton, former Rectors Dan Barker, Darius Mojallali, and Len Cowan, as well as current Saint David's members Deacon Terry Hurlbut and the Rev. Scott Seabury.

The obvious choices were the anniversary of the consecration of our building, yet another Annual Meeting, Saint David's Day, my sixtieth birthday and the fourteenth anniversary of my coming to Saint David's, and our centennial celebration itself on the first Sunday of Advent. I added a couple of additional sermons on the same theme to bring the total to forty.

My goal in these sermons was to celebrate our past and present, as well as to look forward to our next century.

35. Letting Go, and Celebrating[13]

2 Epiphany; January 19, 2025
Isaiah 62:1-5; Psalm 36:5-10; 1 Corinthians 12:1-11; John 2:1-11

Today is the first sermon that is explicitly part of our centennial celebration. The occasion is the anniversary of the consecration of this building, exactly twenty-eight years ago today.

Our building was consecrated at a time of great optimism for our parish. We had outgrown our old building down the street. After a couple of years of worshipping in borrowed space, we at last had a brand-new building that could accommodate us. We were even able to pay it off remarkably quickly.

And our dreams were still bigger. Our original hope had been to use this building as a temporary worship space while we built a separate sanctuary. Then this building would serve as our parish hall.

It was a beautiful vision. But life got in the way. A beloved rector left. The new rector turned out not to be a good fit. The denomination made some decisions that upset people. And within a year or two our numbers were down enough that we had to give up the idea of a separate sanctuary.

All that happened twenty years ago, well before I came to Saint David's. But in this centennial year, it is good to look back at our past to learn what we can as we look forward to our next century as a parish.

And I want to celebrate that time, those first hard years in this building. I know that they weren't easy years. It was

---

[13] I preached this sermon at our 8:00 service. Bishop Scruton preached a centennial sermon at the 10:00 service.

painful and discouraging to let go of our big vision, and to adjust to reduced circumstances.

I certainly don't fault those who left during those hard years. But I celebrate those who stayed, the people who kept our parish going even when it was hard, the people who showed up Sunday after Sunday, and the people who worked through the week to make Sunday worship possible. They, and by 'they' I mean some of you, are our saints.

Our Gospel reading and its aftermath speaks to that time in our parish's history, and to what our saints of that time accomplished. It is Jesus' very first miracle, the beginning of his public ministry. It was a happy occasion, a wedding. And not just any wedding. The best kind of wedding, with wine that never runs out and just gets better and better. John tells us that this was the first of Jesus' signs, and that it revealed Jesus' glory, and that Jesus' disciples believed in him.

As I often do, I imagine what was going through the disciples' heads that day. They had only just started following Jesus. And at that wedding, their decision to follow Jesus looked really smart. Clearly, hanging out with Jesus was going to be great.

And I imagine the disciples looking forward to more miracles, to more days like their day in Cana, to triumph after triumph, as Jesus worked miracles and gathered followers and gradually worked up to establishing his kingdom, all with them at his side.

That day at Cana was surely a day of great optimism and hope. The disciples surely had a big and beautiful vision for what was to come.

But if they had a beautiful vision on that day, they must have been sorely disappointed by what actually happened.

They were right about Jesus, of course. But they were not right about how things were going to unfold.

Jesus kept working miracles. But Jesus also said things that upset people. Powerful people began to resent Jesus. Even some of his followers wavered.

In the single most poignant scene in the Gospel of John, Jesus tells people to eat his flesh and drink his blood. At that, many of his followers dropped away. And Jesus turned to his remaining disciples and asked, do you also wish to go away (6:67)?

Peter responded that they had nowhere else to go, that Jesus and Jesus alone had the true words of eternal life (6:68). Peter and the other disciples we remember today all stayed. And Peter and the other disciples who remained faithful began the long and hard process of letting go of their own big visions, of adjusting to their new and reduced circumstances.

And, most importantly, they kept following Jesus, listening to Jesus, learning from Jesus, being formed more and more in Jesus' image and likeness over time. And that is why they are our capital S Saints, the saints who kept the Church going through the discouraging moments in Jesus' public ministry and the much more discouraging days immediately after Jesus' crucifixion.

What they learned, those faithful disciples who stayed, is that the Christian life is not always easy. Sometimes the Christian life really does involve taking up the cross. The faithful disciples learned not to put too much weight on their own vision of what the Church should be, and instead to keep following Jesus through the ups and downs. The faithful disciples learned to rely on Christ's presence with them and on God's strength, rather than their own.

Those are lessons that every Christian has to learn, one way or another. Those are lessons that we can learn from the difficult parts of our own history. Those are lessons that will stand us in good stead as we look ahead to our next century.

We need to plan for our future. We need to dream, and to dream big. But in the end, and all along the way, too, it's not our dream that truly matters. It is God's dream for us, and for our world. Our task as Christians is to bring our dreams, our visions, into alignment with God's, no matter what God has in store for us. That is the way to be truly faithful, and therefore also the way of true life and true joy.

But I want to return to the wedding at Cana.

I am pretty sure that at Cana the disciples formed wrong-headed visions of what following Christ was going to be like. But the disciples were right to rejoice with Christ in what was happening in that moment. Weddings really are joyful, especially when Christ is present!

And that, too, is a lesson for us. From where I sit, things are going pretty well here at Saint David's in early 2025. I see reasons for hope and optimism about our future. Of course, I also see reasons to worry.

But our Gospel reading invites us not to dwell on what might be coming, good or bad, but rather to focus on the good things that are happening all around us right now. It invites us to pay attention to the way God is at work in our midst. It invites us to celebrate with joy Christ's presence with us. After all, we are about to share our own Eucharistic feast. Just with less wine!

And so, on this anniversary of the consecration of our building, I thank God for the people who had an ambitious vision for Saint David's, and who worked hard to make it happen. I thank God for our saints, the people who stuck it out through the hard times over those next few years. Mostly I give thanks to God for working with and through us every step of the way.

And, as I look ahead to our next century, my prayer is that God will continue to lead us, and to accompany us, and to strengthen us for whatever comes, helping us always to be discerning and faithful disciples.

And I pray that in Christ's name. Amen.

36. Feast, Share, Rejoice
3 Epiphany; January 26, 2025; Annual Meeting
Nehemiah 8:1-3, 5-6, 8-10; Psalm 19; 1 Cor 12:12-31a;
Luke 4:14-21

Today is our Annual Meeting, and I'll come to that. But I want to begin with a passage I have never preached on: our reading from Nehemiah. Out of curiosity, I checked to see how often Nehemiah comes up in the lectionary, our three-year schedule of readings, and this is it. Nehemiah comes up just this once. And I have always neglected Nehemiah in favor of the more obviously relevant readings from Paul and Luke.

But our reading from Nehemiah is perfect for Annual Meeting Sunday. Indeed, Nehemiah describes the Old Testament version of an Annual Meeting.

As usual with the Old Testament, we need to start with a little context.

When the events of our reading happened, the people of ancient Israel were having a bad century.

At the beginning of the sixth century BCE, their kingdom was conquered by Babylon. The Babylonians devastated the countryside, destroyed much of Jerusalem, including the Temple, and forced the Israelite leadership into exile. That's how the century began.

At the end of the century, Israel's new overlord, Persia, allowed the people in exile to return to the Promised Land and rebuild their shattered institutions. That sounds great.

But rebuilding proved difficult. Partly it was a problem of limited resources. When they laid the foundation for a new temple, those who remembered the grandeur of the first Temple "wept with a loud voice" to see what they were reduced to (Ezra 3:12).

Worse yet, their non-Jewish neighbors were actively hostile to the rebuilding program. While they were rebuilding the walls of Jerusalem, the governor, Nehemiah himself, had to keep armed men at the ready the whole time for fear of attack (Nehemiah 4:16-17).

Worst of all, the Jews who had remained in the land were demoralized and not particularly faithful. For example, they routinely violated the Sabbath (Nehemiah 13:15).

Nehemiah and Ezra decided they had to do something. As we just heard in our reading, what they did was gather all the people together to renew their covenant with God. That's their version of an Annual Meeting.

But they renewed their covenant in a big way. Ezra began by reading and interpreting the Old Testament law to them for hours—from early morning until midday. After that, he and Nehemiah sent the people home.

That's all we get in our reading, but the covenant renewal wasn't anywhere near over. They all came back for more the next day, and for the next seven days. Then they returned again a couple of weeks later for yet more listening to the law and more praying and more repenting. At the end of all that, the people committed, in writing, to observe everything they had heard and been taught. That is renewing your covenant, Old Testament style!

Terry suggested that we should do all that for our Annual Meeting. But eight days and more seemed a little much to me, so I convinced Terry that we could just renew our baptismal covenant and then meet for an hour.

What struck me even more than the length of their meeting, and what I want to focus on this morning, was the reaction of the people to their covenant renewal. We are told "all the people wept when they heard the words of the law."

It is true that the people had good reasons to weep that day. They may have been distressed at their situation, which wasn't great. They were dominated by a foreign power, surrounded by hostile people, and struggling with only limited success to rebuild their homeland.

They may have felt guilty as they listened to the requirements of God's law and reflected on their own failures, which were also real enough. When they gathered a few weeks later for the final stage of their covenant renewal, they "assembled with fasting and in sackcloth, and with earth on their heads" (Nehemiah 9:1), so we know guilt was an issue for them.

And/or, they may have been afraid, afraid of what the future held in store for them, and afraid of how God might punish them for their sins and failures.

Whatever their reasons, the people reacted on that first day with weeping. That day, the people heard God's word as bad news.

And in that, they were mistaken.

Nehemiah the governor, and Ezra the priest, and the Levites, which is to say the deacons, all told the people, "This day is holy to the Lord your God; do not mourn or weep....Go your way, eat the fat and drink sweet wine and send portions of them to those for whom nothing is prepared, for this day is holy to our Lord; and do not be grieved, for the joy of the Lord is your strength."

This day is holy. Feast. Share. Rejoice. That is what covenant renewal should be.

I am happy to report that our prospects are considerably brighter than what the people of ancient Israel faced when they renewed their covenant in the book of Nehemiah.

The challenges we face are certainly real. Once again, our nation needs to come together as fellow Americans after a divisive election and recommit to our founding values and to the common good. That has been hard for us after each of the last several elections. I'm guessing it will be hard after this one, too.

Saint David's is not surrounded by hostile people as the ancient Israelites were. Our problem is closer to indifference. Today a higher percentage of the American people identify as entirely non-religious than at any point in my lifetime.

And, here at Saint David's, our resources, financial and otherwise, are limited enough that it is tempting to turn inward, to devote our time and talent and treasure to maintaining the status quo. Even that isn't easy.

Our challenges are real, and they can be daunting. Given them, how can we be expected to do all the things we commit to doing in our baptismal covenant? If we pause long enough to let the words of our baptismal covenant sink in, if we consider exactly what it is we are called to do, if we compare the magnitude of the challenges we face with the limited resources at our disposal, we, too, may feel like weeping.

That's when we need to hear Nehemiah's words. This day is holy. Feast. Share. Rejoice.

That's when we need to remember that our God is a great and glorious God. That we are the body of Christ and individually members of it. That, like Christ himself, we are filled with the power of the Spirit and sent into the world to bring good news.

Later this morning, we will have our Annual Meeting. And we'll do the things we do in Annual Meetings: elect new leadership; discuss our budget; review our ministries.

That's not as bad as listening to 613 laws for several hours, but it may seem like petty stuff to some. But it's not petty at all. What we do at Annual Meeting is reflect on our recent past, prepare for the year to come, and recommit to serving as God's hands in the world. There is nothing more important than that. That's why this day is holy. That's why we feast, and share, and rejoice.

I thank God for our calling to be God's people in this time and place, for the mission God has entrusted to us, and for the many ways God equips us to fulfill that mission. And I pray that we can continue to hear and to respond to God's call with the joy that comes from doing God's will.

In Christ's name. Amen.

37. Do the Little Things

Last Epiphany and Commemoration of Saint David,
March 2, 2025
Exodus 34:29-35; Psalm 99; 2 Cor 3:12-4:2; Luke 9:28-43a

Yesterday was Saint David's Day and, particularly in this centennial year, I want to commemorate our patron saint. Thankfully, Saint David turns out to be surprisingly relevant, with much to teach us about living as Christians in our time.

Unfortunately, Saint David is not well known. I have a degree in Church History, but I had never heard of him when I first came here. I guessed that Saint David was the great Old Testament king from whom Christ is descended. In case you have wondered the same thing, I am here to tell you that they were not the same person. Our Saint David is the patron saint of Wales, by which I mean part of the British Isles, not the large animal that swims in the ocean!

I have tried, without success, to discover why our founders chose Saint David as our patron when our parish was established back in 1925. But even if Saint David is not a household name, not even here at Saint David's!, Saint David has been part of our history.

Not too long after I arrived, I found a large stone under our altar. The Altar Guild knew all about it, but I doubt many other people did. Apparently, Father Tyler, our priest in the nineteen fifties and sixties, brought it back from a pilgrimage he made to Saint David's Cathedral in Wales. I was intrigued, but didn't think much about it.

But when we got our new altar and decided to bring the stone out, I was startled to see that it was carved. It's a fragment from the Cathedral itself! I would like to think that Father Tyler got permission to take it, but this is one of those cases where it is probably best not to ask.

In a post 9-11 world, hauling stone on airplanes is tricky, but I also brought back a stone from a pilgrimage to Saint David's Cathedral a couple of years ago, which now sits on my altar at home. Getting my stone back was not a problem because it is about the size of a quarter, and I just picked it up off the ground. That makes me less impressive, but probably more legal, than Father Tyler!

In my first year here, I also learned that we were part of a network of Saint David's Episcopal Churches in the United States that supports Saint David's Cathedral in Wales. I have no idea when that started, but I send them a little money every year in the name of our parish to maintain the connection.

I say all that to show that we have paid attention to Saint David in different ways throughout our history.

But Saint David can help us in our particular moment, too.

Saint David was a Celtic Christian living at a time when Celtic Christianity was in retreat. Pagan tribes from Germany were overrunning England, pushing the Celtic Christians to the margins, places like Wales in the west and Scotland in the north.

Saint David was part of the Celtic Christian resistance. (So was the historical King Arthur. I briefly fantasized that David and Arthur knew each other, but they lived at different times and in different places.)

In one famous story, Saint David advised the Welsh fighting men to wear leeks to distinguish themselves from their Saxon enemies. That way they would know who to attack and who not to attack when things got confusing.

Saint David also participated in the wider Church. In another famous story, David was preaching at a Church Council, but no one could hear him. So, God raised up the hill on which David was standing and, at the same time, the Holy Spirit came upon him in the form of a dove. You can see an image of that moment on our banner. The Dove has been a symbol of Saint David ever since, including on our Saint David stained glass window.

David's role in the Celtic resistance and at the Church Council remind us that Christian people are called to look beyond our immediate environment, to have an impact on our world, and to join with our brothers and sisters in other places to discern God's will. That's an important reminder when Christianity seems to be in retreat in our time and place, as it was in David's.

But mostly Saint David was a monk. David himself lived at the monastery where Saint David's Cathedral now stands, and he founded other monasteries all along the western coast of Wales.

And there are lessons in his monastic practice as well.

Saint David was strict in his monasteries. He wouldn't let his monks eat meat, drink anything other than water, or use domestic animals for labor. As you might guess, those rules were NOT popular. At one point, David's monks grew so angry that they tried to poison him. David prayed over the poisoned water and food, then ate and drank without harm.

It's fun to imagine what meals were like after the failed poisoning. I'm guessing they were a little tense! But Saint David continued to serve as abbot of the monastery, and it appears that some or all of the monks involved in the foiled assassination attempt stayed on. If so, they all must have gone through a process of reconciliation. I wish we knew more about that.

David's rules were strict even by the standards of monastic houses of that period. I certainly have no interest in following his rules!

But, especially in challenging times, we need to double down on our spiritual practices, on our ongoing formation and growth as Christian people. And for many of us, that may well mean simplifying our lives or practicing some form of self-denial.

As it happens, Lent, the season of self-denial, begins next Wednesday. Saint David invites us to be intentional about things we might give up or take on in an effort to eliminate some of the distractions in our lives and draw closer to God.

But what David and his monks mostly did, what monks have mostly done in every time and place, was pray. And that is probably the best lesson of all.

Despite his occasional forays into the larger world, Saint David mostly lived outside of the major currents of his time. Day after day, he and his monks prayed and worked and did their best to get along with each other. And that seems to have been what mattered most to Saint David. His dying words of advice were, "do the little things, the small things you've seen me doing."

In that, David was like us. We mostly don't have a big impact on the world around us. We mostly try to be faithful out of sight in our little corner of the world.

But David did have an impact. His monasteries were like Christian seeds that ultimately bore rich fruit when Christianity began to spread through England once again.

I think the same thing may be happening now. There are certainly plenty of problems in our nation and in our world. But, for the first time in many years, the younger generation is more religious than their immediate elders. It may be that revival has begun.

Whether or not that turns out to be right, Saint David reminds us that our task is to stay faithful in the little things, to engage the wider world as we are able, and to trust that God is at work through it all. I pray that God will help us here at Saint David's to heed our patron's reminder! In Christ's name. Amen.

38. Pressing On

5 Lent; April 6, 2025
Isaiah 43:16-21; Psalm 126; Philippians 3:4b-14; John 12:1-8

In our Gospel reading, Mary of Bethany pours a pound of expensive perfume on Jesus' feet. That's a LOT of perfume! I suspect it was an understatement to say that the house was filled with the fragrance. I'm guessing the odor was suffocating. Then Mary wipes Jesus' feet with her hair. It's a beautiful act of love that must have also been a little awkward for everyone involved.

But we'll be hearing about the washing of feet again next week, on Maundy Thursday, so I'll focus on our other readings this morning. They certainly have plenty for us!

Speaking on behalf of God, Isaiah says in our Old Testament reading, "Do not remember the former things, or consider the things of old. I am about to do a new thing; now it springs forth, do you not perceive it?" That's God acting.

The Apostle Paul makes a similar point about his own action in response to God. "Forgetting what lies behind and straining forward to what lies ahead, I press on toward the goal for the prize of the heavenly call of God in Christ Jesus."

Forget the old, embrace the new, press on.

People will hear that message differently.

For many, it sounds great. We are a culture that wants the new and improved, the next big thing. My children, ages twenty-eight and twenty-five, love the new. Nicholas tells me, for example, that the newest version of technology is virtually always "objectively better." I am sure he is right. But that is NOT how I experience updates to my computer.

I was once like my sons. I used to like the new.

At the risk of violating everything Isaiah and Paul said about forgetting what lies behind, I reread the first sermon I ever preached, which was on these very readings.[14] It was in the spring of 2007, and I was working my way towards ordination. To fulfill the remaining ordination requirements, my family and I were preparing to move to Massachusetts that fall.

I began my sermon by confessing that I had had an anxiety dream about preaching a few days earlier. Although I didn't mention it in my sermon, I was even more anxious about all the other new things that would soon be coming my way: moving to New England, returning to school, serving as a hospital chaplain, and beginning my priesthood.

But I was also excited about the new thing I was experiencing, the new thing God was calling me to. I was eager to press on towards my goal. The readings we just heard spoke directly to where I was in my life at that time. They were good news for me, and they felt like good news.

But that is not true for me in the same way at this stage of my life. I am settled, comfortable, content with things as they are.

I do look forward with hope. But I certainly don't want to forget the past. I enjoy studying history. I enjoy reflecting on my own journey to this point. Particularly in this centennial year for our parish, I enjoy celebrating the last hundred years.

And I am no longer big on embracing the new. In my house, we joke that if everyone were like me, human

---

[14] So was my third sermon here at Saint David's, also included in this book. See sermon three from October 2, 2011.

beings would still be living in caves. Straining forward to what lies ahead is not who I am, particularly at this stage of my life.

But that makes our readings even more important for me and for people like me. These readings are a challenge and an invitation that we need to hear.

It is easy to get stuck in ruts. That is true for many people, particularly as we age. And it is certainly true of the Episcopal Church.

I'm guessing many of you have heard the jokes about how many people it takes to change a lightbulb from this group or that. How many Episcopalians does it take to change a lightbulb? Change?!

We rightly love our traditions. And, if we get too stuck in our ways, we run the risk of stagnation or worse.

The Apostle Paul, in the years before he became a Christian, was an extreme example of that risk.

Paul loved the traditions of his people, and Paul lived them. Paul claimed that "as to righteousness under the law" he was "blameless." Paul did it all.

And so, when God did a new thing, when God came in the flesh, when a new movement arose preaching a Gospel of love and inclusion, Paul reacted with extreme hostility. Paul was, as he says, "as to zeal, a persecutor of the church."

Thankfully, Christ shook Paul out of his complacency, his self-righteousness, his persecuting zeal. Christ helped Paul to see and understand the new thing God was doing. Christ called Paul to embrace that new thing and to become an agent of further change in the Church. Paul became the apostle of a law-free Gospel to Gentiles at a time when many even of the other apostles weren't prepared to go so far.

And Paul kept pushing forward right to the end of his life. Paul wrote this letter from prison, probably in Rome, probably in his fifties, which was old in the first century, and probably within a year or two of his execution. Even then, in prison, as an old man near the end of his life, Paul, who had been so attached to the old ways before he met Christ, Paul kept straining forward to what lay ahead, pressing toward the goal for the prize of the heavenly call of God in Christ Jesus.

That is our calling, too, hard as it can be for people like me to hear it.

God keeps moving forward. What God did in the past, those things that we have captured in our traditions, is not always a good measure of what God is doing now or will do in the future. Our task, our challenge, the task and challenge of every generation, is to see God's hand at work in the world around us, however new it may be, and to get involved.

Unfortunately, I don't always see God's hand as clearly as I would like. And these readings are a warning that part of my difficulty may come from the very fact that I am comfortable and content with things as they are and have been, that I am not inclined to look for the new thing God is doing.

But if I want to see God's new thing, I do know more or less where to look.

God's new things seem often to happen among people who are struggling: people like the Hebrew slaves in Egypt, to whom God sent Moses; or the people of Israel laboring under Roman domination in the first century, when Christ himself came among them; or people like us during the pandemic, when many of us experienced isolation and loss, but also when Churches embraced technologies that have dramatically enhanced our capacity for evangelism.

It may well be the same in our day. God is doing something, and God's new thing is likely happening among those who are hungry or afraid or oppressed, the "least of these," the people Christ tells us to help if we want to help him.

My prayer for us, especially in this centennial year when we look back at our first century but also forward to our next, is that we can appreciate the surpassing value of knowing Christ, that we could willingly accept the loss of all things if necessary, that we can and will press on toward the goal for the prize of the heavenly call of God in Christ Jesus. And I pray that in Christ's name. Amen.

39. Made at Saint David's

13 Pentecost; September 7, 2025
Jeremiah 18:1-11; Psalm 139:1-5, 12-17; Philemon 1-21;
Luke 14:25-33

This is a shocking thing to admit, but I turn sixty today. Also amazing for me to think about, Thursday will be the 14th anniversary of my arrival here at Saint David's.[15] Time flies when you are having fun!

I had hoped for upbeat readings this morning. That's not exactly what we have. But as I sat with our readings, I came to appreciate them as more encouraging than I first thought.

I begin with our Psalm. It is called a Psalm "of David," but we can think of these as our words, too.

"I will thank you [God] because I am marvelously made; your works are wonderful, and I know it very well…Your eyes beheld my limbs, yet unfinished in the womb; all of them were written in your book; they were fashioned day by day" (139:13, 15).

We are the wonderful works of God in the Psalm. We are marvelously made. Beginning even before we were born, God had a plan for us. Even now, God fashions us day by day.

That's a great start.

Then Jeremiah gives us a picture of God fashioning us. God is the potter working away at the divine potter's wheel, and we are the clay God is working on, fashioning

---

[15] I recently learned that we have another anniversary this week as well. On September 10, 1953, Bishop Appleton consecrated the Church building we used before moving to our current location.

our limbs, shaping our characters, molding us into the kind of people God invites us to be and to become.

That image can make it sound like we don't have any role in how we turn out. After all, as Jeremiah says, clay can't protest to the potter that it doesn't like what the potter is doing with it.

But as Jeremiah keeps going, he makes it clear that our choices matter. If we are on an evil path, but repent, God says, "I will change my mind about the disaster that I intended to bring on [you]" (18:8). What we do, how we respond to God, determines in part what our final shape will be.

So, God is fashioning us, and God is working with us in the process of fashioning us, into the marvelous works that we are becoming, with God's help.

Our Gospel reading describes that same process in a slightly different way. As we draw closer to God, we go through a process of stripping away anything that might hold us back. That stripping can include the people we love, our possessions, our desire for life itself. We have to let go of whatever prevents us from becoming the people God invites us to become.

One of the great sculptors of all time, Michaelangelo, described what I think Jeremiah and Luke are getting at.

When Michaelangelo was sculpting an angel from a block of marble, this is how he described what he was doing: "I saw the angel in the marble and carved until I set [the angel] free."

The angel was already there, in the uncarved block of marble. But the angel was concealed, covered, trapped, until Michaelangelo carved away the excess layers on top to reveal, that is, to set free, the angel within.

That is how God works on us. We start as a block of unformed clay or marble. And God, the great potter in the sky, gets to work on us, giving us form. And part of that process of divine formation is stripping away the layers on top of the marvelous work there in the clay, stripping away the stuff that prevents us from being the people God invites us to become, freeing us from even the apparently good things that actually imprison us.

That's a beautiful way to describe the Christian journey from spiritual birth at our baptisms all the way through the process of sanctification, when God makes us holy enough to stand in God's own presence as God's creation and as God's beloved child.

I love that way of describing the Christian journey, but it is particularly relevant to me today. Turning sixty feels like a milestone. That and the anniversary of my first Sunday here at Saint David's makes me ponder the place of Saint David's in my spiritual journey.

I think first about our children. Our sons were entering 7th and 9th grade when we arrived. They are now 26 and 28, and off adulting, more or less. But in important ways, this is where they grew up. This is the first Church they remember with any clarity as their Church. This is where they began to make choices for themselves about their faith.

As for me, I was in my forties when I arrived here, firmly mid-life. Now I'm entering my senior years. That change is visible in all sorts of ways, starting up top. I arrived with a relatively full head of hair. You see where that stands today. This is the place where that transition has happened.

This has also been my Church home for longer than any other single place. Six other Churches have been important to my journey, but none for as long a time or as deep an involvement as Saint David's.

God has used this place, God has used you, to form me, to shape me, to free me from the things that keep me from being who I am called to be.

I will always be grateful to this parish particularly for two things.

First, Saint David's provided roots for my family and me when we first moved to Massachusetts.

I was anxious about leaving my family, friends, and career in Georgia to embark on a new life as—think about what this means for a southerner—as a Yankee. That is not easy!

When we arrived in Massachusetts, I needed community. And almost immediately you became my primary community. You are the people who supported me in that important transition in my life journey.

This is also the place where I first truly lived into my priesthood.

I was fortunate in my mentors along the way. But when I was ordained, I remember thinking about one of them in particular that he was a priest straight through. He wasn't just filling a role or doing a job. He truly lived as priest. I don't mean that he was always saintly. He was a truly good man, but of course he botched it sometimes. But even when he botched it, he was still a priest.

I wanted to be like that. I wanted to be a priest straight through. But I definitely wasn't when I arrived here. At that time, I didn't think of myself as a priest so much as a teacher who had gotten ordained and could do priest things. When I met people, that was often how I introduced myself: as a teacher who was also a priest

Gradually that changed. I can't remember a particular moment when it happened. But over my time here, I got comfortable being a priest. I even got used to introducing myself to strangers as a priest, although I can tell you, that is often a conversation-stopper at parties.

Living into my priesthood has probably been the single most important development in my spiritual life during the time we have lived in Massachusetts, as I was finishing mid-life and preparing to become an elder. And that happened here, largely thanks to you.

As I enter this new stage of life, as I begin my next decade and my fifteenth year here at Saint David's, I thank God for this parish and for you, its people, for the many ways God has used you to form me. And I pray that we can all continue our journeys, continue being shaped by God, through the rest of our centennial year and beyond. In Christ's name. Amen.

40. Honoring Our Past, Embracing Our Future, Savoring Our Present

1 Advent; November 30, 2025
Isaiah 2:1-5; Psalm 122; Romans 13:11-14; Matthew 24:36-44

Today is both the final sermon in our centennial preaching series and the first Sunday of the new Christian year. As you might guess, that is not a coincidence.

From the very beginning of our centennial planning, we wanted to do two things, both named in our centennial slogan. We wanted to "honor our past," and we wanted to "embrace our future." We wanted to look back in gratitude and forward in hope.

That's why we scheduled this centennial sermon for this day. In Advent, all Christians do on a grand scale what we have been doing all year here at Saint David's.

In Advent, Christians around the world prepare themselves to celebrate the birth of our Lord two thousand years ago, to remember with gratitude the good news of great joy that Christ was born, Immanuel, God with us. That's honoring our Christian past.

Advent is also a season for looking forward. We get that in our readings about the second coming of Christ, which may be a time of suffering and certainly a time when things get shaken out, but which will also be a time of joy and the establishment of God's kingdom. As Christian people, we embrace that future.

That combination of looking back and looking forward makes every Advent a complicated and busy time.

For me personally, Advent is probably the most challenging season of the Christian year.

There's all the Church stuff, as we do Advent and prepare for Christmas.

And there is normally a fair amount of non-Church stuff, too. Carrie finishes her semester this week, after which our family will swing into Christmas action. That means we will once again have to navigate the challenging fact that I am busy with work at a time when Carrie is not and there is a lot to do on the home front. I emphasize, Challenging!

This year there is more than usual here at Saint David's. In addition to everything it always is, this Christmas Eve is our actual centennial, the day our parish turns one hundred. On Christmas Eve we won't emphasize our centennial since we'll be busy celebrating Christ's birth. But our year-long centennial celebration culminates a week from Monday with a festive meal. I hope you will all come if you can.

All that busyness is great. But I hope we can also pause long enough to enjoy the season and particularly to enjoy our celebration.

I think back to the single busiest time of my life. As I was turning thirty—exactly half a lifetime ago—I was finishing my education (finally!), moving to a new city, starting a new job, and anticipating the birth of our first child.

My last academic requirement, the actual end of my education, was an oral defense of my dissertation. I had to present my research to my professors and any students who wanted to be there, and answer their questions about it. Then the other students and I had to leave the room while the faculty voted on whether I had done well enough to pass.

The stakes were high. If I passed, I would graduate and could start my new job in the next week or so. If I didn't pass, I wouldn't graduate, and my life would get very complicated.

Going in, I was confident enough that I invited friends to meet me after the defense for a celebratory beer. But time was tight because Carrie and I also had a three-hour birthing class that evening. That was my life at the time— one big thing after another, with not much break in between.

So, during my defense, I did my best in front of the faculty. Afterwards I felt good about my performance. I figured the faculty vote would take about thirty seconds. My professors would look around at each other, all give the thumbs up, and come out to give me the good news.

That is not what happened. The minutes clicked slowly by as I waited anxiously. Friends reassured me that all would be well. I waited some more. I got more anxious. Apparently, I had not done as well as I thought.

After what seemed like a very long time but probably wasn't, my professors finally came out to tell me I had indeed passed. Relieved, I headed to the pub with friends. My main mentor came with us to join in the celebration.

But at the pub, I was not in celebratory mode. I was still all business. I didn't have much time before our birthing class, and there were things I wanted to know, like what my professors had been talking about for so long after my defense, and, looking ahead, what I needed to do to publish my dissertation. After thirty years, my education was done, and I was moving forward.

Thankfully, my mentor slowed me down. He pointed out that I had been working for this moment for a long time. He told me to pause in gratitude for all the help I had received along the way and in pride for what I had accomplished. He was telling me to take a moment to honor my past.

He also understood that my future was coming at me fast and hard, and he assured me that we could talk another time about the faculty conversation after my defense, and about my own next steps. He knew that I needed to embrace my future.

But at least for a few minutes, he said, I should savor the present, enjoy a beer and time with friends.

My mentor never got around to telling me what they had talked about while I waited outside for the verdict. We also never had a conversation about publishing my dissertation. But I appreciated his advice then, and now.

It would be a LONG time before I had another opportunity for genuine leisure! In the next few weeks, I would move, start a new job for which I felt poorly prepared, and become a father, for which I was definitely poorly prepared. Going forward, I wouldn't often see my fellow students, my friends and companions of the previous seven years.

So, as best I could, I took my mentor's advice. I enjoyed a little time with my friends and the chance, brief as it was, to look back at the journey we had been on together. In my own way, I was honoring my past, as well as embracing my future. But I also paused to appreciate the present moment.

I hope that we can do the same over the next week, and especially at our centennial meal. For the last year, we have tried to honor our past in different ways. Always we look forward in hope. But it's good to pause every once in a while to savor the present, to count our blessings, and to enjoy each other's company.

Of course, we can't simply pause forever, just as I couldn't celebrate with friends forever. The future is coming, and we have to move into it with courage and faith. Today begins a new Christian year. Next month we begin our second century as a parish.

I don't know what the future holds for Saint David's. But right now, we are in a good place. I thank God for that. I thank God for you. And I pray that God will richly bless us in the years to come as God has richly blessed us in the past and as God is richly blessing us now. In Christ's name. Amen.

www.ingramcontent.com/pod-product-compliance
Lightning Source LLC
LaVergne TN
LVHW052023080426
835513LV00018B/2124